Phenomenology of Communication

PHENOMENOLOGY OF COMMUNICATION

Merleau-Ponty's Thematics in Communicology and Semiology

Richard L. Lanigan

Duquesne University Press
Pittsburgh, PA

Published in the United States of America
by Duquesne University Press
600 Forbes Avenue, Pittsburgh, PA 15282

First Edition

Library of Congress Cataloging-in-Publication Data

Lanigan, Richard L.
Phenomenology of communication.

Bibliography: p.
Includes index.
1. Communication—Philosophy. 2. Merleau-Ponty, Maurice, 1908–1961—Contributions in philosophy of communication. 3. Phenomenology. 4. Semiotics. I. Title.
P91.L34 1988 001.51 87–24587
ISBN 0–8207–0185–8
ISBN 0–8207–0199–8 (pbk.)

Contents

A teacher who can arouse a feeling for one single good action, for one single good poem, accomplishes more than he who fills our memory with rows on rows of natural objects, classified with name and form. Goethe

In Philosophy, my teacher,

HUBERT GRIGGS ALEXANDER

Professor Emeritus of Philosophy
University of New Mexico
Director, U.N.M. Aesthetics Institute at Taos

And, his teacher,

WILBUR MARSHALL URBAN

Professor of Philosophy
Yale University

In Communicology, my teacher,

THOMAS JENNINGS PACE

Professor and Director of Graduate Studies in Speech Communication
Southern Illinois University

And, his teacher,

ELWOOD HUEY ALLEN MURRAY

Professor Emeritus and Director of the School of Speech
University of Denver
Director, Institute of General Semantics
Founder of the International Communication Association

List of Tables and Figures

Tables Page

Figures Page

Preface

Phenomenology and Communication have been related closely in the recent history of ideas. Yet, the association usually has "communication" located in the guise of linguistics, expression, perception, or cognate views of aesthetics. This is largely the unintentional result of professional disciplinary lines in which the daily practice of Phenomenology as First Philosophy tends to exclude in practice Phenomenology as a modality in the Human Sciences. In this context, the research reported here as a *Phenomenology of Communication* is an affirmative phenomenological hypothesis in the spirit of Maurice Merleau-Ponty's philosophy. The hypothesis is that philosophy is phenomenology, and, that phenomenology is a rigorous human science in the mode of *Communicology*—as it is in other disciplinary modes such as Psychology and Sociology. Indeed, the work of Merleau-Ponty stands as a paradigm case of this hypothesis. However, there is an earlier story to tell.

The introduction of *phenomenology* into the English speaking world began with the scholarly interest of communicologists, the persons whose concern is speech and meaning in the lived-world. It was, after all, C.K. Ogden and I.A. Richards who in 1923 first announced phenomenology in their classic work *The Meaning of Meaning: A Study of the Influence of Language upon Thought and the Science of Symbolism*. This volume in its famous "Appendix D: Some Moderns" lists as the first modern, the first person of the contemporary scene, one Edmund Husserl. Ogden and Richards go on to report a very brief précis of Husserl's *Logische Untersuchungen* and *Ideen zu einer reinen Phänomenologie und phänomenologischen Philosophie*. This appendix entry is abstracted from the syllabus for the course of lectures on the "Phenomenological Method and Phenomenological Philosophy" that Husserl gave during June 1922 at London University. Ogden and Richards quote Husserl's own programmatic words: a series of lectures to explicate "a transcendental sociological phenomenology having reference to a manifest multiplicity of conscious subjects communicating with one another".

And we should recall, as does Herbert Spiegelberg in his monumental *The Phenomenological Movement: A Historical Introduction*, that Wilbur

Marshall Urban in his 1929 *The Intelligible World: Metaphysics and Value* was the first person to introduce the American (USA) discussion of Alexius Meinong's "*Gegenstandtheorie*" in comparison to Husserl's logic. But as Spiegelberg fails to note, it is Urban's *Language and Reality: The Philosophy of Language and the Principles of Symbolism* published in 1939 that provides American readers with the first systematic discussion of the *Logical Investigations* and their bearing on the emerging science of symbolism (communication). This favorable presentation of Husserl's phenomenology of communication comes some four years before the more frequently remembered Harvard University Press publication of *The Foundation of Phenomenology* by Marvin Farber in 1943.

While Husserl was the focus of early work on the phenomenology of communication, it is Maurice Merleau-Ponty who figures in the contemporary discussion. We may recall that Georges Gusdorf's *La Parole* was one of the early works chosen as a representation of phenomenological thought for translation into English. It is a work that highlights the many threads of the phenomenology of communication that have their grounding in Merleau-Ponty, Husserl, and Roman Jakobson (the first communicologist to study with Husserl). Merleau-Ponty again receives focused attention in the two Duquesne University Press volumes by Remy C. Kwant, *Phenomenology of Language* in 1965 and *Phenomenology of Expression* in 1969.

It is in this context that I began my own work on the phenomenology of communication as a subject matter in both the disciplines of Communicology and Philosophy. As an undergraduate and then graduate student at the University of New Mexico, I was fortunate to study under a student of Wilbur M. Urban, Professor Hubert Griggs Alexander. He first introduced me to Merleau-Ponty and to the philosophy of communication recorded in his own works: *Time as Dimension and History* (1945), *The Language and Logic of Philosophy* (1967; 2nd ed. 1972), and *Meaning in Language* (1969). I then completed my doctoral dissertation (published as *Speaking and Semiology*) under the direction of Professor Thomas J. Pace. Pace was a postdoctoral student of William Earle at Northwestern University and did his own doctoral work under Professor Elwood Murray at the University of Denver. I should note as an aside that Professor Murray once taught an undergraduate student as a communication major who, in addition, was on the collegiate debate team. That student was Nathan M. Pusey who became president of Lawrence College and was the first supporter of one of his philosophy faculty members who wanted extensive release time to write a book. The faculty member was Herbert Spiegelberg and the book was *The Phenomenological Movement*.

During past years, I have had occasion to write several papers that are both a context and an interconnection for the book length discussions that appeared as *Speaking and Semiology* (1972) where I compare phenomenology and phenomenalism, as *Speech Act Phenomenology* (1977) where I compare analytic philosophy of language with phenomenology, and as *Semiotic Phenomenology of Rhetoric* (1984) where I suggest the emergence of semiotic phenomenology in the work of Merleau-Ponty and his student Michel Foucault. The best of these papers are collected in the present volume.

The chapters were edited to serve a number of purposes. As a whole collection, the book represents a systematic research program—both in philosophical theory and in human science application. It can be read as such by the newcomer to the phenomenology of communication. On the other hand, a certain amount of overlap is retained in each essay so that it can be read independently of other chapters by the scholar already familiar with phenomenological thought and procedure. A balance is struck between introductory and technical analyses, as well as between eidetic and empirical projects. There is extensive cross-referencing between the chapters so that the reader knows immediately when and where a particular point is treated in detail elsewhere in the text. Figures are used generously to assist the reader in following many of the more complex relations under discussion and analysis. While many of these concepts could be accommodated more easily by using a formal calculus, such a procedure in spirit would do violence to the essence of phenomenology. Human language diagrams and figures better represent the lived-experience of communication analysis. The author-date system of reference is used to assist the reader in finding quickly and easily the work under discussion in the text.

Let me close this Preface in the tradition of Professor Spiegelberg's Preface by noting that as we approach two decades of phenomenological research in the Department of Speech Communication at Southern Illinois University, a debt is owed to a series of departmental chairs for their sympathetic and continuing support: Dr. Ralph Micken, a Cicero scholar who championed the place of communication in the humanities, Dr. Richard Paul Hibbs, a distinguished teacher who exemplified the beauties of the English language in performance, Dr. Edward McGlone, a rare combination of humanist and statistician who likes to quote Husserl's *Cartesian Meditations*, and Dr. Marvin D. Kleinau, an administrator whose genuine priority is the education of students through a meaningful dialogue with motivated faculty—a priority he personally displays in person, in the classroom, and in the television studio. These gentlemen have chaired a faculty that is uniquely distinguished by the mutual respect and tolerance for one another that they bring to the department. The faculty is in its own way is a genuine example of the phenomenology of communication.

I also want to note the generous and affirmative support of former

President Dr. Albert Somit, Dr. John Guyon, Acting President and Academic Vice President, and Dr. Keith Sanders, Dean of the College of Communications and Fine Arts, for the faculty pursuing phenomenological research at Southern Illinois University. The result has been the emergence of a Southern Circle of Phenomenology within the normal structure of the university. The vitality of this interdisciplinary effort is due to my colleagues Thomas J. Pace (Speech Communication), Garth J. Gillan and Stephen Tymann (Philosophy), Hans Rudnick (English), Jnanabrata Bhattacharyya (Community Development), and Thomas O. Mitchell (Psychology). I owe a particular thanks to the graduate students whose dialogue is a constant stimulation in the *Phenomenology Seminar I: French Communicology* and *Phenomenology Seminar II: German Communicology*.

Acknowledgements

The following chapters are reprinted (with modifications and additions) by permission from publishers as noted. Chapter 1 from *Philosophy Today*, *23*(1), 1979, 3–15; Figure 1 in Chapter 1 from "Talking: The Semiotic Phenomenology of Human Interaction", *International Journal of the Sociology of Language*, *43*, 1983, 105–117 (Hawthorne, NY: Mouton De Gruyter & Co.); Chapter 2 from *Communication Yearbook 3*, ed. Dan Nimmo (New Brunswick, NJ: International Communication Association & Transaction Books, 1979), 29–49; Chapter 3 from *Philosophy Today*, *14*(2), 1970, 79–88; Chapter 6 written with the partial assistance of Dr. Rudolf L. Strobl [see Note 5], from *Handbook of Political Communication*, ed. Dan Nimmo & Keith Sanders (Beverly Hills, CA: Sage Publications, 1981), 141–167; Chapter 7 from *Communication*, *7*(2), 1983, 241–261 (New York, NY: Gordon and Breach Science Publishers); Chapter 9 from *Central States Speech Journal*, *21*(2), 1970, 108–116; Chapter 11 from *Review Journal of Philosophy and Social Science*, *11*(2), 1986, 55–70 (Meerut, India: Anu Books); Chapter 12 and the Appendix from *Encyclopedic Dictionary of Semiotics*, 3 Vols., ed. Thomas A. Sebeok (Berlin: Mouton De Gruyter & Co.); Chapter 13 from *Journal of Applied Communication Research*, *10*(1), 1982, 62–73; Chapter 14 from *Semiotica*, *27*(4), 1979, 293–305 (Hawthorne, NY: Mouton De Gruyter & Co.); Chapter 15 from *Dégres*, *1*(2), 1973, 1–7 (Belgium); Chapter 17 from *Semiotica*, *41*(1–4), 1982, 221–245 (copyright, the East-West Center, Honolulu, Hawaii).

The following chapters are printed here for the first time. Chapter 4 is from a paper presented at The Merleau-Ponty Circle, Concordia University, 29 September 1984, Montréal, Canada; Chapter 5 is from a paper presented respectively at The Merleau-Ponty Circle, State University of New York, 12 October 1979, Stony Brook, New York and as revised at the International Communication Association Conference, 26 May 1984, San Francisco, California; Chapter 8 is from a paper presented respectively at the Midwest Sociological Association, 19 April 1984, Chicago, Illinois and as revised at the Conference on Research Practice in the Human Sciences, 13 July 1984, Pennsylvania State University; Chapter 10 is from a paper presented in various stages of development at the Semiotic Society of America Conference on 9 October 1983, Snowbird, Utah, at the Society for Phenomenology and Human Sciences on 23 October 1983, St. Louis, Missouri, and at the symposium on "Oral History: Theory and Practice" held on 2 March 1984 at the State University of New York at Buffalo; Chapter 16 was presented respectively at the International Human Science Research Conference, 16 May 1984, West Georgia College, as revised at the Semiotic Society of America Conference, 12 October 1984, Atlanta, Georgia, and as revised at the conference on "Worldly Phenomenology—The Continuing Influence of Alfred Schutz on North American Human Science," 30 June 1986, Ohio University, Athens. Schutz conference papers are being published in book form (Lester Embree, editor) by the Center for Advanced Research in Phenomenology & University Press of America; and Chapter 18 is from a paper presented respectively at the Southern Speech Communication Association Conference, 13 April 1979, Biloxi, Mississippi (edited by S. Deetz) and as revised at the International Communication Association Conference, 26 May 1985, East-West Center and University of Hawaii, Honolulu. This Chapter 18 is an empirical illustration of Merleau-Ponty's theory of ideology as developed previously in Chapter 9 (1970), in a 1977 paper entitled "Critical Theory as a Philosophy of Communication" (see Note 4), and in Chapter 7 (1983). With regard to Chapter 9, I wish to note in particular the work (both published and unpublished) on ideological formation produced by my S.I.U. colleague, Prof. Jnanabrata Bhattacharyya, who is a specialist on politics and peasant cultures, and, Prof. Mark Hickson III, a fellow doctoral graduate from S.I.U., which has been a substantial influence on my own thinking about this subject.

Most of the research reported here was supported departmentally by assigned time for research at Southern Illinois University and by direct grants for research by, respectively, the S.I.U. Office for Research Development and Administration (1974 grant), the East-West Center Institute for Communication and Culture (1980 grant), the Mellon Foundation (1981 and 1984 grants), and the Danforth Foundation (1981 grant, with Dr. Randall Bytwerk). In addition, much of the research has been supported indirectly through my associations with the Merleau-Ponty Circle, with The Center for Advanced Research in Phenomenology, directed by Lester Embree (Duquesne University), the center's Committee on Cultural Studies and Institute for Human Sciences, directed by Algis Mickunas (Ohio University), with The Center for the Study of Cultural Transmission, directed by Madeliene Mathiot (SUNY-Buffalo), with the Graduate Program in Semiotics [Departments of Anthropology, Communication, Liguistics] directed by Paul Garvin (SUNY-Buffalo), with the Research Center for Language and Semiotic

Studies, directed by Thomas A. Sebeok (Indiana University), and, with the Simon Silverman Phenomenology Center at Duquesne University whose directors are Amedeo Giorgi, Edward L. Murray, Richard Rojcewicz, and André Schuwer.

Part One:

Philosophy of Communication

Chapter One

The Phenomenology of Human Communication

The Collège de France is a popular, yet respected, French institution. The college embodies an attitude of social consciousness that appeals to the citizen and the intellectual alike. The French government maintains various academic chairs at the college and on the death of a colleague, the collegium elects a new *professeur* to assume the vacant place of honor. But, such a professor does not teach according to our usual expectation. He or she is admitted into the college for purposes of research, dialogue and, from time to time, public lectures free to those who follow the intellectual life of Paris.

A new professor at the Collège de France is for me an exemplar of the familiar "fact"-versus-"value" paradox in human communication that the speech communication discipline has historically referred to as *rhetorical ethics*—or is it *ethical rhetoric* that we question? Maurice Merleau-Ponty (1963a, pp. 4–5) sensed this historical and existential paradox when he assumed the chair of philosophy at the Collège de France. At that time he said to his Parisian audience:

> The philosopher is marked by the distinguishing trait that he possesses *inseparably* the taste for evidence and the feeling for ambiguity. When he limits himself to accepting ambiguity, it is called equivocation. But among the great it becomes a theme; it contributes to establishing certitudes rather than menacing them. Therefore it is necessary to distinguish good and bad ambiguity.

In short, the speech communication discipline has in "rhetoric" a "taste for evidence" and in "ethics" a "feeling for ambiguity." The conjunction of these two elements in the communication process becomes the necessary and sufficient ground for certitude or doubt in conscious experience. The result of good ambiguity is therefore a *theme* for living and the counterresult is equivocation or bad ambiguity.

GOOD AND BAD AMBIGUITY

I find the problem of good and bad ambiguity present in the communication theory and praxis that we, by custom, label "rhetorical ethics." This is a generic reference, which has as its counterpart the predication "ethical rhetoric." In the present context, I take *rhetoric* to be pragmatic discourse where a social value is ascribed to the explicit behavior of persons. In a specifically phenomenological sense, rhetoric is speaking that creates an *object for consciousness* that speaker and listener perceive. In parallel fashion, I view *ethic* as a value generated in discourse that is implicitly a condition of personal conscious experience. For the phenomenologist, an ethic is the authentic choice made by a person in a world of other persons. Speaking, here, is an *object of consciousness*. I do not, therefore, accept the often popular notion that rhetoric is a value-free method (has no ethical constraint) nor that an ethic is factually indeterminate as method (has no rhetorical context).

The problematic issue with us since the Greeks is the *ratio* to be discovered between a rhetoric and an ethic. Or as Merleau-Ponty contemporizes the problem, the *ratio* in human communication is a matter of praxis: good or bad ambiguity is chosen in discourse.[1] That is to say, good ambiguity is "rhetorical ethics"; rhetoric as speaking *refers* to ethics as human values. By contrast, bad ambiguity is "ethical rhetoric"; ethics as value choices *predicates* diction (Habermas 1984a; Searle 1969). The conceptual grounding of the linguistic turn from rhetorical ethics to ethical rhetoric requires a phenomenological analysis that will uncover the relational presuppositions in human communication. As Frederick Sontag (1969, p. 185) argues:

> In its existence between the actual and possible worlds, ethics as a theoretical enterprise is doomed both to contingency and to the same lack of finality that characterizes all existence. The value norms involved are

1. Recall that ambiguity is a condition where two or more equally useful explanations are available; ambiguity is not synonymous with paradox, as we are often led to believe in various historical analyses of rhetoric and ethics beginning with Plato (see chap. 17, below). The nature of this "linguistic turn" is discussed by Derrida (1976, pp. 216ff.) and is included in the general discussion of "epidictic genre" by Perelman & Olbrechtes-Tyteca (1971, pp. 47ff.).

> neither contingent nor subject to change, but the context for their application is. Ethics transcends the actual world, and, just because it does, it eludes fixed expression. The number of ethical norms is actually finite and stable, but the possibles to which they apply are not. This indicates both the fixed [rhetorical ethics] and the unstable [ethical rhetoric] element in all ethical pronouncements.

I propose to accomplish a phenomenological analysis of the conscious relationship that unites *rhetoric* and *ethic* in the human act of speaking by entertaining three basic questions that bear directly on the fact-value *ratio* in human communication (Zaner 1975).

The questions that I set myself are these: (1) What is phenomenology?, (2) What is a phenomenology of communication? (3) What is a phenomenology of human communication? The progressive answer to each of these questions reflects a research method practiced by such existential phenomenologists as Jean-Paul Sartre, Maurice Merleau-Ponty, Karl Jaspers, and Martin Heidegger among others. It is a method with an American tradition as well and includes what William James called *pragmatism* and later radical *empiricism* (Merleau-Ponty 1963a, p. xi). The phenomenological method is what Charles Peirce (Brinkley 1960) referred to as *semiotic* and what I call *semiotic phenomenology*. All these perspectives echo Edmund Husserl's (1970a, b) quest for a return to "rigorous science" where analysis (*acta*) focuses on conscious experience (*capta*), rather than on hypothetical constructs (*data*), which by definition promote ethical crisis in a worldview (*Weltanschauung*). This failure of "data" is best known in the philosophy of science as Thomas Kuhn's (1962) notion of "paradigm crisis" and in social philosophy as Jürgen Habermas's (1975) thesis on "legitimation crisis."

It may be helpful at this point to recall the historical metatheory and methodology relationships operating in the philosophy of science among the concepts *capta*, *data*, and *acta*, and their respective methodological implications (Figure 1). *Capta* or "what are taken" are formally known as the Q.E.I (*quod erat inveniendum*; which was to be found out). It is a method for *systemic* analysis consisting of four steps: (1) the process of discovery or *hypothesis*; (2) the testing of possibilities or *verification*; (3) the description of results or *explication*; and (4) the achievement of understanding or a *proposition* (*Verstand*). On the other hand, *data*, or "what are given," are the formal notion of the Q.E.D. (*quod erat demonstrandum*; which was to be demonstrated). It is a method for *systematic* analysis consisting of four steps: (1) the process of invention or *hypostatization*; (2) the testing of probabilities or *versimilitude*; (3) the prediction of results or *explanation*; and (4) the achievement of knowledge or a *statement* (a *Verstehen*).

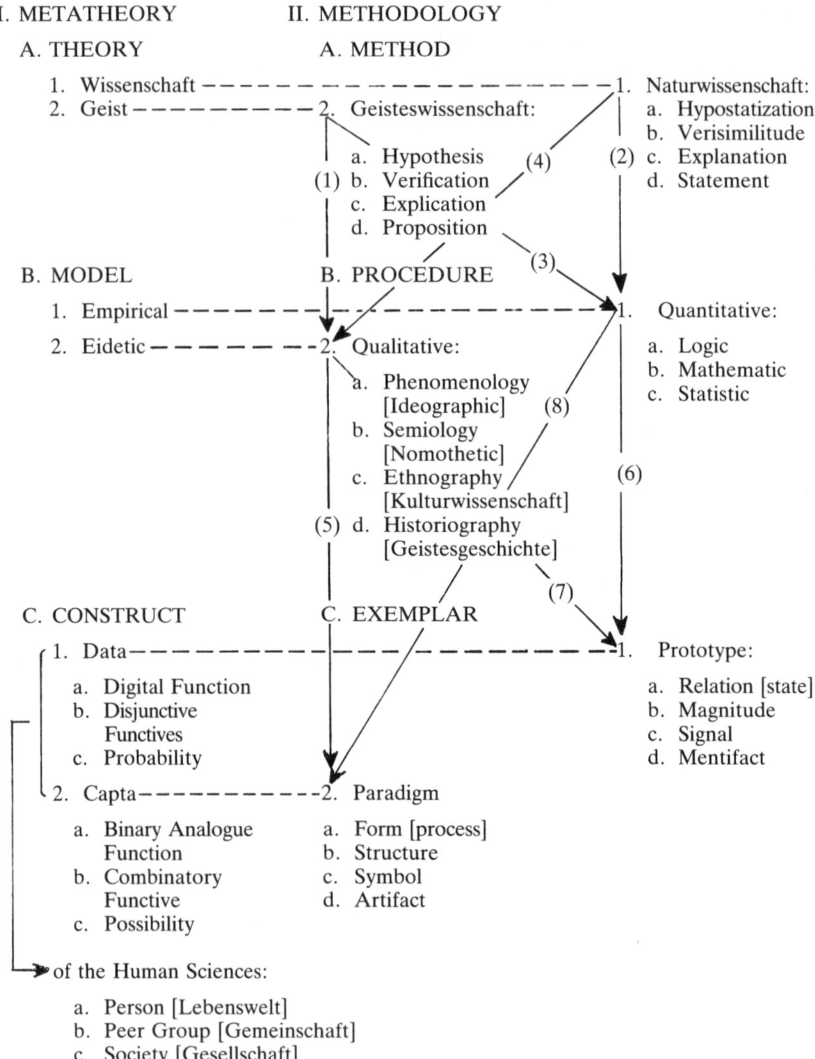

Figure 1. Metatheory and methodology in human communication

Key to relationships: 1. Q.E.I. (*quod erat inveniendum*: which was to be found out); 2. Q.E.D. (*quod erat demonstrandum*: which was to be demonstrated); 3. Praxis and 4. Application, Q.E.F. (*quod erat faciendum*: which was to be done); 5. Synthesis (synthetic judgment); 6. Experiment (experimental judgment); 7. Analysis (analytic judgment); 8. Speculation (experiential judgment; 'thought experiment')

In general, the human sciences (*Geisteswissenschaften*) study *capta* whereas the physical sciences (*Naturwissenschaften*) study *data*. The unifying force in both cases is *acta* or "what are done." Our modern view of *acta* is "science" where the analogue structure of *capta* and *data* forms a *ratio* or praxis. Here we have a theory-construction theorem where opposition (a digital *ratio*) between *capta* and *data* is used to validate their categorical identity. An illustration of this point is the familiar proposition that all communication is metacommunication. Hence, the digital *ratio* is the grounding for an analogical practice—that is, both *capta* and *data* are the practice of science because one set is the context for the other in *acta*. *Acta* as this metatheory procedure are formally known as the Q.E.F. (*quod erat faciendum*; which was to be done) (Apel 1967, 1972a, b, 1975; Orth 1973).

To summarize my point, the historical notion of "crisis" in the work of Husserl and the contemporary view of "crisis" offered by Kuhn and Habermas is a scientific concern with the bifurcation of *capta* and *data* in *acta*. That is, the human sciences are incorrectly seen to be or are treated as *methodologically* different from the physical sciences, rather than *essentially* different.[2] In consequence, phenomenology emerged and is now reviving as philosophy of science the attitude that all science consists in a methodological progression from (1) *capta* to (2) *data* to (3) *acta* and (4) the progressive repetition of the process in the accumulation and communication of research findings and applications. The "rigor" of science is thereby achieved by making the conceptual whole (that which is systemic) a dialectical function of its parts (that which is systematic) and conversely (the familiar logics: coherence, correspondence, performance, etc.).

PHENOMENOLOGY

Phenomenology is the name for a historical movement born in Germany with Husserl, Jaspers, and Heidegger, sustained in France by Merleau-Ponty, Sartre, and de Beauvoir, and complemented by a growing community of American scholars in the human sciences. This movement locates its purpose and direction in the theory and praxis we call *con-*

2. The "methodological" issue is literally one of *method* and *logic*, or in contemporary terminology, *praxis* and *theory*. The issue has two modalities in my discussion: (1) rhetorical ethics or personal communicative attitudes, and (2) ethical rhetoric or norms of social behavior. The essential, but not functional, issue is one of conscious experience—i.e., the differentiation and integration of (1) rhetoric(s) or rational action in society, and (2) ethic(s) or norms of personality in the social world (*Umwélt*). For a discussion and critique of Max Weber's notions of "differentiation" and "integration" as they apply to "act," "action," and "acting," see Schutz (1967) and chap. 16, below. On the relationship of theory and praxis as they apply to social behavior, see Habermas (1971a, b) and chap. 6, below.

scious experience—that is, the relationship between a person and the lived world (*Lebenswelt*) that he or she inhabits (*Zeitgeist*). As a theory, phenomenology concerns itself with the nature and function of consciousness. Inasmuch as consciousness is a human phenomenon, phenomenology is properly described as an attitude or philosophy of the person. In short, the descriptive adjective "existential" is now implicit in the term "phenomenology." As praxis, phenomenology operates with an investigative method that explains experience. The application of the method has the same range of explication that the problematic of "experience" has. In short, phenomenology is a historical movement; it is a philosophy in the existential tradition, and it is a research method exemplifying a philosophy of science. In subsequent sections I will take up the nature of that philosophy, especially as it applies to the human science of communication.

Phenomenological method is a three-step process that is synergistic in nature. This is to say, the methodology entails each step as a part in a whole, yet the very entailment makes the whole larger than the sum of its parts. In other words, relationships are created between "parts" and these relationships become new "parts" to be added into the total scheme. All consciousness is synergistic in this way: the moment that you move from step one to step two, you have simultaneously invented (experienced) step three—that is, the relationship between steps one and two. The generated relationship is a *presence* where there was none originally—that is, an *absence* or a contextual infrastructure that promotes the "presence." In a contemporary sense we usually refer to this presence/absence or activity/passivity phenomenon as the coincidence of consciousness (an implicit perception) and experience (an explicit perception), which is metaphor and metonymy, to use a linguistic example (Holenstein 1976). The classical name for this synergistic process is *rhetoric*, where the joining of arguments compels judgment—that is, the joining of the experience, as an object *for* consciousness, and consciousness, as an object *of* consciousness, produces perception and expression for the listener or speaker, respectively.

The synergistic process of perception and expression is formalized by Aristotle in his "syllogism" (Lanigan 1974). But a word of caution here. Aristotle literally formalized conscious experience by making *data* out of *capta*: human utterances are formalized and reified into abstractions—idealizations treated as realizations. In short, *statements* are made to conform to value norms and are thereby constituted as *propositions*. This is why a theory constructionist is always warned about material truth or essential understanding as a "reality check" of conscious experience on the logical validity of argument or formal knowledge. Put another way, the theory constructionist in the speech communication discipline is

THEORY	METHODOLOGY
Phenomenological Description	
1. DESCRIPTION (entails): a. Description; b. Reduction; c. Interpretation.	1. DESCRIPTION: (Thematizing the) 2. Interpretation (of the) 3. Reduction (of the) 4. Description (of the SIGN).
Phenomenological Reduction	
2. REDUCTION (entails): a. Description; b. Reduction; c. Interpretation.	5. REDUCTION: (Abstracting the) 6. Interpretation (of the) 7. Reduction (of the) 8. Description (of the SIGNIFIER).
Phenomenological Interpretation	
3. INTERPRETATION (entails): a. Description; b. Reduction; c. Interpretation.	9. INTERPRETATION: (Explicating the) 10. Interpretation (of the) 11. Reduction (of the) 12. Description (of the SIGNIFIED).

Figure 2. Theory and methodology of semiotic phenomenology (Lanigan 1984)

warned that rhetorical ethics (propositions) cannot be equated with or treated as equivalent to ethical rhetoric (statements). Such an equation in one case creates a "paradigm crisis" or failure of experience in the social world, or in the other case, the equivalence promotes a "legitimation crisis" or failure of consciousness in the personal world. The theory of general semantics is a ready illustration of this point.

The first step in phenomenological method is *description* (see Figure 2). The usual technical name is appropriate, *phenomenological description*. Rather than a mere truism, phenomenologists insist on the adjective "phenomenological" to remind us that we are dealing with *capta*, conscious experience. Singular use of the term "description" allows our thinking to slip into hypothetical constructs, into the creation of abstractions as things, as *constructs*. This bad ambiguity of created abstraction as formal multiplicity can be avoided by intentionally making the description come back to conscious experience. Husserl originally called this procedure the *epoché* or "bracketing" of conscious experience. The idea in this technique is that our thinking should establish brackets around the experience to be described, not so much to isolate the experience "in" brackets as to keep external presuppositions "outside" the brackets from influencing our description. This is to say, an attempt is made to analyze the experience in the context of consciousness and preconsciousness, rather than in terms of assumed boundaries of judgment based on historically generated value norms.

At this point, I believe that we can see that phenomenological description is rhetorical in nature; there is in the *epoché* an intentional control (*acta*) imposed on thinking and that control reflects an objective value, in a word an "ethic." Husserl's rigorous scientist would call this description a truly objective fact of human communication where *data*, *capta*, and *acta* merge.

The second step in the phenomenological method is *reduction*, technically referred to as the *phenomenological reduction*. The overt goal of this step in the method is to determine which parts of the description are *essential* and which are not—that is, merely methodological. In other words, we want to find out exactly which parts of the experience are truly part of our consciousness and which parts are merely assumed. The purpose of this second step is to isolate the object of consciousness—the thing, person, emotion, and so forth, that constitutes the experience we have. The usual technique for accomplishing the phenomenological reduction is called *imaginative free variation* (see chap. 15, below). This procedure consists in reflecting on the parts of the experience that have cognitive, affective, and conative meaning, and systematically imaging each part as present or absent in the experience. By contextual comparison and elimination, you are able to reduce the description to those parts that are essential for the existence of the consciousness of experience (gestalt). The description thus becomes a *reduction* or depicting *definition*, but in the phenomenological sense that my consciousness is based directly on my experience, not a *conception of* what my experience *may be*, which is the consensus method of crisis science. We must also recall that phenomenological method is synergistic so that the phenomenological reduction permits a more precise phenomenological description. In short, there is a geometric logic of inclusion operating as we move from description to reduction in the phenomenological method.

The third step in the method is *interpretation*. In a general sense this step is an attempt to specify the "meaning" that is essential in the reduction and description of the conscious experience being investigated. The technical name for this operation is variously *semiotic* or *hermeneutic analysis*. More recently, it is simply called *phenomenological interpreta-*

tion. Semiology is the study of sign systems or codes, so a hermeneutic semiology is the specification of the value relationship that unites the phenomenological description and reduction. For example, think of a conscious experience of rhetoric—a human utterance. You might describe such an experience as hearing a speech. You may further reduce this experience to your consciousness of being persuaded by the words you heard. Finally, you might interpret this experience as a commonplace belief that you have (consciousness). The commonplace is a code, it signifies the value—conscious experience—that functions as the relationship in the description and reduction: the speech *(acta)* given to you *(data)* that is taken *(capta)* as meaningful—that is, the signification of the language is known because you understand it. Hence, a "rhetorical ethic" constitutes a condition of good ambiguity because it is the conscious experience of the person who constructs the communication situation. In contrast, "ethical rhetoric" is a condition of bad ambiguity because it is the regulation of the conscious experience per se. The social consequence of this regulation is the legitimation of a negative social value (e.g., prejudice by stereotype) or a positive value (e.g., teaching by example) (Hörmann 1971, pp. 109–32). The ambiguity here is "bad" because the value assignment is purely arbitrary; hence the difficulty in assigning a value to a stereotype or exemplar in social situations.

Interpretation entails definition just as definition entails description, so the value or meaning that is the essence of conscious experience accounts for the way in which we are conscious and the way we experience. Put another way, we discover that the conscious experience that each of us knows as subjectivity in being a person is linked to the intersubjectivity of the social world—that is, interpersonal relationships define the person. However, before we can explore this fact of being a person, we need to examine the phenomenological nature of communication.

A PHENOMENOLOGY OF COMMUNICATION

A phenomenological definition of communication necessarily requires that our analysis proceed through a phenomenological description, reduction, and interpretation. First the description. What is communication? At a minimum it is an ecosystem in Anthony Wilden's (1980) sense of the term. That is, communication is the name for the reversible relationship between an *organism* (person) and its *environment* (lived-world), both of which exist in a mutual context or *Environment*. At its most sophisticated level this relationship is one of language (*langage*). Language is, of course, an analogue system in which semantics (*capta*), syntactics (*data*), and pragmatics (*acta*) are constituent parts (a code), each relating to the other as a matter of degree (Edie 1970). In other words, semantics is the meaning in language where language is a function of structure (syntax) and use (pragmatics). Likewise syntactics is the meaning in language where language is a function of content (semantics) and use (pragmatics). Last, pragmatics is the meaning in language where language is a function of structure (syntax) and content (semantics).

Our second step of analysis is the phenomenological reduction of the description we just generated as a conscious experience of "communication." When we consider that language is a key feature of communication and that language is an analogue, we see immediately that the nature and function of communication is one of degree. In fact one can easily imagine the organism and environment reversing natures and functions, for both are contextualized by the same ecosystem. For example, we can take the human personality and the human body as a case in point. Descartes to the contrary, the human body and personality often reverse themselves in life. Personality distress becomes body dysfunction in a psychosomatic state of involuntary paralysis; and conversely, body distress becomes personality dysfunction in a pathogenic state, as in suicide.

In more familiar terms, the language function of degree variation in the lived world of an ecosystem is what we would call a social dialect (*langue*) of language. The social dialect is surely language (*langage*), but it is language in its reversible form of constant degree variation. We are quite aware of this variation when we think about it. Semantic, syntactic, and pragmatic nature and function reverse themselves as Hjelmslevian dependencies. In linguistics these reversals are known semantically as metaphor and metonymy shifts, syntactically as paradigm and syntagm shifts, and pragmatically as diachronic and synchronic shifts (Lyons 1969). Thus the key feature of linguistic communication is that it is a contextual process. More specifically, let me recall that our phenomenological description indicated communication as a language state, but the phenomenological reduction disclosed that language only appears or is conceived of as a state. The language presence in consciousness is a process experience. So we discover that our original description of communication as synonymous with language is an inappropriately assumed abstraction.

Perhaps an illustration of the communication process would be helpful. The conscious experience of communication is always a triadic relationship of semiology among semantics, syntactics, and pragmatics. At any one time and place we focus on one of the three factors, but the other two are ever present as context. In short, we have a variation on the organism/environment theme. A specific linguistic example will help here. In careful discourse we can use the word "statement" to indicate a semantic function, the word "sentence" to indicate a syntactic function, and the word "utterance" to indicate a pragmatic function. All these function names are related by one essential nature, which we usually name by the word "proposition." It does not matter what word we may choose at a given moment, for the others are its context—that is the nature and function of an analogue: to set an essential boundary. The words "sentence," "utterance," "statement," and "proposition" all have the same sense but are capable of distinct reference; each can have the same reference but a different sense, as Frege (1948) demonstrated almost a century ago.

The third step of the phenomenological analysis is interpretation or hermeneutic semiology. At this point we have discovered that our conscious experience of communication is language in its analogue status as a social dialect (*langue*). What is the meaning, the value contained in this description and definition? Jaspers (1970) calls it "the will to communicate"; Merleau-Ponty (1962) describes it as "being condemned to meaning," having critiqued Sartre's (1956) theme of "being condemned to choosing" as a failure of hermeneutic analysis; and Heidegger (1962) calls it simply "talk." Saussure (1966) was the first to call it "speaking."

Most of us would use the word "speech" to describe the meaning state, whereas "speaking" describes the functional character (performance) of the conscious experience we call communication. But we must recall that state and process have an infrastructure, an implicit grounding relationship, which we have previously observed only as the explicit relationship called "language" and "social dialect." The infrastructure of act and action between "speech" and "speaking" is the same as the link between consciousness and experience. So just as we would use the expression "conscious experience," we discover *speaking speech*. Our conventional name for the conscious experience of speaking speech is the speech act or the *act of speaking*. In short, the hermeneutic semiotic of communication is the *speech act*.

We are now ready to take up the question of human communication. It may be noted that, except for two illustrations, human behavior has not been discussed in our phenomenological analysis of communication. I make this point because I, along with Husserl, believe in rigorous science. In other words, the phenomenological analysis of communication I just completed may, on careful analysis, apply to what we know of animal communication (zoosemiotic; see Sebeok 1977) and machine communication (cybernetics; see Wilden 1980 and Fauvel 1975).

A PHENOMENOLOGY OF HUMAN COMMUNICATION

We began this essay by noting that the phenomenological method is synergistic, that the method reflects back on itself in a constant refinement of reflective consciousness. By now it should be apparent that the three questions posed at the start are an explicit use of the phenomenological method—namely, phenomenological description (What is phenomenology?), phenomenological reduction (What is a phenomenology of communication?), and phenomenological interpretation (What is a phenomenology of human communication?). Each of these questions has itself been subjected to description, reduction, and interpretation. This repetition of method is what Merleau-Ponty (1962, p. 369) calls the *radical cogito*, and what Heidegger (1962, p. 27, n. 1) has in mind with his *daseinsmässig*. Simply put, the process is one of reversibility, of converting consciousness into experience and vice versa. In a linguistic example, the process is illustrated by the conversion of one part of speech into another. I think one example will make the point: "speaking." Is it a noun or a verb? To decide your conscious experience becomes the product of a phenomenological description, reduction, and interpretation, which generates the appropriate *answer* in the questioning situation (Fales 1943; Merleau-Ponty 1964b, pp. 3–4).

Now let us take up a specific answer to the question: What is a phenomenology of human communication? At the level of phenomenological description, our conscious experience of human communication is just where our analysis of communication per se ended — that is, the speech act. When the ecosystem of organism and environment is made the object of human conscious experience, we have not organism, but human being, and not environment, but life-world (*Lebenswelt*). A life-world is no less than what, where, when, how, and why a person lives. The discovery of the speech act as a relationship between person and life-world is also the location of a rhetorical ethic. It takes little analysis to perceive that there is a relationship between speech and act, just as there is a ratio between rhetoric and ethic. What we are describing is the highest content and form of communication — namely, the co-presence of digital and analogue relationships.

Let us take the "speech act" example first. As an object of analysis, a speech act is an analogue; any given speech act will be by degree like any other speech act. At the same time any given speech act stands in contrast to any other speech act — a digital relationship exists here. A parallel description exists in the case of a "rhetorical ethic," which is a ratio of action and act. Discourse may be perceived as exemplifying a rhetorical ethic because the rhetoric is in degree like all other ethical behaviors. At the same time the rhetorical ethic is a digital relationship in which the rhetoric (the action) stands apart from the value or ethic generated (the act).

We can now move to the second methodological step, the phenomenological reduction of human communication. Our task at this point is to specify what relationship in conscious experience is essential to both an analogue and a digital form of the speech act or the parallel concept of a rhetoric ethic. In as much as an analogue is always an exemplar in a set, we know that the analogue relationship between one speech act and another is a matter of degree. Whether I focus on "speech" or "act," one is by degree contextual to the other.

In recent years we have discovered this phenomenon as the harmony between verbal and nonverbal systems. In fact, we no longer use the specious digital designation of "verbal or nonverbal communication systems." We merely, but appropriately, use one analogue name: semiotic system. The point is: no matter how I approach the conscious experience of the speech act or rhetorical ethic, it will be an analogue *about itself*. In short, the analogue speech act is always a metacommunication as well as a communication.

What can be said about the digital act? Because a digit is always a self-contained set in contrast to another set or its absence (also a set), we understand that the digital relationship between one speech act and another is a matter of type or kind—that is, a difference of sets or categories. If I focus on "speech," it is not "act," and vice versa. Speech scholars used to call this phenomenon the conviction/persuasion dichotomy. If you have one, you did not have the other. Some persons, philosophers in particular, argue that the same point applies to rhetorical ethics. That is, if you have rhetoric, you do not have ethics and vice versa. Such a position is tenable only if you specify by assumption that rhetorical ethics never states an analogue relationship. In other words, a strict digital logic that disregards material experience compels us to say that rhetoric and ethic are two categories and have two equal combinations; one is "rhetorical ethics" and the other is "ethical rhetoric."

What is interesting in this busy work of digital logic is the discovery that in either combination the category "rhetoric" is *about* the category "ethic," or conversely. Merleau-Ponty expressed this discovery by saying that all human communication, whether verbal or not, is a *gesture*; Sartre on the other hand called it the *gaze*. Put another way, speech is about an act, and an act is about speech; a person lives a world as a rhetoric and the world is what a person lives as an ethic. The digital speech act is likewise always metacommunication (*acta*) about communication (*capta*/*data*).

Our phenomenological reduction of the conscious experience of human communication yields this result: rhetorical ethics as exemplified in speech acts is the relationship between (the "about" of) persons and their lived-worlds. The implications of this reduction—that analogue and digital speech acts are both metacommunicative (both about persons' life-worlds)—leads us to the third methodological step, the phenomenological interpretation.

By attempting to determine the hermeneutic semiology inherent in human communication, we are necessarily asking what value is to be found, what meaning generated, by observing that the speech act (*acta*) defines the person (*capta*) and lived-world (*data*) as "about" each other, as metacommunicative. Let us look at these relationships as conscious experiences. A person communicates and generates a lived-world. Such a person literally expresses a world; the person comes to inhabit the speech uttered—we all believe that *we* say! And, the world in which a person lives communicates to the person—for example, we all know and understand what's happening to us. Such a world expresses the person, or, more appropriately expressed, the person perceives a world. So we find that expression and perception are the same functional analogue relationship specifying degrees of difference in *consciousness*. However, the same relationship separates the expression and the perception as different, digital *experiences*.

The union of consciousness and experience, analogue and digit, expression and perception, person and lived-world, rhetoric and ethic, constitute *human communication*. The Stoic philosophers called this relationship of conscious experience the *lekton*, the sign that held discourse and reason (*logos*) together in all human behavior. We would describe the *lekton* of *logos* as the speech act, the rhetorical ethics, which is the same phenomenon as a person in a lived-world. In summary, human communication is a sign system of conscious experience, and conversely. Such is the phenomenological interpretation of human communications; it is a good ambiguity of rhetorical ethics.

COMMUNICATION LEGITIMATION

By way of drawing to a conclusion, I should like to take up a small portion of classical history that bears on rhetorical ethics. We are all familiar with the Greek *stases* or states of affair. The Greeks invented the *stases* to solve digital problems, to distinguish: what (*data*), how (*capta*), and why (*acta*)—that is, the respective problems of cognitive, affective, and conative meaning. We have retained this mode of thought, this digital logic. We variously call it the Q.E.D., analytic thinking, problem-solving, or "scientific method." However, we do our Greek forebears a disservice because in our fascination with the *stases* we have forgotten the *lekton*, the sign that holds the *stases* together, the analogue containing the digit. The digital logic, as an ethic in use, is rhetorical in application. We analytically ask: What is known? How is it known? Why is it known?

The analogue logic, the missing *lekton* in contemporary thinking, is the ethic—the human value. We call this analogue logic of rhetoric the Q.E.I., synergistic thinking, problem-stating, and "rigorous" or truly empirical science. Thus we need to phenomenologically ask, as did the Stoics in a different context: What do *I* know? How do *I* know? Why do *I* know? A rhetorical ethic is a conscious experience where the method for knowing and understanding that experience is phenomenological and existential (Q.E.F.).

In contrast, an ethical rhetoric starts with an *assumed* value—that is, answers to the questions "What is known by us?," "How is it known by us?," and "Why is it known by us?" always depend on consensus of either experience or consciousness, but rarely reflect conscious experience. A person who attempts to live in such a world of paradoxical consensus encounters what Gregory Bateson (1972) describes as the *double bind*, equally appropriate but conflicting signs in communication. The ethical rhetoric of the double bind drives persons and worlds crazy; we call it respectively "insanity" and "war" where the double bind of bad ambiguity is an agreement (analogue) to disagree (digit). Put another way, perception and expression are communicated as different kinds of experience, rather than the experience of different levels of consciousness (Shinner 1969).

Chapter Two

Theoretical Models in the Philosophy of Communication

Human science is not an invention. Like its counterpart physical science, it is an experiential and experimental discovery process in the empirical world of persons. And in both the human and physical motif, the constitution of research methods embodies the universal laws of thought that the ancients called *philosophy*. These classical formulas for exploring the theory and praxis relationship between human thought and action have their contemporary articulation in the *philosophy of communication* (Lanigan 1979a, b).

Communication models traditionally surface as paradigms in the standard areas of philosophical analysis. A basic reason is that the intimate connection among language, thought, and action leads most philosophers to examine their metaphysics, epistemology, logic and axiology in the context of communicology. In the current state of analysis, in the discipline of philosophy, communication models are progressively emerging as interdisciplinary paradigms in the research applications of the human and social sciences (Lanigan, 1982a). The accessibility of communicative behavior as an object of investigation largely accounts for this philosophic turn. Yet, the significant development of this renewed interest in philosophic models is due primarily to the refined theories that philosophy as a discipline presently offers for testing and evaluation by other disciplines. Not only the field of communicology, but those of anthropology, linguistics, psychology, sociology, political science, and similar fields are turning to philosophy for the theory construction accomplishments that are developed already and awaiting application (Israel 1972).

My purpose in this chapter is to explicate in an introductory manner several constructs and models that dominate the philosophy of communication. First, I indicate the basic harmony that exists between the theory construction process familiar to most communication researchers and the disciplinary parameters of the philosophy of communication. Secondly, I briefly review the major divisions of philosophy itself as a categorical grounding for the discussion that follows. Thirdly, I attempt to pinpoint selected communication theory constructs as they are studied in contemporary philosophy. Lastly, I explore the specific models of communication that function as paradigms in the philosophic schools of existential phenomenology, semiology, conceptual analysis, and German critical theory.

THEORY CONSTRUCTION AND PHILOSOPHY

Theory construction in any one discipline is usually so integrated with subject matter as to be ungeneralizable. The discipline of philosophy is no exception to this problem. However, one perspective that is profitable to explore is the connection of philosophy with theory construction as a problem in itself. In such a context, which is normally the province of the history of philosophy or the philosophy of science, it is possible to articulate construction principles that accommodate our basic interests in the communication discipline (Lanigan 1979b; Deetz 1973a, b).

A typical division of construction possibilities in the development of theory is the distinction among (1) research-then-theory, (2) theory-then-research, and (3) the composite approach combining the first and second approaches (Reynolds 1971). A succinct illustration of these approaches is Kuhn's (1970, p. 23) discussion of the process of *normal science*. The research-then-theory approach is a determination of what Kuhn discusses as *empirical facts*. These facts fit into a sequence that (1) reveals the nature of the object under investigation, (2) formulates the phenomenal description into quantitative laws or qualitative exemplars, and (3) articulates a paradigm for applied research.

The theory-then-research approach illustrates Kuhn's notion of *theoretical facts*. Such a theory construction procedure functions by letting postulates specify which facts are significant. Then the theory determines the ways in which significant facts are matched to necessary causality—that is, to axioms. The theory next articulates a research paradigm—that is, a theorem.

The composite approach simply joins the first two approaches together so that the researchers move from (1) *exploration*, where the phenomenon is located and then appropriately quantified or qualified respectively as *data* or *capta*, to (2) *description*, where an exemplar serves as a limited paradigm—that is, a model, and on to (3) *explanation*, where inferences are drawn from necessary facts to articulate the paradigm as a generalization—that is, a theory per se. In this three-part sequence we have the familiar causality of science: data, model, and theory as invention (see Figure 1).

Now, it is possible to relate the theory construction process to philosophy. The scientist starts research with some experience that is fairly claimed to be a "fact," or if you will, some given phenomenon. The philosopher begins in exactly the same way, except that the primary or brute fact must be justified before being used in valid theory construction. Put more concisely, science is a clear process that hypostatizes a connection from data to model, thereby producing a theory. Philosophy begins with a theory from which a model is abstracted as criteria for locating data. This three-part sequence is the normal causality of philosophy: theory, model, and data as discovery. Obviously, theory construction and philosophy are two names for the same cumulative research process that moves differentially among theories, models, and data, and is communicable as such. Some specific comparisons help exemplify this point.

The three approaches of theory construction have their equivalent conceptual processes in philosophy (Alexander 1972). Research-then-theory has its equivalence in the philosophic notion of a *necessary condition* (p. 273). Simply put, a necessary condition announces the minimal conceptual characteristics required for a fact; this condition is sometimes referred to as the discovery process in which an observation can be made. With the use of a necessary condition, we assert *that* something is, thereby making a metaphysical claim. By contrast, a *sufficient condition* is like the theory-then-research approach in theory construction. A sufficient condition indicates the minimal empirical characteristics that a fact can have; this condition is often designated as the invention process in which a conceptualization is made from experience. A sufficient condition tells the observer *what* something is, thereby making an epistemological claim. The composite approach has its parallel in the combination of necessary and sufficient conditions that constitute several possibilities of verification—that is, a truth function that is a logical claim. We should note that the research *application* of necessary and sufficient criteria produces axiological effects by creating sociocultural norms— for example, the study of law.

The philosophy of communication per se is important in the comparison of theory construction with the process of philosophic inquiry. The importance emerges with the realization that the articulation of a theory requires another higher order theory. That is, a philosophy of communication is a metatheory in the area of theory construction. Likewise, the articulation of any philosophy of communication is a metatheory where philosophy (or one of its subdivisions) is itself the object of analysis. In a historical sense, metaphilosophy consists in the interconnection among the major divisions of philosophy. Each division of the study of philosophy provides the necessary and sufficient conditions by which that particular division can be communicated—that is, expressed and perceived as a system of thought and action.

MAJOR DIVISIONS OF PHILOSOPHIC ANALYSIS

Philosophy as a discipline is usually categorized into four main subareas according to the type of justification that can be accommodated by an answer to the basic questions: What do I know? How do I know it? Am I sure? And, am I right? More formally, these questions relate to systematic inquiries that are known, respectively, as the study of metaphysics, epistemology, logic, and axiology. For our introductory purposes, some arbitrary limitations need to be imposed on the definitions and explications of these major divisions.

Metaphysics is a study of the nature and function of theories of "reality." With particular regard to communication theory, metaphysics concerns such issues as (1) the nature of a person and the individual contextual relationship to other realities in the universe; (2) the nature and evidence for purpose, cause, rule or intentional behavior; and (3) the problem of choice, specifically, freedom versus determinism in human behavior. These metaphysical issues are particularly illustrated in the communication model of existential phenomenolgy with its focus on "intentionality."

Epistemology concerns the acquisition of knowledge and, more fundamentally, the criteria for judgments of truth and falsity. It is appropriate to associate epistemology with the usual sense of the term *methodology*. Most methods follow the general pattern of factual (1) location, (2) definition, and (3) valuation. That is, the knowing process constitutes the origin, organization, and verification (validity) of content. Semantically the process is frequently specified as the progressive movement from cognition to affection to conation.

Particular epistemologies rely on one or more theories of truth. There are four standard theories: (1) *correspondence*, in which the identity or equivalence of facts is tested, (2) *coherence*, in which the systemic or systematic consistency of facts is measured, (3) *pragmatic theory*, in which causal prediction is the standard of decision, and (4) *performative theory*, in which consensus is the criterion. In many respects, these epistemological themes are the chief elements in the semiology model of communication with its focus on information boundaries and code conditions.

The third basic area of philosophy is logic. The nature of reasoning and the rules for correct or right thinking constitute the study of logic. A basic historical separation is normally made between rhetorical logic and symbolic logic. *Rhetorical logic* subdivides into deduction (rule + case = result), induction (case + result = case), and abduction (rule + result = case). *Symbolic logic* is occasionally called formal logic and consists of propositional calculus (either analytic or synthetic) and mathematical calculus (either differential or integral). Most logics, however, can be reduced to a set of necessary and sufficient conditions that operate with a predetermined number of values. In this sense, rhetorical logics are usually two-valued systems, which most communications theorists would recognize as a digital system, whereas symbolic logics are normally multi-valued and resemble an analogue system. The conceptual analysis model of communication is a good illustration of a logic-based theory of rule-governed linguistic behavior.

Axiology, the fourth major category of philosophy, is the study of ethics and aesthetics. That is, axiology is the examination of what human values are and the ways in which they can be symbolized or expressed. My primary concern in reviewing the German critical theory approach to human communication is its focal concern with ethics; yet the presence of social norms as symbolic artifacts—that is, institutions—requires an equal concern with aesthetics when the communication medium is a central factor in the human valuing process in society.

Given this brief review of philosophy as a discipline in the context of theory construction, I can now suggest the specific constructs utilized by the various models in the philosophy of communication. Certain schools of philosophy take as a focal point one of the traditional divisions of philosophy as the theory by which to locate data for a communication model. Having located these data, a particular construct is hypostatized as a key proposition in the model by which a theory can be articulated with the goal of achieving a paradigmatic philosophy of communication (Apel 1972).

COMMUNICATION THEORY CONSTRUCTS IN PHILOSOPHY

All the philosophic models of communication share a systematic concern with certain problematic features of human communication. I have selected four of these features and will treat them, for purposes of explication, as constructs in an overall communication theory context. Each construct has a dual function. First, it suggests the particular focus that a given model offers for analysis. Secondly, the given construct exemplifies one of the major divisions of philosophy as a research perspective. However, please be cautioned that the coherence of the communication theory context that I am constructing as a review and commentary is achieved at the expense of the particular philosophic models being discussed. Thus, my selection of certain propositions in the philosophic models represents a selective description and interpretation rather than a complete exposition of the given philosophies.

In particular, the construct *intentionality* is a key item in the existential phenomenological model and allows us to examine a metaphysical approach to research problems. The construct *punctuation* or system-code is a main theme of semiology and undertakes an epistemological approach. And, the approach of conceptual analysis locates the construct *convention* or rule use as a logical program of formation and transformation. Finally, the construct *legitimation* figures in the critical theory approach, which concerns the use of axiology in the creation of social norms.

With this summary view of competing models in mind, we can now begin a more detailed study of each construct as located in the general background of the relevant model. After this initial definition process, the analysis can then shift to a discussion of the models proper, which will be the next section of this chapter. It is necessary to review these individual constructs prior to a complete explication of the various individual models, for all the constructs are featured in each model. But, three of the constructs will always contextualize the fourth, primary, construct.

INTENTIONALITY

As with all the constructs I shall be discussing, there is both a usual reference for the construct meaning and a technical referent suggesting the philosophic model being discussed. In the case of "intentionality," the usual meaning is a sense of purpose or motivation in thought or action. Occasionally this purpose is built into the communication itself as a sort of thought in action. For example, the verb *promise* provides such a performative utterance. When I say that "I promise to meet your train," I utter a sentence that both announces my purpose and is itself an action—the act of promising.

In a more precise sense, intentionality points to and includes the object receiving the action of my speaking. From the phenomenological perspective, intentionality refers to that *object of consciousness*. This is to say, I as a person am a conscious being engaged in the communicative activity of perception and expression. Part of my inventory of experience is the unique human feature of reversibility. I can quite objectively convert my perception into an expression, and conversely. My principal vehicle for this feat is speech communication. Speech captures and sediments my perceptions in a form that can be expressed and shared with another. In reverse fashion, my speech is a system of perceptions learned from others in the form of their expression. Speech communication allows perception and expression to blend together and be the cause of one another, even to the point of experienced synesthesia, where one is the direct stimulus for the other (Lanigan 1970)—for example, as in oral narrative.

Normally a communication theorist speaks of encoding and decoding a message in order to distinguish "purpose" from "object of consciousness" in a discussion of intentionality. Both coding processes indicate a reified item: the message as intention. In most cases, the message is assumed to be a static construct that can be manipulated and examined for its salient features. One parameter for making this feature determination is the nontechnical sense of intention. That is, a message suggests one of its distinctive features through its characteristic purpose. This perspective is the well-known "effects" approach to message analysis.

By contrast, the phenomenologist as a philosopher inquires about the dynamic nature and function of the message. The message is not assumed to be a static construct. Indeed, no assumption is made about the message. The message is examined as part of its context or situation of use. The message is rigorously matched to its empirical condition of occurrence. It may well be determined that a major description of the message relates to its purpose or concomitant effect. Yet, the phenomenologist withholds that assumption as an initial criterion of analysis; the conceptual assumption of purpose is *bracketed*—that is, initially marked as a theoretical presumption that should not influence the analysis.

Given the communication context, the phenomenologist sees several values for the message as an object of consciousness. The message is an expression (one type of object) for the speaker, for the listener (a second typology), or for both (a third typology), or the message is a perception for the speaker (a fourth typology), or for the listener (a fifth typology), or for neither the speaker or listener (a sixth typology), and so on.

It is quite obvious that the typologies are extensive in what may be judged as their *typicality*. Hence, the nature and function of intentionality will vary with the essential features of the communication situation and the connection to the researcher making the analysis (Brandt 1970; Ihde 1977). The phenomenological approach to intentionality can stimulate a rethinking of many communication theory assumptions. For example, communication researchers whose orientation to intentionality is the assumed "purpose" approach tend to study the viewer in front of the television as participating in a "mass" media situation, when in fact (as a matter of phenomenal logic) it is an "interpersonal" media typology: one viewer listening (or expressing?) to one newscaster, for instance.

One of the key features of intentionality for the phenomenologist is the condition of *reversibility* between perception and expression (Ihde 1976). Here is the interest in speech communication. The ability of human communicators to switch back and forth between speaking and listening, to do both simultaneously, to remove the spatially real into memory, or project the conceptually real into memory, or project the conceptually real into time as a future expectation—all suggest the way in which communication is an object of consciousness and not the mere announcement of purpose (Lanigan 1977).

PUNCTUATION

A consistently problematic variable in communication theory is coding, or the nature and function of transactional boundary setting—that is, the problem of communicative punctuation. Punctuation as a technical term in semiology (Barthes 1968; Wilden 1980) derives from the theoretical practice in linguistics of distinguishing syntagmatic and paradigmatic elements in the formation of natural languages. For our purposes, these elements are best illustrated at the level of the sentence.

If you take a simple declarative sentence like "John ate the turkey," you will immediately notice certain features about this sentence based on your knowledge of the English language. First, it is easy to substitute another noun or pronoun for "John." For example, you could say "Sam ate the turkey" or "He ate the turkey." In all cases the noun or pronoun subject substitution has a paradigmatic relationship; each can substitute for the other in that place and function in the sentence. It is helpful to think of a paradigmatic substitution as being a "vertical" rearrangement of similar items. By contrast, syntagmatic relationships are the linear or "horizontal" relationships of typicality. In our example sentence, "John," "ate," "the," and "turkey" are all in a syntagmatic relationship. Thus, you can say that "John *hit* the turkey" because of your knowledge of English, which tells you that verbs follow subject nouns, and verbs are interchangeable given the linear context of the sentence originally used. In a different perspective, you might be childlike in using an unexpected, but legitimate, syntagmatic shift and say, "The turkey ate John."

Normally, there would be nothing interesting or unusual about these paradigmatic and syntagmatic shifts, but their presence in speech communication makes them a transactional variable that goes beyond mere language description. First, we discover that one shift is the context for the other. Paradigmatic elements contextualize and permit syntagmatic elements, and vice versa. Two static linguistic elements can now be seen as a dynamic control element in communication (Lanigan 1973).

Punctuation in its technical sense in semiology refers to the typological continuity or discontinuity that communication theorists usually describe as systematic and systemic features, respectively. Systematic features are essentially atomistic; they are constituents in a system. In this context, continuity relates to the syntagmatic function, for one type of speech communication used in a given situation suggests the ways in which similar communications can be made. Likewise, the idea of *discontinuity* (the French term *rupture* is more often used [Lemert 1981]) reflects the paradigmatic function. That is, one type of speech communication indicates certain transactional boundaries that by definition suggest what is and is not appropriate. Remember that punctuation is a boundary relationship that simultaneously indicates the technical condition of *information* as a systematic boundary or *context* of choice, and *communication* as a sytematic boundary of *choice* of context (Wilden 1980).

Convention

Rules that define the transactional boundaries of speech communication are conventions (Lewis 1969). Conventions are a logical outgrowth of both intentionality and punctuation. This connection relies on two key ideas in the conceptual analysis approach to communication. First, we must distinguish between natural and nonnatural meaning (Grice 1967; Lanigan 1977, p. 51). Next, regulative rules have to be compared to constitutive rules (p. 36).

We may refer to Grice's now famous distinction between natural and nonnatural meaning in discourse as the intentional theory of meaning. This theory is based on the description of meaning as the effect intended to be produced in a listener by a speaker through the listener's recognition of the speaker's purpose in attempting to communicate (Lanigan 1977, p. 53). Put more simply, natural meaning occurs where the speaker by means of speaking purports to act.

For example, my utterance, "I will meet your train," has a natural meaning—that is, the declarative sentence I just used has one purpose: to inform. Natural meaning suggests what the message has to do. In comparison, nonnatural meaning indicates what has been done by the message. Following the same example, my rephrasing of the commitment by the sentence "I promise I will meet your train" is a case of nonnatural meaning. In this second example, the meaning of the sentence is contained in the listener's recognition of my intention as embodied in my action: to promise.

The next step is to locate nonnatural meaning in the communication situation. Searle's (1969, p. 33) discussion of rules does just this. The so-called *regulative rules* are conventions that govern a preexisting condition or situation. That is, a communication exchange has certain boundaries that suggest a natural meaning. Social manners serve as a frequent example in the literature. Norms of appropriateness suggest what should be talked about and how the communication should proceed. Regulative rules often have the form: "if Y do X" or simply "Do X." With regulative rules a boundary already exists and, hence, is merely applied as needed. Eliminating the rules does not logically eliminate the meaning—for example, bad manners do not destroy etiquette.

On the other hand, *constitutive rules* bring a situation into being. The conventional practices indicate what must be done for the meaning to exist. Again, a frequent example is a game. For example, certain rules indicate what a game of chess is; eliminate the rules and you eliminate the game—that is, its meaning. There is a logical necessity between the rule and the meaning that is created thereby. Constitutive rules create nonnatural meaning. In the case of constitutive rules a boundary is brought into being; it is created. Constitutive rules create the possibility of behavior and typically have the form: "X counts as Y in context Z."

LEGITIMATION

In a simple sense, legitimation is the process by which facts and values are linked together. The opposition between conditions of fact and value is one of the classic problems in philosophical analysis. The basic difficulty is one of perspective, which counterposes the individual against society in the determination of norms of behavior or belief (Gellner 1974). The issue of legitimation is a central topic in all the philosophy of communication models with which we have concern.

In particular, there is the apparent connection between conventions of discourse and the facts or values that consensus creates by the use of that discourse. In a well known assertive argument, Searle (1969, p. 175) links the development of values out of facts to the communicative situation in which speech acts are self-legitimizing. Searle's argument is fairly straightforward. He contends that speech communication is an institution in society. Thus, a speaker participates in and thereby appreciates the institution, whether positive or negative in consequence. Participation that is factual in nature has the simultaneous function of giving value to the institution. Searle further argues that the meaning of language as a socio-cultural institution determines the ways in which a person is committed by the act of speaking.

As a conceptual analyst, Searle is concerned with legitimation only as a secondary consequence in the determination of speech act conventions. However, legitimation is the focal point in the German critical theory approach to communication, as suggested in the work of Karl-Otto Apel (1967) and Jürgen Habermas (1970a, b). For example, Habermas suggests that in a rational society a fundamental distinction can be drawn between (1) *instrumental action* (variously called "purposive-rational action") and (2) *communicative action* (Habermas 1971b). Both types of action emerge in the communicative situation where an individual legitimizes a social institution by the action of speech communication (Mueller 1973; Pateman 1980; Habermas 1979b).

Instrumental action is the product of "technical rules" that are derived from empirical knowledge—that is, empirical facts in Kuhn's sense of normal science. Every person develops certain "strategies" for making rational choices. These are based on conditional predictions about observable events, whether physical or social. Persons can then make choices that derive from "preference rules" and decision procedures in the value system they hold. In short, technical rules are implied deductions that can be tested as correct or incorrect. Hence, the action is or is not instrumental (institution) in that a purpose (individual) coincides with a reason (social purpose) or does not. Technical rules are either empirically true or analytically correct propositions—that is, legitimized beliefs (Habermas 1971b, pp. 91–92).

Communicative action, by comparison, is symbolic interaction among persons, or at least between two acting persons. "Consensual norms" direct such actions that indicate, in a definitional manner, the reciprocal expectations about behavior that communicators must understand and recognize. Consensual norms become objectified in everyday speech communication and are simultaneously enforced by means of social sanctions on misuse. Communicative actions thereby result in Kuhn's version of theoretical facts as legitimized behaviors. In sum, consensual norms are grounded exclusively in the mutual understanding of intention by the persons in symbolic interaction and are secured by the obligation of the persons who are in communication with each other as a shared act.

Habermas's theory of instrumental and communicative action suggests a new perspective for comparing the empirical infrastructure of the physical sciences (*Naturwissenschaften*) and the theoretical infrastructure of the human sciences (*Geisteswissenschaften*). On the one hand, we have a conjunction betwen nomological and instrumental knowledge and on the other we have hermeneutic and reflective knowledge (Wellmer 1971). Yet, in both cases there is the legitimation or valuing process that categorically forms facts, whether physical or social. Regardless of whether or not the valuing process is positive or negative, institutions are affirmed by the use made of them. Hence, individual communicative performance legitimizes certain norms of social competence.

In summary, my analysis thus far has taken up the general issue of fact versus value, consisting in a subdivision into intention and punctuation on the factual side, and convention and legitimation on the value side. I have also treated of the relationships among intention and metaphysics, punctuation and epistemology, convention and logic, and legitimation and axiology.

THE INTERPERSONAL COMMUNICATION PARADIGM IN PHILOSOPHIC RESEARCH

Intention, punctuation, convention, and legitimation as communication constructs are among the key elements in a theory of human communication. As such, this theory is a base upon which all the contemporary models in the philosophy of communication build from an interpersonal to a social level of explanation for communicative behavior. In the discussion that follows, I describe each model in terms of those four theory constructs. In this way, a parallel discussion emerges that allows for comparison and the contextual location of construct emphasis that makes each theory unique by contrast with the others.

THE MODEL OF EXISTENTIAL PHENOMENOLOGY

Phenomenology is a rigorous *form* of empirical research applied to human consciousness and experience (Schmidt 1967; Lanigan 1984). Originally suggested by Edmund Husserl (1970a; 1965; 1969) as a reaction *against* subjective psychologism in the early twentieth century, phenomenology represents a logical perspective in the social sciences (Natanson 1973; 1974) and natural sciences (Kockelmans & Kisiel 1970) that competes as a theory in both scientific and applied research. Husserl's work is known as descriptive or transcendental phenomenology. It bears the label *descriptive* from its early contrast with the intuitive theories of psychologism. In time Husserl's method became known as the transcendental form of phenomenology because he argued for an ultimate and ideal (nonempirical) form of logical description (1931); 1960; 1964; 1967).

Intention. We may for convenience subsume all of Husserl's descriptive phenomenology under the heading of intentionality, as a special form of the construct "intention." That is, *intentionality* is the location of an object of consciousness through a series of logical analyses that Husserl called *reductions*. There are three such reductions, typified as categories containing secondary reductions. The first category is the *phenomenological epoché* or bracketing of previous experience—that is, the correction of an objective attitude (often called the "natural attitude"). Husserl argues that the "rigorous science of phenomenology" requires a bracketing at three levels:

1. A *philosophical reduction*, in which the researcher removes epistemological presuppositions about the project—that is, does not prejudge the best method for research.
2. A *scientific reduction*, in which logical presuppositions are removed—that is, a particular logic and its values are not assumed. Instead, all possible values are manipulated in order to arrive at the appropriate logic system. This procedure is often called the technique of "free imaginative variation" (see chap. 15, below).
3. A *phenomenological reduction*, in which the researcher is sensitive to the ontological presuppositions being made—that is, the investigator does not assume a certain type or degree of "reality" before it is described.

Further, the phenomenological reduction is a demand for empirical experience as it is logically known to consciousness. Our normal sense of "testing" our experience captures this idea. The researcher does not hypostatize the ideal objectivity of the research observation, but puts the observation in context as a logical hypothesis.

The second category reduction that follows directly from the *epoché* is the *eidetic reduction*. This reduction is a procedure designed to locate, in a literal sense, the realistic elements of the description generated under *epoché* conditions. Husserl suggests two stages of analysis for accomplishing the eidetic reduction:

1. Focus on the abstract and general properties of, ideas about, or forms of the phenomenon under investigation.
2. Avoid the uncritical use of analysis that leads to differentiating and particularizing the description. A good illustration of this process is the development of a postulate from a research phenomenon we have empirically observed or logically described.

The third category reduction, which completes Husserl's method, is the *transcendental reduction*. At this stage, Husserl attempts to move from a philosophic position of realism to idealism. He suggests that the transcendental experience has three levels of description. Before detailing these levels it will be helpful to suggest that by "transcendental" Husserl does not mean an illusory or spiritual progression beyond the empirical. Rather, his meaning is closer to a communication theorist's notion of *transaction* or *encounter* as a logical structure of conscious experience. Schmidt (1967) provides a detailed discussion of the special logical meaning that phenomenologists attach to the term "empirical." An excellent review of transaction as a fundamental unit of communication in a sense that is compatible with Husserl's is the discussion by Smith and Williamson (1977), although these authors ignore the historical contribution of Husserl and phenomenology to interpersonal communication theory.

A transcendental reduction consists in the following levels of analysis:

1. A focus on the *Lebenswelt*—the "life-world"—of the person in which consciousness and experience combine into a sense of reality in both a preconscious/prereflective and conscious/reflective modality.
2. The process of an attempted "total bracketing" in which self, other, and world are explicitly describable.
3. The manifestation of "pure Ego" as a culmination of the reductions.

The transcendental reduction led Husserl to formulate the theorem that *subjectivity is intersubjectivity*. Thus, Husserl deserves credit for the discovery of encounter or transaction as the fundamental unit of analysis in communication theory (1960; 1967, p. 90).

Punctuation. With the historical context of Husserl's descriptive phenomenology complete, we can now turn to the work of Maurice Merleau-Ponty as a formal illustration of the modern existential focus in phenomenological research. Merleau-Ponty's existential phenomenology consists in three methodological steps: (1) phenomenological description, (2) phenomenological reduction, and (3) phenomenological interpretation (also called "hermeneutic or semiotic phenomenology") (Lanigan, 1972; 1984). In the continuing parallel style of my analysis, I shall examine phenomenological description as a form of punctuation, phenomenological reduction as a form of convention, and phenomenological interpretation as a form of legitimation. However, a brief comment should be made about the label *existential* in the present discussion.

Merleau-Ponty's work is an advance upon the work of Husserl. In many respects it is an attempt to correct several of the idealistic tendencies in Husserl's work that took phenomenology away from the empirical experience embodied in the person. Existentialism as a basically solipsistic philosophy of the subject was not uncritically incorporated into phenomenology. Rather, existentialism (historically) raised many issues that allowed phenomenology to explore the empirical nature and function of the person. Hence, existential phenomenology is best viewed as a form of "empiricism" whose object of analysis is the consciousness and experience of the person as part of the interpersonal encounter. In this sense, Merleau-Ponty is responsible for the communication theory theorem that the object of analysis in communication is always the person—that is, the lived-body (*corps propre*) experience. This theorem lies at the center of all research in the human and social sciences (Merleau-Ponty 1964a, b, c).

Merleau-Ponty's *phenomenological description* as a form of punctuation consists in three elements. (1) Perception assumes a primacy in the reflective process. (2) Consciousness is located in the *Lebenswelt*—that is, consciousness of the person (*corps propre*) is the discovery of subjectivity in intersubjectivity (Merleau-Ponty 1962). (3) A person becomes capable of the lived-body experience by means of consciousness, which is the informed connection among self, others, and the world (*être-au-monde*). In short, a person's perceptions set the expressed boundaries of transactions. A good linguistic illustration is the structural concept of language (*langage*) as the formal symbolization of a natural language such as English but devoid of personal or cultural use—as one finds in a grammar book. A more familiar example, perhaps, is our experience of learning a so-called dead language like Latin or classical Greek. In both examples, the speaker brings meaning to the language and brings the language into the world of pragmatic consciousness. Language is an empty shell before it envelopes the *Lebenswelt.*

Convention. Merleau-Ponty's second methodological step is the *phenomenological reduction* that illustrates the communication construct of convention. Here also there are three levels of analysis constituting the reduction. First, The traditional notion of the *epoché* derived from Husserl. That is, the researcher suspends disciplinary theory construction presuppositions deriving from a special interest point of view. Second, there is the creation of a *radical gestalt* perspective in which the research observer and subject are the focal point of the description. This process is frequently referred to as locating the *thematic* in the data from the description. Third, the researcher attempts to locate the prereflective source of the theme as derived in the description. That is, the researcher finds out what the conscious experience was prior to reflections and judgments about it.

Again, a typical linguistic example is the social or dialect level of language (*langue*) in which language carries a cultural meaning that is uncritically assumed and used by persons. Such a meaning is not the product, initially, of reflection. Early language acquisition by infants is also a good illustration of this linguistic phenomenon. In both cases, the investigator must discover the prereflective connotation that exists prior to the denotative use.

Legitimation. The third step in Merleau-Ponty's method is *phenomenological interpretation* as a form of communicative legitimation. There are four stages in this hermeneutic procedure:

1. The principle of reversibility is used—that is, locates those elements of the description that are present to experience and those that are not. These elements form in consciousness as a *radical gestalt* of self-other-world.

2. A *radical cogito* is produced as a result of the reversibility. The normal cogito function of "I think," which produces the reflective phenomena present to consciousness, reverses itself as absent to consciousness (removed in space and time), thereby becoming a function of prereflective capability, of "I can, I am able to. . . ." Ability and capability become contextual referents for each other in an ongoing process of transaction.

3. The result is the manifestation of preconscious phenomena. These phenomena are part of everyday experience, which is displaced in time or space for various situational reasons. Such phenomena emerge from the preconscious/prereflective state to become part of the here-and-now consciousness of reflective experience. Our usual sense of speaking (*parole*) is a linguistic example. The psychoanalytic technique of verbal free association, for instance, relies on the ability of preconscious themes to emerge in language before they are reflected upon by the speaker.

4. The end result is a hermeneutic judgment or specification of existential meaning—that is, the meaning of the phenomenon as the person lived it in the *flesh* (Merleau-Ponty 1968; 1973a; Lanigan 1972; 1984).

In short, existential phenomenology utilizes the paradigm of interpersonal communication to articulate its metaphysical starting point for research by focusing on the conscious experience of the person (intention), which allows epistemological boundaries to be set at the individual level of description (punctuation). By the use of logical inference, reductions of conscious experience (convention) allow the researcher to locate those elements of meaning that are empirically present in the situation as perceived or expressed (legitimation).

The Model of Semiology

Semiology or semiotics is the study of sign systems and philosophically has its classical roots with Stoic philosophers. Yet, most contemporary work bases itself on the extensive logic system developed by the American logician Charles Sanders Peirce and Swiss linguist Ferdinand de Saussure. We will not be concerned with Peirce's existentialism or very technical logic work, but we should note in passing that his systematic logic of perception and expression provides an often forgotten link (see chap. 12, below) between the intentionality construct of the existential phenomenology model and the punctuation construct of modern semiology (Freeman 1934; Brinkley 1960; Coward & Ellis 1977).

Intention. Saussure (1966) first argued that natural languages could be viewed with two conceptual values. One is associated with the "plane of content," which is the *signified*. It is usually helpful to think of the linguistic context, where we can generally suggest with caveat that the signifier is a "word" and the signified the "referent" for the word. However, we should be careful to note that the "word" can occur in three modalities: (1) as a sign in an abstract system (*langage*), (2) as a sign in a diachronic (historical) system (*langue*), and (3) as a sign in a synchronic (current) system (*parole*).

Given these qualifications, Saussure argues that linguistics is properly the study of language (*langue*), whereas the study of speech (*parole*) is semiology. This original distinction is now generalized to the extent that semiology includes all forms of communication, whether animal, human, or machine (Culler 1977). Yet, the focus of much research is on the ways in which signifiers and signifieds combine into specific sign systems. The special importance of semiology is its focus on punctuation that derives from the special theories of sign-production. Production occurs where signifiers and signifieds form syntagmatic and paradigmatic relationships—that is, they code contextual boundaries.

Punctuation. The conjunction of signifiers and signifieds as system values of expression and content (perception) formally constitutes the Theory of Codes (Eco 1976). Morris (1971) popularized a behavioral version of the theory with his well-known distinction among semantics, syntactics, and pragmatics. In brief, semantics is the code between signs and their referents, syntactics is the code between signs and other signs, and pragmatics is the code between signs and their application.

However, the sign systems advocated by Barthes (1968) are the stimulus for much of the current research in semiology (see chap. 17, below). He suggests that in a syntagmatic connection (recall the horizontal connection) signifiers are coded to signifieds at three levels: (1) a *real system* or reality level in which the signifier and signified are the same—for example, the word is the thing; (2) a *denotation* or metalanguage level, which is one degree of abstraction away from the real system where a *new* signifier is attached to the signified of the real system—for example, the use of a verbal synonym for an item already mentioned in conversation; and (3) a *connotation* where the signifier is used without any signified—for example, a specialized proper noun—lose the name and you lose the constituted meaning.

Reversing the code relationships is also important. Connotation can exist with the singular use of the signified. Where this is the case, Barthes refers to the communication as an example of the system of *ideology*. In contrast, the singular use of the signifier is the system of *rhetoric* (see Figure 41, chap. 17, below). Of course, both systems presume a paradigmatic condition (recall the vertical connection). That is, rhetoric has a paradigmatic code consistency of the signifier through the three levels of reality, denotation, and connotation. Ideology has the same consistency through the levels of the signified (Barthes, 1968, p. 89).

Convention. The combined paradigmatic and syntagmatic systems that Barthes calls rhetoric and ideology represent two examples of convention as a communication construct in semiology, but there are an infinite number of possible systems that signifiers and signifieds can produce within the context of communication (Barthes 1972; Leach 1976; Lanigan 1979b). These possibilities of sign production have been explored chiefly by Wilden (1980), Eco (1976), and Lyons (1977).

For our purposes, the best explanation of convention is the combined Theory of Codes and Theory of Communication that Eco discusses. The theory of codes begins with a context of *experience* that divides into (1) *content*, consisting in interpreted units (tokens) and a semantic system (types); and (2) *expression*, consisting in produced units (tokens) in a syntactic system (types). Both expression and content are connected by a *code* that results in *stuff*—that is, phenomena produced by the code condition. A theory of communication is then derived in which experience becomes a *source* converting content into *meaning* and expression into a *sign-vehicle*. The code is now a *message* produced in a *channel* by which the phenomena are known. The theories of code and communication provide, in Eco's work, the basis for a Theory of Mentions and a parallel Theory of Communicational Acts. Taken together these theories constitute a form of legitimation.

Legitimation. The social and empirical presumptions of semiology are apparent in the development of Eco's theory of mentions. For a clearer explication, I must reverse the linear presentation of elements for the theory of mentions, as compared with the format used above in the theories of code and communication. For Eco, the specific channel (theory of communication) in a theory of mentions is an *utterance* having the explicit form of a *sentence*. The sentence is a production form of behavior such that *mentioning* suggests a *proposition* drawn from a *world*. World, then, is parallel to *source* in communication theory and to *experience* in code theory. In the theory of communicational acts we begin with an overall *pragmatic process* in which a *sender* creates a *message* for an *addressee*.

Eco's semiology presents a straightforward philosophic model of communication by beginning with the epistemological considerations of a code theory (punctuation) leading to a metaphysics in the theory of communication (intention). The theory of mentions as a logical element (convention) grounds the theory of communicational acts as an axiological phenomenon (legitimation). In short, the semiology model of communication emphasizes punctuation as a starting point for theory construction with interpersonal communication as the basic research paradigm.

THE MODEL OF CONCEPTUAL ANALYSIS

Conceptual analysis is a collective name for the work of the Anglo-American philosophers who have their historical roots in the *ordinary language movement* that grew out of logical positivism in post–World War II Britain (Roche 1973, p. 39). As the name implies, the focal procedure in this model of the philosophy of communication is to analyze the conceptual nature and function of interpersonal communication.

Intention. In an attempt to further clarify the initial work of Grice (1967) with respect to intention and convention in speech acts, Strawson (1971, p. 150) suggests four issues that are the heart of the conceptual analyst's approach to interpersonal communication. Strawson first indicates that any account of intersubjective communication raises a "question as to *how what was said was meant* by the speaker, or as to *how the words spoken were used*, or as to *how the utterance was to be taken* or *ought to have been taken*." Secondly, the locutionary act *of* saying something is distinguishable from the illocutionary act performed *in* saying something—that is, natural and nonnatural meaning. Third, explicit performance verbs in the first person present indicative name *kinds* (types) of illocutionary acts. This issue is usually taken to be a truism.

Fourth, the illocutionary act is a conventional act—that is, an act done as conforming to a convention. These issues concerning intention emerge more explicitly in the interplay among punctuation, convention, and legitimation.

Punctuation. A fundamental discovery about the purposeful use of sentences in verbal discourse was made by the late John Austin (1962). He noticed that some sentences are factual in nature and function to the extent that they describe phenomena easily confirmed or denied by experience. That is, some sentences are simply true or false to experience. Austin called such statements *constatives*.

Yet again, Austin found that many statements that deal with questions of value, whether they be ethical or aesthetic in scope, are not simply true or false, because it is inappropriate to experience to make such a judgment. Rather, our judgment is more on the order of being *sincere* or *insincere*. Such a judgment occurs because the utterance of the sentence is itself an action and is merely appropriate or not. Such sentences Austin called *performatives*. For example, saying the words "I swear" as a witness testifying in a courtroom performs a particular *institutional action* by the very utterance of the words. In a similar sense, a performance sentence illustrating a *personal action* is the use of the verb "promise" in an utterance. We may judge oaths or promises as sincere or insincere, but not as true or false in a logical sense. Yet, the constative/performative distinction left Austin with as many questions as answers, for there is too much of the interpersonal situation being ignored in the simple utterance classification.

Convention. Searle (1969) expands on Austin's work by making the theory of performative utterances match the theory of nonnatural meaning in a new theory of *speech acts*. First, we should note that Austin provides a technical division of performative utterances into three classes. Initially there are *locutions* that belong to a natural language, but are devoid of context. Second, Austin suggests that some locutions take on a semantic *force* and become *illocutions*. That is, the action performed by the mere utterance of the statement has a communicative impact, although it is not necessarily a behavioral reaction or response. Where there is such a reaction as a feedback element or behavioral effect in the situation, you have a *perlocutionary act*.

Searle argues that there is no logical differentiation in Austin's classification. In fact, Searle maintains that all utterances fit the category of illocutionary acts and are what he calls *propositional acts*. His formal theory is beyond the scope of this chapter. However, he does present a simplified version as a set of propositions that indicates the position held by most conceptual analysts working with language.

The theory of speech acts (Searle 1967) consists of the following set of postulates:

1. Speaking a language is engaging in a rule-governed form of behavior.
2. The minimal unit of communication is the illocutionary act.
3. Saying something and meaning it involves saying it plus:
   (a) intending to produce certain illocutionary effects [force] in a hearer (which effects are a function of the rules governing the sentence uttered);
   (b) intending to produce these effects by getting the hearer to recognize intention "a," and
   (c) intending to get him to recognize intention "a" by means of his knowledge of the rules governing the sentence uttered.
4. Whatever can be meant can be said.
5. Systems of semantic rules are constitutive and not regulative.

Legitimation. Searles argues that language is a rule-governed form of behavior that must be analyzed in "idealized forms of speech behavior" (1967, p. 120). In this context he says that the constitutive rules that naturally exist as part of any language combine with Grice's theory of nonnatural meaning to result in propositional acts. That is, the meaning of an utterance by a speaker is the listener's recognition of a particular purpose on the part of the speaker in making a given utterance. The speech act thereby has an explicit meaning whose value is the proposition that the speaker and listener mutually recognize. This theory seems to work only when cast in an ideal, hypothetical situation and is consequently limited in its application to actual conversational analysis (Lanigan 1977), although it has stimulated a great deal of theoretical work, like that of Sadock (1974).

In short, the conceptual analysis model begins with a logical approach to speech communication (convention) as a basis for its idealized metaphysics of nonnatural meaning (intention). By distinguishing types of utterances on a fact-versus-value basis, an epistemological priority (punctuation) is assigned to performative speech acts that have the special quality of being neither true nor false, but sincere or not (legitimation) as an axiological condition.

THE MODEL OF CRITICAL THEORY

The critical theory model of interpersonal communication derives from a long historical tradition in German philosophy and sociology that is essentially neo-Marxist in orientation (Jay 1973; Schroyer 1975; Adorno 1976). Because much of that tradition applies to the problems of speech communication at a social level in a way suggested by Jürgen Habermas (1971a, b; 1973; 1976; 1979b; 1984), I shall deal exclusively with selected portions of his theory of universal pragmatics, with special attention to the issue of *communicative ethics*. Limiting the analysis in this manner provides a direct connection between critical theory and the speech act theory of conceptual analysis just discussed (Giddens 1976).

Intention. Habermas (1970a) locates intention as the object of consciousness in the general theory parameters of psychoanalysis. Explicitly he argues that psychoanalysis gives the researcher: (1) a preconception of the structure of nondistorted ordinary communication, (2) an attribution of the systematic distortion of communication to the confusion of two developmental levels of symbols organization, the prelinguistic and linguistic, and (3) a theory of deviant socialization to explain the origin of deformation.

On this psychoanalytic base, Habermas builds a parallel set of theoretical propositions that indicate the meaning parameters in *normal communication.* First, in the case of nondeformed language games there is a congruency of all three levels of communication as presented in the psychoanalytic model above. Second, normal communication conforms to intersubjectively recognized rules; it is public in this sense. Third, speakers are aware of the categorical difference between subject and object in normal speech. Fourth, normal communication provides a contextual situation in which an intersubjectivity of mutual understanding, which guarantees ego-identity, develops and is maintained in the relationship between individuals who acknowledge one another. Finally:

> Normal speech is distinguished by the fact that the sense of substance and causality, of space and time, is differentiated according to whether these categories are applied to the objects within a world or to the linguistically constituted world itself, which allows for the mutuality of speaking subjects [Habermas, 1970a, p. 212].

Punctuation. The boundary limitation for the analysis of normal communication results from two postulates that Habermas draws from his set of five propositions. He argues that psychoanalysis in the study of communication relies on a genetic connection beyond successive phases of human symbol organization. First, "the archaic symbol-organization, which resists the transformation of its contents into grammatically regulated communication, can only be disclosed on the basis of the data of speech pathology and by means of the analysis of dream material" (1970a, p. 212). Second, the symbol organization that the psychoanalyst utilizes is a theoretical construct in that it genetically precedes language. In brief, Habermas goes on to suggest that such a theoretical construct presumes a theory of communicative competence modeled on Chomsky's model of linguistic competence/performance.

Habermas's theory of communicative competence is a combination of the problem as defined by psychoanalysis and the method of ordinary language analysis suggested by the conceptual analysts: Austin, Grice, and Searle. In particular, Habermas (1979b) adopts Searle's (1967; 1969) general formulation of the speech act theory and applies it in the *social* context of communication (Sullivan 1978). That is, an interpersonal model of communication at the performance level is generalized to a model of social discourse (as a legitimation process) at the competence level. In this generalization of social levels from the individual to the mass, Habermas maintains the ideal speech situation as a construct. Let me simply indicate that there are serious problems in maintaining such an ideal in the analysis of empirical social research (Wellmer 1976).

Habermas offers the following set of theoretical propositions, which correspond at the social level to those that Searle (1967; 1969) presents for the interpersonal speech act:

1. The personal pronouns and their derivatives form a reference system between potential speakers. The identity of meanings, the foundation of every communication, is based on intersubjectively valid rules—that is, at least two speakers understand the meaning of a symbol on the basis of reciprocal recognition.
2. The deictic expressions of space and time, as well as articles and demonstrative pronouns, form the reference system of possible denotations.
3. Forms of address (vocative), forms of social contact (greeting), forms of speech introduction and speech conclusion, indirect discourse, questions and answers, are performatory in that they are directed at the act of speaking as such.
4. The performatory speech acts form a system that finally enables us to mark the basic differentiations fundamental for any speech situation. Thus system relationships are formed between:
   (a) being and appearance;
   (b) being and essence; and
   (c) fact and value—what is and what ought to be (Habermas 1979b).

Convention. The summary result that Habermas's model of communication achieves is a specification of the social levels of communication and the parallel validity claim that can be based on speech acts as rule-governed behavior with social import. By examining the formation and transformation of speech acts, Habermas (1976) arrives at two levels of communication. First, the level of intersubjectivity at which speaker and hearer, through illocutionary acts, bring about an interpersonal relationship that allows them to achieve mutual understanding. Secondly, the "level of objects in the world, or states of affair about which they would want to achieve a consensus in terms of the communicative role as laid down in the level of intersubjectivity" (p. 159).

In principle, therefore, every competent speaker has the responsibility of choosing among three modes of social communication (Habermas 1979b, p. 58). First, communication to state a proposition that can be illustrated in the propositional attitude of a nonparticipating third person who hears a speech act. Second, communication to stress an interpersonal relationship as such, as illustrated in the performative attitude of a participant conforming to the expectations of a second person. Third, communication to express an intention as such—that is, a speaker presents himself before others. Each form of communication carries a claim to validity that is situationally recognized for its value (Hooft 1976).

Legitimation. Habermas makes an explicit connection between communication and axiology, both in terms of how human communication leads to ethical judgments about persons and in terms of the social aesthetic values that dominate personal existence. Ultimately, his concern is with the special connection in communication by which personal ethics and social aesthetics form into political norms of existence—that is, social legitimation.

In careful propositional language, Habermas (1975) suggests that "only *communicative ethics* guarantees the generality of admissible norms and the autonomy of acting subjects solely through the discursive redeemability of the validity claims with which such norms appear" (p. 89). We should recall that communication is an action that deals with theoretical facts—values that have a pragmatic effect because they are formed in speech acts. In this context, Habermas advances three basic *pragmatic universals* derived from the linguistic universals apparent in all speech communication.

First, "each specific language offers a reference system which permits a sufficiently reliable identification of something in the world about which one would want to make propositions." Second, "each specific language offers a *system* of personal pronouns and a system of speech acts with the aid of which we can bring about interpersonal relationship." And third, "each particular language offers a *system of intentional expressions* for the self-presentation of subjectivity which, in spite of the degree of variation of its expression in particular languages, reflects the system of ego-deliminations" (Habermas 1975, p. 161).

For Habermas, then, social and political legitimation of personal and public action, whether technically instrumental or communicative, results in the formation of a communication ethic. That is, the rational society that manifests a universal pragmatics is a transformation of "the communication community (*Kommunikationsgemeinschaft*) of those affected, who as participants in a practical discourse test the validity claims of norms, and, to the extent that they accept them with reasons, arrive at the conviction that in the given circumstance the proposed norms are 'right'" (p. 105). A parallel argument in non-Marxist terms is made by Apel (1967; 1980).

In short, the critical theory model begins with an axiological pragmatics (legitimation) of speech communication, based on the logical notion of ideal speech acts (convention). For Habermas, as a critical theorist, speech acts are part of the symbol formation process (punctuation) that derives its epistemological stages of development from the metaphysical approach of Freudian psychoanalysis and its theory of consciousness (intention). Thus, a theory of a rational society is an ideal generalized from a theory of normal communication in the rational person (Habermas 1979b, pp. 67–68).

CONCLUSION

Throughout this chapter, I have demonstrated a theoretical parallel among the major divisions of philosophy (metaphysics, epistemology, logic, axiology), the key constructs in communication theory (intention, punctuation, convention, legitimation), and selected models in the philosophy of communication (existential phenomenology, semiology, conceptual analysis, critical theory). Although I emphasize the particular format that each philosophic position takes in respect to the various communication constructs, the positions do share a common reliance on the interpersonal aspects of Communicology as a general philosophic project in the human sciences.

The best articulation of the contributions of each model in the philosophy of communication is, I believe, the following set of theorems. They may be regarded as a preliminary attempt to state .the fundamental constructs required by a theory of communicology with a well-founded philosophical base.

THEOREMS

1. The theorem of intentionality. *Conscious experience is the minimal unit of meaning in communication*. This theorem derives from Husserl's proposition that subjectivity is intersubjectivity. It is associated with Merleau-Ponty's, Schutz's and Foucault's proposition that the person is the object of analysis in conscious behavior.

2. The theorem of punctuation. *The reversibility of expression and perception is the minimal system-code for communication*. This theorem is drawn from the proposition advanced by Peirce, Saussure, Hjelmslev, and Barthes that speech entails levels of expression and content individually and jointly the result of sign-production. Eco's construction of the theory of communicational acts on the basis of sign-production further supports the theorem.

3. The theorem of convention. *The transaction is the minimal rule-governed behavior required for communication*. This theorem expresses the logical elements in discourse discovered by Austin, Grice, and Searle. The analogue nature of communicative performance provides analytic

insights about the constitution of speech communication—insights obscured by simple linguistic description.

4. The theorem of legitimation. *Interpersonal speech competency is the minimal norm in society for communication.* This theorem formulates a key relationship in which historical fact/value and individual/mass bifurcations are resolved as a ratio of communicative actions. For Apel and Habermas, the conjunction of hermeneutic and normative actions explains the community achieved by persons in society.

These theorems suggest certain implications for research and the consequent refinement of communication theory utilizing the philosophic paradigm. First, the philosophy of communication is a form of rigorous theory construction. It provides a systemic and systematic review of the theoretical propositions that describe communication. Secondly, these propositions explicitly provide a context for qualitative and quantitative analysis and synthesis in the *human science* of *communicology*. Such a critique provides, in addition, a problem-centered investigation and explication of communication behavior that avoids disciplinary limitations based on preconceived methodological paradigms for theory and praxis. In short, the philosophic models may permit us to encounter a basic empirical discovery: the philosophy of communication discloses a phenomenal logic of the person in which consciousness constitutes a world of others in experience.

Part Two:

Communicology

[Section One: EIDETIC RESEARCH]

Chapter Three

Merleau-Ponty's Phenomenology of Communication

During his inaugural lecture on January 15, 1953, at the Collège de France, Maurice Merleau-Ponty asserted that "the more energetic our intention to see the things themselves, the more the appearances by which they are expressed and the words by which we express them will be interposed between the things and us" (1963a, p. 20). With this remark he emphasizes the philosophic concern with language in its modalities of expression and perception. It is a major theme of those French philosophers of the Paris school of existentialism who have developed projects beyond the pioneering work of the founder of modern phenomenology, Edmund Husserl (see chap. 12, below).

In particular, Merleau-Ponty's philosophic regard for language and reality as existential styles of expression and perception is a central issue in his phenomenology. His original and provocative philosophy emerges in a process that turns the freedom of phenomenological method—that is, description, reduction, and interpretation—to the service of existential ontology in a rigorous attempt to locate meaning as the human situation. This is to say, Merleau-Ponty presents the process nature of personal and interpersonal *Being* by examining the lived-encounters of perceptive and expressive *signs* that are experienced as communication. As he (1962, p. 50) puts it, "the recognition of phenomena, then, implies a theory of reflection and a new *cogito*."

In this chapter I wish to suggest that Merleau-Ponty's original and distinct formulation of phenomenology is a semiotic system or synergic theory of signs founded on an interplay of: (1) the recognition of the *presence* of phenomena by description—that is, a "primacy of perception";

(2) the reflective location of meaning by structural reduction—that is, a "primordial expression"; and (3) the new *cogito* of intentionality or lived-experience in which one recognizes the "I am able to," the "I can," rather than the Cartesian formula, the "I think," the "I feel."

In short, I want to argue that Merleau-Ponty's theory of communication or theory of intercorporeal Being is the precise formulation of a semiotic phenomenology of human existence-as-lived. In this sense Merleau-Ponty (1963a, p. 57) correctly hypostatizes that "each philosophy is also an architecture of signs. It constitutes itself in close relation with other modes of exchange which make up our historical and social life." Hence, the immediate task is to examine respectively the modes of semiotic exchange that are perception and expression: (1) the primacy of perception as method; (2) expression as the primordiality of Being; and (3), semiology as a phenomenology of communication.

THE PRIMACY OF PERCEPTION AS METHOD

Merleau-Ponty regularly defines phenomenology as the study of essences. And as previously noted, the study consists in the description, reduction, and intentionality of phenomena to determine, respectively, content, structure, and existential meaning-as-lived. He states:

> But this also means that one does not go beyond the world except by entering into it and that the spirit makes use of the world, time, speech, and history in a single movement and animates them with a meaning which is never used up. It would be the function of philosophy, then, to record this passage of meaning rather than to take it as an accomplished fact [1963a, p. 9].

In the case of human communication, Merleau-Ponty's phenomenology concerns itself with the essences or signs of personal perception and expression that combine acts of consciousness and sensitive awareness into public encounters. Such public encounters become fixed as personal and intersubjective history. This is to say, essences are signs reflecting and constituting meaning-as-lived. Put another way, communication among persons is a holistic system of signs moving through the synergism of individual perception and expression toward a state of equilibrium that is personal or shared meaning. Thus, Merleau-Ponty's phenomenology requires a study of the essence of communication—that is, a study of signs, as three progressive, yet simultaneous steps of reflection.

According to Merleau-Ponty one is first required to engage in the phenomenological description of the communication act as the propagation and reception of signs-as-meaningful. This initial analysis of the simultaneity of expression and perception requires a fundamental understanding of the personal experience of self, human embodiment. The consciousness of embodiment is precisely an awareness and understanding of the unitary *presence* of mind and body *living* in the acts of expression and perception that are the synoptic acts of *doing* that create *speaking* and *silence*. The human person as Body-subject (an unhyphenated existence!) achieves intersubjectivity or communication because he lives the simultaneous separation and union of perception and expression *in* himself and *with* others. This is to suggest that I think and I feel or I conceive and I sense, but such a separation and union of mind and body is descriptive only of *living*. Living is a synoptic whole greater than the sum of its parts and not divisible into its parts. As Merleau-Ponty (1963a, pp. 28–29) formulates this idea, "in order to be themselves, freedom and spirit must witness themselves in matter or in the body; that is to say, they must express themselves."

In the descriptive process of specifying the signs that constitute the communication *Gestalt*, there is a "primacy of perception" for Merleau-Ponty. The content of communication is experienced as a *perception of*, a *consciousness of*, what is expressed by oneself or others. The phenomena of perception allow one to "see" the essential modality or so-called objectivity of lived-experience, which is communicated. The descriptive procedure allows the Body-subject to be conscious of the reality that is lived in the many acts of personal becoming. That is, meaning takes on reality by functioning as an orientation in a person's life-world (*Lebenswelt*). Persons come to discover and recognize their Body-subject as an instrument of the ability to live authentically. Thus, the human personality senses and knows the direction of its very Being as s/he arrives at the threshold of an intentional object. In short, phenomena become meaningful when experienced-as-lived, experienced-as-signs, rather than as conceived, as sensed symbols.

Description, then, captures and encloses the meaning present in the consciousness of myself and others that constitutes a shared history of inhabitants. As Merleau-Ponty (1963a, p. 11) explains, "communicative life" is history in the existential sense of human *immanence*. Description in the phenomenological sense is precisely the location of immanent signs that are expressively and perceptively co-present in lived-behavior.

The second step in philosophic analysis for Merleau-Ponty is a "radical reduction" or the specification of the structure of phenomena—in a phrase, the phenomenological reduction of the essential *Gestalt*. The process is "radical" because it is synergic rather than synthetic in the Hegelian sense. The structural estimation of personal lived-experience is descriptive of both self-realization and the empathy acknowledged in relations with other persons. For example, speakers encounter the structure of communication when they are conscious of the meaning that listeners infer precisely when listeners' responses or lack of response is also determinate of speakers' perceptions of their own expression, and indeed, perception of their ability to further engage the communicative act. As Merleau-Ponty (1964c, p. 97) concisely states, "to the extent that what I say has meaning, I am a different 'other' for myself when I am speaking; and to the extent that I understand, I no longer know who is speaking and who is listening."

Yet, one must go beyond the superficial designation of essential structural relationships to the existential structure of meaning. That is, one must "bracket" one's experience as a conscious act. By bracketing one engages in the process of analysis devoid of the influence of personal lived-experience as an "objective" orientation. In particular, investigators should suspend their analytic, philosophic, sensual, and other prejudices or predispositions as to the nature of perception or the phenomena to be perceived. With the completion of bracketing—as far as it be possible—one is able to recognize the essential structures of phenomena as reductive to existential phenomena. For example, one witnesses and engages in private behavior that is universal to one's interpersonal experience with others, as opposed to situationally dependent behavior (see chap. 9, below).

At this level of inquiry, meaning emerges as a structural unit independent of affective or rationalized content borne by a person or a person's situation. Put another way, the transcendent signs of phenomena compare and contrast with immanent signs thus specifying the phenomenal presence. What is essentially given as signified unites with what is transcendentally given as signifying; thus emerge meaningful, significant phenomena. This is by way of saying that the phenomenological reduction allows an experiential structure to become knowable as the existential fiber or style in a person's lived-experience. Indeed, one comes to the genesis of meaning, which is the sign-to-signification; it is the "sedimentation" of personal experience into intersubjectivity.

If one fails to bracket one's perspective inquiry, an inability to distinguish *structure* and the *consciousness of structure* arises, where in fact the consciousness of structure functions as a content for structure, an "objectivity." In consequence, structure (the existential) is perceived incorrectly as a sole function of content (the essential). In other words, the phenomenological reduction involves the suspension of the consciousness of phenomenal content (sign-to-signification) and the realization of the phenomenal structure that is the preconscious (sign-as-signification) or existential meaning. This process method of perception links the immanent phenomena of description to the transcendent phenomena of reduction to discover or create a presence that is existential per se.

The process can be exemplified in one's everyday experience of awakening from sleep. One wakes up, so to speak, by progressing in perceptive awareness, with varying degrees of meshing, from (1) corporeal awareness of self to (2) mental or conscious recognition of self to (3) the actual synergic point where one is fully aware of one's lived-behavior as a unitary body-mind (Body-subject) *able to act* in fulfillment of preconscious capabilities—capabilities that are not merely physical or mental, but both. One is alive, not merely breathing or thinking.

In the brief period before one is fully aware of being awake, there is the beginning of a conscious awareness of how things really are—prior to any conceptualization, cognition, or affection about the things "being as they should be." One in point of fact is perceiving the content of ambient phenomena prior to one's consciousness of it—that is, prior to the structuring or designating of phenomena as meaningful. There is an existential, lived-meaning to phenomena before they are named as essential, as "objective." In short, the sign meaning is a priori to the act of signification.

The third and final step in Merleau-Ponty's phenomenological method is the "radical *cogito*" or *intentionality*. At this juncture Merleau-Ponty directly moves his phenomenology to an existential project. For one is now concerned with pure intentionality devoid of consciousness and absent from the structural phenomena that are hidebound to the preconscious as sign-to-signification. This is to suggest that one progresses beyond bracketed experience or "operative intentionality," which marks the first and second phase of phenomenological inquiry—that is, description and reduction. In the third step one arrives at the process of "thetic intentionality."

Thetic intentionality means the lived-experience or act of perception that contains meaning precisely because it is not dependent on the calculated maneuver of the bracketing experience; one transcends one's "consciousness of" phenomena to the phenomena themselves. Thetic intentionality or existential meaning is the preconscious perception of self prior to the interpersonal perception that is communication. As Merleau-Ponty (1964c, p. 90) says, "for the speaking subject, to express is to become aware of; he does not just express for others, but also to know himself what he intends." Existential meaning is the knowledge base from which "I" realize that "I am able to" or "I can" perceive and express, as opposed to the bracketed or essential meaning in which "I think that" and "I sense that" perception and expression are engaged. In brief, bracketed experience is operative intentionality at the empirical level (a history of phenomena), whereas thetic intentionality is existential experience (primordial phenomena). In consequence, the existential creates the essential in the process of perception. Indeed, says Merleau-Ponty (1963a, p. 63), "the philosopher is the man who wakes up and speaks."

Merleau-Ponty's phenomenological method is in fact the very process of perception. This is to say, perception is marshaled to determining the essential *constructa* of experienced phenomena as a key to interpreting existential meaning. The counterpart to perception is, of course, expression, and in this conjunctive role expression is the phenomenon of perception. The expression of factual knowledge presents a ready-made lived-structure of meaning (signification) in the language used (signs). By applying phenomenological techniques to articulated language (speaking), one arrives at an understanding of the semiotic meaning force of communication acts. Merleau-Ponty summarizes it well:

> What we have now understood is that symbolic matrices, a language of self to self, systems of equivalences built up by the past, effect groupings, abbreviations, and distortions in a simple act and which analysis reconstitutes more and more closely" [1969, p. 83].

EXPRESSION AS THE PRIMORDIALITY OF BEING

An examination of the levels of expression helps to further clarify distinctions promoted by a phenomenological method. Expression at the level of descriptions, according to Merleau-Ponty, should be designated as language (*langage*). At this initial stage of communication analysis Merleau-Ponty follows the explanation of the linguist Ferdinand de Saussure (1966) and defines language as the synoptic presentation of two structural subunits that compose any given "word" in relation to other contextual signs (verbal and nonverbal)—namely, the *signifier* and the *signified*. The signifier means simply the value category (logic typology) of the sound-image of a word; the signified (another value category) is the concept as implied or as understood. Thus, one narrows down a given communication act to the ordinary language (*langue*) used and within that utterance the distinct words articulated, which are indentifiable by the holistic sound-image and concept. Yet, such a description still leaves the analyst far short of determining the *intended* meaning of a message. In short, linguistic structure is a behavioral factor of linguistic content as perceived, not an expressed structure of lived-experience.

Investigators should move to the second phase of inquiry by bracketing their perceptive experience of the language used in the message. Language should be approached in its neutral structural sense, much as one might attempt to do in defining a new word for a young child: unadorned structure to be filled in by lived-experience. Here language emerges as a structure devoid of historical content—that is, removed from the public situation in which it is uttered and reuttered. Bracketed language and its meaning are what might be called *cultural* or *social significations*. The French use the word *langue* (roughly meaning a society's current spoken tongue) as opposed to *langage* (a symbol code and grammar) to get at this distinction. In terms of meaning analysis, a crude American equivalent might be the denotative or consensus meaning of language as opposed to the connotative or personal meaning. In any event, the task is to find the language structure implicit in a tongue or cultural signification. As Merleau-Ponty (1963a, p. 30) suggests, "expression presupposes someone who expresses, a truth which he expresses, and others before whom he expresses himself. The postulate of expression and of philosophy is that it can simultaneously satisfy these three conditions." Once the meaning, as a hermeneutic of the *Weltanschauung*, of a message is ascertained at the structural level, one can move to the third area of phenomenological analysis. That is, one can examine intentionality in meaning, which is the penetration of the lived-experience (*Lebenswelt*).

Merleau-Ponty argues that the act of speaking (*parole*) is at the core of the "radical *cogito*." He stresses the primordiality of embodiment in communication. As he says, "expression is a matter of reorganizing things-said, affecting them with a new index of curvature, and bending them to a certain enhancement of meaning." That is, "speaking to others (or to myself), I do not speak *of* my thoughts; I *speak them*, and what is between them—my afterthoughts and underthoughts" (Merleau-Ponty 1964c, p. 19).

For example, when one speaks, there is an expression that is at the preconscious level of the speaker at the moment the words are uttered and thus rendered perceptible to myself and other conscious body-subjects. One might readily object that the speaker thinks before speaking and hence is conscious of the words spoken. This objection can be granted, not as existential speech (sign-as-significations), but as a description of bracketed speech or the use of a cultural meaning, an "objectivity" of sign-to-signification. When the conscious, rational scrutiny of language is absent—for example, in the impromptu speech—one is speaking at the existential level or preconscious level of expression. There is in the impromptu speech experience an awareness of personal communication with self and others through language and body that is the felt or lived-awareness of primordial self-expression—a fact exploited by the psychologist in the verbal technique of "free association."

One can therefore express oneself at the level of existential awareness that is properly preconscious and revelatory of one's private reality. Being, in the metaphysical sense, is recognizable in expression as the human structure of verbal and nonverbal behavior that is embodied lived-intentionality. In the existential modality of expression, a personal act of communication can indeed reveal one's "real" self at the interpersonal level of perception. Speaking is an existential risk, for "at the moment of expression the other to whom I address myself and I who express myself are incontestably linked together" (Merleau-Ponty 1964c, p. 73). Our great care (or the lack of it!) in the use of language before other persons is demonstration enough of this point.

Merleau-Ponty indicates the primordiality of being entailed by expression in his definition of speech:

> Speech, as distinguished from language, is that moment when the significative intention (still silent and wholly act) proves itself capable of incorporating itself into my culture and the culture of others—of shaping me and others by transforming the meaning of cultural instruments [1964c, p. 92].

This is to say, *speaking* displays a preconscious structure of private, existential meaning that becomes frozen by its verbalization—frozen into a cultural pattern that is the tongue we speak and the reality we inhabit. The interpersonal perception of existential expression (primordial signs) sediments into empirical speech (empirical signs) allowing its reuse by anyone. Thus, speech removed from its value or social context of private or public lived-experience is mere language; it is a symbol code barren of any personal awareness in the absence of human utterance and social perception. This is precisely the distinction between *speech speaking* and *speech spoken* (Merleau-Ponty 1962, p. 197).

SEMIOLOGY AS A PHENOMENOLOGY OF COMMUNICATION

Having examined the parallel structure of perception and expression as reflected in communication analysis, an explanation of the semiotic system or sign theory underlying Merleau-Ponty's existential-phenomenological method is particularly relevant. He uses an explicit system of signs to explain both the lived-experience of perception and expression. Again emulating Saussure, Merleau-Ponty argues that meaning is a product of the conjunction of signs. It is the synergic connection of signs, not the individual sign, that produces meaning. Even in the case where there is a void or "chasm," one encounters meaning, for the specific absence of a sign is also a sign to be linked to other signs. For example, the force of speaking derives in part from silence—meaning is the communication of what is said and what is not said.

Put another way, the occurrence of meaning is not a sign-to-signification structure, but a sign structure in which the signs *are* the signification. The existential signs are by structure primordial and self-definitive, whereas empirical signs are historical and definitive only in the congruence of structure with usage content. Existential meaning consists of signs in which signifiers and signifieds (sound-image and concept in expression, or, immanent and transcendent perspective in perception) are synergic and inseparable: the sign is the signification. Meaning is the same as expressed and perceived at either the intrapersonal level or the intersubjective level. In contrast, empirical meaning consists of signs in which the signifier or immanent perception is variously joined synthetically (not synergically) to an intended signified or transcendent perception, respectively. Thus, empirical expression or perception is a sign-to-signification structure where meaning as semiotic structure depends on semiotic content (Lanigan 1984).

The encompassing *Gestalt* nature of the semiotic process can be illustrated with two visual examples. Empirical signs are observed in the perception of a painting where the foreground is apparent in comparison with the background precisely because the perceived plane of the background is itself devoid of a "foreground." Similarly, the plane of the foreground is clearly perceptible with its equally lacking "background." The two planes join synthetically to posit one foreground and one background; the structure (signs) is a function of its content (significations). On the other hand, existential signs are equally obvious in most so-called optical illusions where foreground and background as sign structures on *one* plane are identical and thus erratically reverse themselves to observers' consternation in attempting to focus their perspective on *two* planes. Here content must be a function of structure, for content is structure—the signs are the significations. In the "illusion" one is a constant witness to the birth of a visual object.

In both perception and expression several semiotic relationships operate at the verbal and nonverbal levels of communication. The most common system is of course linguistic semiology, which provides a structural model for multilevel perception and expression in a given communication analysis. Thus, speaking is semiotically divisible into language as immanently and transcendentally *expressed* or as immanently and transcendentally *perceived*. In this sense, Merleau-Ponty (1964c, p. 67) correctly asserts that "all perception, all action which presupposes it, and in short every human use of the body is already *primordial expression*."

To explain briefly, immanent language is both expressed and perceived as a "tongue" spoken in a speech community or cultural-social signification. This is the level of empirical speech and meaning. On the other hand, transcendent language is speaking (*parole*) in the existential sense of language that creates personal lived-experience. By a process of historical approval, disapproval, or modification, certain existential expressions or perceptions become sedimented. They assume a public meaning content that can be used over and over again as an immanent sign structure for personal content meaning. In short, transcendent signs become sedimented into one or two possible immanent signs—that is, only one or two possible significations-for-signs.

For example, immanent signs in expression form a sediment or cultural meaning that allows communication at an empirical level. Speakers, however, in their use of communication elements (language, voice, gesture, etc.), can express transcendent signs that form an existential meaning not dependent on empirical meanings. Indeed, language that is eloquent to our ears is of this order. Yet, such existential speech may well sediment to affirm, alter, or replace empirical speech at the personal or social level. A similar structure of signs exists in the act of perception. The cultural orientation to given perspectives is on the level of empirical perception. An original and existential perception that transcends the empirical can still occur. Such a perception is generally classified as an "insight." Indeed, how many such existential "insights" are now sedimented as "accepted" or even as the "only way" of doing and saying certain things? Wise sayings and epigrams are exemplary of this perceptual phenomenon.

By way of caution, one should note that the immanent and transcendent elements of Merleau-Ponty's semiology are reversible at the interpersonal level when expression and perception constitute intersubjective communication (Lanigan 1972). This is to say, for example, that one's personal articulations using language considered to be immanent may be perceived by another as transcendent for various reasons. Similarly, a speaker uttering existential or transcendent speech may be perceived as using empirical speech. The point to be made is that the proper understanding of the synergic union of perception and expression as a single agency can be achieved only by a phenomenological analysis of communication acts based on a semiotic division of elements.

Interpersonal structures must lead back to personal structures when perception and expression are explored for their meaning, whether at the empirical or the existential level. Yet, an existential-phenomenological examination of communication is by definition limited to finding the meaning present in the elements of a lived-experience that is strictly speaking a subjectivity born of intersubjectivity (Husserl 1960). To separate the intrapersonal from the interpersonal in the hermeneutic analysis of perception and expression is to deny the possibility of a phenomenological reduction to the existential. On the contrary, meaning is a determinate lived-experience manifest in the communication act.

THEOREMS

Several communication theorems can now be drawn from the present analysis of Merleau-Ponty's semiotic phenomenology (see chap. 2, above).

1. Communication is a synergic process of perception and expression, which is both intrapersonal and interpersonal.
2. Communication is a synergic process (a) of empirical and existential speech, and (b) of immanent and transcendent perception.
3. Existential-phenomenological analysis utilizes a semiotic system to

distinguish empirical and existential modes of perception and expression.

4. The semiotic integration of description, reduction, and intentionality allows for an existential hermeneutic of communication acts.

By way of final comment, we should note that Merleau-Ponty's existential-phenomenological approach to communication analysis is by definition a project in intersubjective semiotics as a function of personal expression and perception. It is a philosophic approach that utilizes the semiotic model as a paradigm for an approach to locating meaning in personal and public encounters with being and reality. As Merleau-Ponty (1964c, p. 21) remarks, "in a sense, the highest point of philosophy is perhaps no more than rediscovering these truisms: thought thinks, speech speaks,the glance glances. But each time between the two identical words there is the whole spread one straddles in order to think, speak, and see."

Chapter Four

Freedom and Field

Merleau-Ponty's Sinngebung as the Essence of a Semiotic Phenomenology of Human Communication

The phenomenological thematic of field and freedom finds its problematic expression in Merleau-Ponty's major work, the *Phenomenology of Perception* (1962). On the one hand, the Preface to the book marks out in a general communication to the public reader what the field of phenomenology is. It is *Sinn*, a sense-giving expression discovered in perception. The field is marked by a method. The field sets eidetic boundaries, which are methodological for philosophy rigorously conceived as phenomenology. In this Preface, Merleau-Ponty announces the synergism that he makes of the Husserlian reflections on becoming. For Merleau-Ponty, the phenomenological method takes its existential turn in the world by moving progressively from the phenomenological description, to the phenomenological reduction, and then to the phenomenological interpretation. We all come to the realization that the field of expression is the choice made in the process of perception.

On the other hand, the final chapter of the book marks out in a specific communication to the person as reader what the freedom of phenomenology is. It is *Gebung*, the act-character of perception discovered in the process of expression. As with the field, freedom is marked by a method. Freedom sets the empirical boundaries that are methodological for the human sciences rigorously conceived as phenomenology. In this final chapter devoted to the subject and freedom, Merleau-Ponty articulates the syncretism that he makes of the Sartrian reflection on being. For Merleau-Ponty the existential method takes its phenomenological turn in conscious experience by moving progressively from the human situation to a direction (sense) of history, and to a historical truth (commitment). Each of us comes to the instantiation of *freedom* as the perception constituting *choice*. In short, Merleau-Ponty (1962) signals the ambiguity of the *Sinn-Gebung*, the problematic of field and freedom, of choice and context, when he says:

> By defining ourselves as a universal power of *Sinn-Gebung*, we have reverted to the method of the "thing without which" and to the analytical reflection of the traditional type, which seeks the conditions of reality. We must therefore resume the analysis of the *Sinngebung*, and show how it can be both centrifugal and centripetal, since it has been established that there is no freedom without a field [p. 439].

By making the *Sinn-Gebung* the existential problematic of field and freedom (see Figure 3), Merleau-Ponty constitutes the *Sinngebung* as the phenomenological thematic of field (see Figure 4) and freedom (see Figure 5). This thematic of the empirical and eidetic moment is precisely human communication as lived.

In the analysis that follows, I suggest the way in which Merleau-Ponty relies on certain eidetic characteristics of communication theory in order to argue that the *synergism* (see Figure 4) of field and freedom is an empirical phenomenon—namely, *tolerance*. In this instance, tolerance is my reflexive capability of seeing in the choice not made the ability of the other to choose. Tolerance is the field in which freedom can be lived as conscious experience. Second, I explore the reflexive moment of this argument by which Merleau-Ponty establishes several empirical characteristics of communication theory as the *syncreticism* (see Figure 5) of field and freedom. This coming together of field and freedom as an eidetic phenomenon constitutes an existential *style*. Style is the freeedom within which the field of conscious experience is the ontological capability that Heidegger (1984, p. 205) calls *ek-stase*. Last, I affirm in this dialectic examination that Merleau-Ponty's analysis of freedom and field is a semiotic phenomenology of the person.

Merleau-Ponty suggests that the *Sinngebung* "can be both centrifugal and centripetal." In this short phrase, he utilizes the substance and structure of modern communication theory (Lanigan, 1970; 1979a, b; 1982a, b; 1983a; 1984). The combinatory opposition between the centrifugal and centripetal directions of experience is the substance of consciousness existentially lived. The communicative structure of combinatory exchange records equally well the categorical force of the centrifugal and the centripetal together with the syncategorimatical terms "both"/"and" that announce a binary analogue logic. Just as Saussure's sign emerges always in the context of other signs, and just as the signifier is always connected to the signified in a reflexive moment, so too the

○ → Centrifical

○ ← Centripical

Figure 3. Static communication [○ = *nexus*]

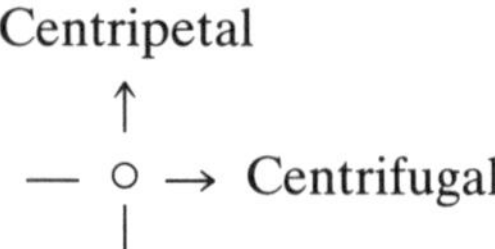

Figure 4. Orthogonal static communication

Figure 5. Orthogonal dynamic communication [Helix]

centrifugal and centripetal moments of human action are reflexive to one another. In the centrifugal moment of communicative behavior, we witness consciousness form itself into an extensional dimension of signification. Choices always secure their own context. In parallel fashion, it is also the context that gives definition to the choice. The centripetal moment of communicative behavior constitutes experience as an intentional dimension of meaning in consciousness. Hall (1969, p. 108) provides an empirical confirmation of this analysis of centrifugal/centripetal meaning in his parallel discussion of sociofugal/sociopetal behavior.

The force of Merleau-Ponty's analysis is all the more persuasive as we realize that his argument parallels that put forth by Jakobson in his early critique of Saussure's linguistic structuralism. Holenstein (1976) provides a convenient summary schema of Saussure's language theory where *parole* and *langue* are counterposed in information theory terms. This is to say, the analyst must choose either *parole* and its static features or *langue* and its static features. The choice offered by such a structural description is digital and has its coherence in the operation of disjunction. Thus, the Saussurian static model (Holenstein 1976, p. 160) offers:

	langue		***parole***
(1)	linguistic norm	(1)	linguistic utterance
(2)	language as supraindividual, social endowment	(2)	language as individual, private property
(3)	the unifying, centripetal aspect of language	(3)	the individualizing, centrifugal aspect of language

Jakobson effectively shows that the Saussurian static concepts of *langue* and *parole* are an inadequate description, reduction, and interpretation of human communicative practice. Jakobson's solution is the suggestion of a dynamic conception in which the concept of *code* replaces that of *langue*, and *message* is used in place of *parole*. As a communicologist, Jakobson is aware of the principle that communication theory entails information theory. That is, the ability of the *poetic function* to make static oppositional distinctions with a digital logic of disjunction is contextualized by the prior ability to make dynamic differentiations with the binary analogue logic of conjunction (Holenstein 1976, p. 163).

It is quite true that *langue* and *parole* can be distinguished in many cases. But it is equally important to note that in essence this is not true. Where we are sensitive to the fact that a person in the practice of discourse is simultaneously a speaker and a listener, the static conception gives way to the dynamic practice. Although the speaker encodes discourse by relying in a primary way on the paradigmatic features of speech as articulation (eidetic), the listener decodes discourse primarily on the basis of the syntagmatic features of language as silent deconstruction (empirical). In short, the communal features of *langue* as the centripetal force of discourse that unites persons, and the individualizing aspects of *parole* as the centrifugal force of discourse that separates person from person, are dynamic lived-elements of conscious experience.

Here we must remind ourselves that consciousness is displayed in the paradigmatic function whereas experience is contained in the syntagmatic function of discourse. The fact that "conscious experience" and the "paradigmatic/syntagmatic" axes are individually and jointly combinatory is precisely why Jakobson insists on *code* in place of *langue*, and *message* for *parole*. Nonetheless, Jakobson's analysis falls short in one way that is critical for our understanding of Merleau-Ponty's position. Jakobson still identifies the code with a centripetal function in discourse. Language as code unifies theory and practice by assuming that the level of analysis is intersubjective. Thus, the code becomes a characteristic of dynamic society and messages are created as social norms. By comparison, this view holds that the message is an aspect of the dynamic individual. Language as message is deictic by assuming a subjective level of analysis—for example, as pronouns are deictic in place of naming nouns. The centrifugal function of discourse separates person from person in dynamic interaction. Put in communication theoretic terms, Jakobson uses a binary analogue logic (both/and) to join the code and message functions together, yet he also permits any one description of either code or message to stand as a digital logic (either/or) representation of the discursive process.

Merleau-Ponty's position is corrective. Not only do code and message combine in a binary analogue logic, that very logic is an entailment of the digital function, not of one, but of both the code and message (or their dialectic absence) as presentations in the communicative process. It is in this sense that what is not present in the disjunction is more meaningful than what is, when considered in the context of conjunction as an originary analogue boundary. Merleau-Ponty put the issue this way:

> In all uses of the word *sens*, we find the same fundamental notion of a being orientated or polarized in the direction of what he is not, and thus we are brought back to a conception of the subject as *ek-stase*, and to a relationship of active transcendence between the subject and the world [1962, p. 430].

Thus in certain key respects, Merleau-Ponty's discussion of the *Sinn-Gebung* and *Sinngebung* opposition displays the sense in which the law of noncontradiction formulates the communication theory entailment of information theory. The opposition of field and freedom in which the conjunction of the two allows their praxis disjunction is an empirical illustration of the eidetic thematic. And I might add that this very methodology is exploited to great advantage by Michel Foucault (1970; 1972; see Lanigan 1984) in his studies of freedom and field.

For Merleau-Ponty as semiotic phenomenologist, then, a centrifugal phenomenon is an act of expression that moves outward from the person and thereby comes to constitute a perception for others. This centrifugal construction of expression and perception is a signifier with extensional consequence. Discourse and gesture are expressive insofar as they can be so lived by an other, and insofar as an act of communion becomes a lived-world. By comparison, the centripetal phenomenon is an act of perception that moves inward from the other and thereby comes to constitute an expression of self. This centripetal construction of perception and expression is a signified with intentional purport. Gesture and discourse are perceptive insofar as an act of communication becomes a world of living. The centrifugal communication becomes an exemplar of the phenomenological constitution of the *Sinngebung*. That is, expression as an act-character (*-gebung*) entails the sense-giving (*Sinn-*) trait of perception. As the communicologist would summarize, choice is always a choice of context.

But what of centripetal communication? It also becomes an exemplar, yet it is an existential exemplar of the *Sinngebung*. This is to say, perception as sense-giving (*Sinn-*) entails the act-character (*-gebung*) of expression. Again in strict communication theoretic terms, choice in context is always grounded in the originary choice not made. The ontological point is explicit in Merleau-Ponty's (1962, p. 454) thesis: "We choose our world and our world chooses us." This is to say that the centrifugal and centripetal moments of expression and perception are the reflexive substance of human communication. Expression entails perception just as perception entails expression; freedom and field are a dialectical discourse. Communication emerges as the eidetic phenomenon in which consciousness entails experience as the condition of the World (intersubjectivity) and in which experience entails consciousness as the condition of Self or the absent Other (subjectivity).

And so we discover the human *situation* that is the result of *phenomenological description*. The centrifugal moment of human communication constitutes a field of expression and perception within which freedom is both choice and the capability of choosing. Choice becomes the necessary condition of experience and the sufficient condition of consciousness in the act of choosing as an empirical phenomenon. Field and freedom form a *synergism* of conscious experience in which freedom instantiates human choice (the empirical) as the capability of choosing (the eidetic). The name of this synergism is *tolerance*.

Recall Merleau-Ponty's proposition that the *Sinngebung* "can be both centrifugal and centripetal." The analysis of the communicative situation in which the substance of the centrifugal and centripetal moments constitute a phenomenological description allows us to move to a phenomenological reduction of the *Sinngebung*. The binary analogue (both/and) logic of the proposition suggests an eidetic structure for communication that accounts for the unlikely combination of the countervailing empirical moments so precisely named "centrifugal" and "centripetal" by the human sciences.

The answer to the empirical paradox lies in Merleau-Ponty's suggestion that, just as phenomenological reduction follows on the description, we discover existentially that upon every human situation there follows a sense of the "direction of history." Just as the human situation is valued as an act-character (*-gebung*), so too is the sense-giving (*Sinn-*) essence of history. Of course, this is to recall with Benveniste (1971b, p. 206) that discourse and history are already present in the phenomenological reduction as an existential syncretism in the very empirical condition of *parole* (*l'histoire* as lived) and *langue* (*l'histoire* as text).

The "truth of history" as the phenomenological interpretation of freedom derives from the *Sinngebung* as the field of capability. Recall that the *Sinngebung* "*can* be both centrifugal and centripetal." Signification can signify, just as expression can become perception in the outward movement of the centrifugal sign. The signifying act can be a signification, just as perception can become expression through the inward moment of the centripetal sign. As a semiotic phenomenology of communication, the binary analogue logic uses the syncategormatic "both/and" terms to combine the empirical signifier and signified elements of a sign (experience) into an eidetic signification (consciousness). The centrifugal movement of human communication becomes a signifier signifying—that is, an expression of perception: Merleau-Ponty's *parole parlante*. The reflexive moment of centripetal communication is thereby a signified signifying—or perception of expression: Merleau-Ponty's *parole parlée*. In other words, the Saussurian stylization of the human communicator as an auditor who listens in order to understand is a false synthesis. Rather, Merleau-Ponty argues, the human communicator is a person whose expression and perception are existentially reflexive. Communication is a syncretic synergism—that is, a hyper-reflection. Signifier and signified as a sign constitute the syncreticism of expression and perception, yet the very combination of signs is a synergism—the synergism we live as conscious experience. This conscious experience is the *Sinngebung* in which the sense-giving-act-character of communication is signification signifying—that is, a semiotic phenomenology. The vertical structure of consciousness combines with the horizontal essence of experience as an orthogonal nexus. Just as the semiotic structure of signs is an orthogonal synergism of the paradigmatic and syntagmatic elements of discourse, so too the phenomenological essence of conscious experience is an orthogonal syncretism of freedom and tolerance in history (Holenstein 1976, p. 31). With this insight, we complete the hermeneutic helix (see Figure 5).

As Merleau-Ponty argues in his Preface to the *Phenomenology of Perception*, the phenomenological description, reduction, and interpretation are three ways of saying the same thing about the field as *Sinngebung*. So too in the final chapter of his book, the human situation, a direction of history, and the truth of history are three ways of perceiving the same thing about freedom as *Sinngebung*. There is no better hyper-reflection than Merleau-Ponty's (1962, p. 455) own words: "I am a psychological and historical structure, and have received, with existence, a manner of existing, a style."

Chapter Five

Communication Science and Merleau-Ponty's Critique of the Objectivist Illusion

Commentary is thematic in the work of Maurice Merleau-Ponty. We recall with familiar ease that his inaugural lecture at the Collège de France is a commentary on the philosopher as a person and as an agent provocateur in human communication. With dialectic explication, Merleau-Ponty's lecture describes the philosopher's consciousness of good ambiguity in the personae of Lavelle, Bergson, and Socrates, and in the human encounters we know as the discursive institutions of religion, history, and philosophy. "But," as he remarks (1963a, p. 27), "it is not merely a question here of confronting ideas but of incarnating them and making them live, and in this respect we cannot know what they are capable of except by trying them out. This attempt involves a taking of sides and a struggle" (cf. Lingis 1979). And we might recall the more poignant version of human communication that R. D. Laing (1967, p. 44; cf. Ruesch 1972; Leach 1971) offers—namely, that the struggle is the "estranged integration we call sanity." It is in this hermeneutic sense that Merleau-Ponty struggles with communication science by taking sides and making conscious experience as lived the horizon of discourse.

I should like to characterize the position that Merleau-Ponty takes on the practice of communication as the critique of the objectivist illusion in therapeutic philosophy. In my analysis I want to rely initially on Merleau-Ponty's (1973a, p. 147) view of the objectivist illusion that one finds in the last pages of the *Prose of the World*. He says, "Nowadays we encourage every form of illusive and allusive expression, especially pictorial expression, and in particular the art of the 'primitives,' the drawing of children and madmen, as well as every genre of involuntary poetry, the 'testament' or spoken language." Second, I briefly characterize the behavioral notion of therapeutic philosophy that Levin and Koestenbaum counterpose to Merleau-Ponty's method of philosophic consciousness as a phenomenology of encounter bracketed by communication science—that is, his hermeneutic of positive ambiguity. Having set the context in this way, I shall then return to the passage from the *Phenomenology of Perception* (p. 291) that grounds my analysis.

THE OBJECTIVIST ILLUSION

As Merleau-Ponty remarks,

> The objectivist illusion is firmly established in us. We are convinced that the expressive act in its normal or fundamental form consists, given a signification, in the construction of a system of signs that, for each element of the signified, there corresponds a signifying [signifier] element in other words, in *representation* [1973a, p. 148; cf. Haymond 1967].

Thus, in the spirit of Saussure, Merleau-Ponty reminds us that discourse analysis is not the illusory world of acoustic images and concepts—that is, the objective illusion of words and things. For the apparent objectivity of the historical connection among persons, words, and referents is an illusion; it is the natural attitude writ general. "Here, as everywhere, it seems at first sight true that consciousness can find in its experience only what it has itself put there. Thus the experience of communication would appear to be an illusion" (Merleau-Ponty 1962, p. 178). Rather, discursive analysis must seek a return to the speaking subject and the rediscovery of philosophic consciousness as a "rigorous science" of communication (Dreyfus 1979; Foucault 1970; Searle 1982; 1983; 1985). "Speaking, in the speaker, does not translate ready-made thought, but accomplishes it" (Merleau-Ponty 1962, p. 178). Here the expressive arts, and discourse in particular, become the gesture that articulates and embodies in place of the sedimented representations of a text.

The very perception of the semiotic unity of signifier and signified for Merleau-Ponty is good ambiguity:

> The philosopher is marked by the distinguishing trait that he possesses *inseparably* the taste for evidence and the feeling for ambiguity. When he limits himself to accepting ambiguity, it is called equivocation. But among the great it becomes a theme; it contributes to establishing certitudes rather than menacing them. Therefore it is necessary to distinguish good and bad ambiguity [1963a, pp. 4–5].

Positive ambiguity is the diachronic and synchronic synergism of diacritic values produced in the labor of discourse—that is, what Jakobson defines as the "poetic function" in human communication. Speaking (*parole parlante*) and speech (*parole parlée*) are not to be confused with representation, with the objectivist illusion of language (*langage*) and meaning (*langue*). Indeed, as "idle talk" in the Heideggerian sense (1962; see Dreyfus & Rabinow 1982) begins to take hold of our being-in-the-world, we confuse gesture (practice) and its text (*l'histoire*). Speaking lapses into language, things become rooted in the body, and sanity becomes my exclusive space, for in pathology only I am in-sanity. Only my philosophic consciousness offers to disclose the "oneness of man and the world, which is, not indeed abolished, but repressed by everyday perception or by objective thought" (Merleau-Ponty 1962, p. 291).

But where can I find the philosophical consciousness that "protects the sane . . . against delirium or hallucination" or defends against the natural attitude or myth or the objectivist illusion? This question should be carefully compared with the diagnostic question: Am I embodied? Or in a more lived, albeit Heideggerian, sense, am I in-sanity? Or finally in its communicative typicality as a clinical question for the patient: "Can't you hear my voices?" The answer to both questions may be found in the problematic that Levin characterizes as the therapeutic process and that Koestenbaum advocates as clinical philosophy.

THERAPEUTIC PHILOSOPHY

As Levin (1979, pp. 2–3) describes his own philosophic analysis, its primary goal is "to open up new fields for thinking to play and deepen our experience of life." Or more specifically, he notes that "we need not only to question his [Merleau-Ponty] working notions of sanity and madness, but also to explore the hint that there are *alternative ways of structuring space and inhabiting its world*." In my view, Levin is proposing and carries out a project in clinical philosophy in which the object of analysis is not Merleau-Ponty's philosophical position, but rather that Merleau-Ponty's text (like the discourse of a patient) is a clinical condition in need of remedy (Poole 1966). At this point it may be helpful to review several selected criteria that Koestenbaum offers as communicative ingredients in the practice of clinical philosophy:

> Clinical philosophy operates within the following parameters: a. The atmosphere is sincerely and profoundly supportive. Even confrontation exists in an atmosphere of support. b. The initial complaint is not nearly as significant as the need to explore the undisclosed and originary projects of the patient or client. c. Regardless of contrary claims, the *only* problems are (i) the patient's inadequacy in (or resistance against) taking charge of his or

> her own life, and (ii) lack of contact with the world or not reaching toward the future (self-transcendence). . . .
>
> Diagnostic procedures: a. Symptoms are essentially ignored. Although they may help to initiate therapy by saying "help," symptoms are mostly *objects* whose function is to prevent access to the transcendental ego. b. Diagnostic measurement can be taken only by the inwardness (or unconscious) of the therapist. Traditional tests and techniques are at best only peripherally relevant. . . .
>
> Therapeutic strategies: The sense of individual identity of *Existenz* and self-transcendence can be encouraged to grow in the following ways: a. Identify existing strengths; b. Repeatedly use accurate "universality-to-individuality" fantasy; c. Encourage anger, protest—including anger-at-self—perhaps through confrontation; d. Be an example of a self-made person [1978, pp. 535–36].

Thus when Levin's analysis of such questions as "Is this repression necessary for sanity, for health?" and "What is the experiential significance of this repression?" with regard to the passage (in the chapter section below) in the *Phenomenology of Perception* (p. 291), he illustrates two points. First, the text is taken to be an inadequate attempt to take charge of the problem of sanity and spatiality. The text is seen as a case of Merleau-Ponty's lack of contact with the experiential world and the communicative extrapolations that are possible. Second, the text as cited by Levin constitutes a paradigmatic case of the objectivist illusion. Rather than focusing on the text as the philosophic consciousness recovered from a clinical condition cited in a patient (with a structural affinity to mythology), which is in fact Merleau-Ponty's procedure, Levin takes the detached text as a *representation* of the transcendental ego.

Recall Merleau-Ponty's explanation of the objectivist illusion:

> We are convinced that the expressive act in its normal or fundamental form consists, given a signification, in the construction of a system of signs such that, for each element of the signified, there corresponds a signifying element—in other words, in *representation* [1973a, p. 148].

THE MERLEAU-PONTY TEXT

Many of the issues that I have raised can now be illustrated by going back to the Merleau-Ponty (1962) text in question. Let me stress that I begin two sentences ahead of the citation that Levin uses for his analysis. These two sentences clearly entail communication science as part of philosophic consciousness:

> No appeal to explicit perception can arouse the patient from this dream, since he has no quarrel with explicit perception, and holds only that it

> proves nothing against what he experiences. "Can't you hear my voices?" a patient asks the doctor; and she comes resignedly to the conclusion: "I am the only one who hears them then." What protects the sane man against delirium or hallucination, is not his critical powers, but the structure of his space: objects remain before him, keeping their distance and, as Malebranche said speaking of Adam, touching him only with respect. What brings about both hallucinations and myths is a shrinking in the space directly experienced, a rooting of things in our body, the overwhelming proximity of the object, the oneness of man and the world, which is, not indeed abolished, but repressed by everyday perception or by objective thought, and which philosophical consciousness rediscovers [p. 291].

What Merleau-Ponty accomplishes in this passage is a specification of a pathological human communication. Here there is not only a failure of authentic being-in-the-world (*être-au-monde*), there is even a failure of the natural attitude as an ego defense. The critical power of the patient is dysfunctional in the natural attitude inasmuch as the patient's explicit perception cannot match the doctor's perception in at least typicality. The patient's existence becomes inauthentic in the appeal to experience, for the pathological experience is precisely a representation where primordial presence should be. That is, the patient has constructed a system of signs in which the referential values (signifieds) consistently point back to her clinical experience as lived. The patient has an illusion of objectivity, which is confirmed when it does *not* match that of the doctor. The classic symptomatology of schizophrenia is thus displayed. The patient's explicit perception is pathologically maintained by associations, ambivalence, autism, and altered affect (Koestenbaum 1978, pp. 450ff.).

Merleau-Ponty (1962, p. 291) captures this complete pathological condition in his epigrammatic example: "Can't you hear my voices?" a patient asks the doctor; and she comes resignedly to the conclusion: "I am the only one who hears them then." We witness delirium in the question "Can't you hear my voices?". And in the statement "I am the only one who hears them then," we are party to hallucination.

But what of the doctor, the sane person who is protected from delirium and hallucination—that is, from pathological expression or perception? Why, in Merleau-Ponty's example, does the doctor remain silent? Without speech there is no discursive connection to the patient. The doctor sees the paradox of legitimation that the patient's behavior presents. For the doctor to respond by speaking is to equivocate, to live in bad ambiguity (Merleau-Ponty 1963a, pp. 4–5; 1962, p. 339; cf. Virasoro 1959). The utterance of an affirmation ("Yes, I hear the voices") or denial ("No, I don't hear the voices") becomes complicity. To affirm the patient in discourse is to join the clinical representation of pathology; it is to hallucinate with the patient. To deny the patient's experience is to concede delirium, to admit to confusion where there is none on the doctor's part. The doctor does understand that the patient hears voices that he does not hear, but to say so is to participate in the objective illusion of the patient (Merleau-Ponty 1962, pp. 289, 337; Ledermann 1970). As Natanson concisely notes:

> The pathology of communication itself involves a different dimension of human reality. What is at issue here is the meaning of there being a world in which ego and alter ego share an experiential order in virtue of normalcy and lose that communality in mental morbidity. The psychotic's world can be understood but not shared [1969, p. 103].

What protects the doctor, the sane person, is the *structure of space*, according to Merleau-Ponty. This is a complex answer within the horizon of communication science. However, we can achieve a certain amount of clarity and understanding by initially differentiating between the concepts "structure" and "space." In this philosophic pair, I should like to begin with "structure" because it seems to be fundamental to Merleau-Ponty's discussion in a way in which "space" is not. Indeed, I concur with Kockelmans, who argues:

> Nevertheless, I think one should recognize that the problem of space as such cannot be called one of primordial importance for Merleau-Ponty. The chief concern of his works lies in the query about the very Being of man and about the fundamental significance of our body-subject; he explains and justifies his views on these issues by means of reflections utilizing human behavior and perception as primary themes. In these reflections the space problem is recurrent, but only as a touchstone for the general theses he wants to defend [1970, p. 280].

First, then, the problem of "structure." For Merleau-Ponty there are two senses in which we can explore the idea of structure relevant to our analysis. One is the semiotic structure diacritically manifest in the diachronic and synchronic movements of speaking, or more generally as the behavioral reversibility of expression and perception (see chap. 3, above). The other is the hermeneutic structure in the sense of good ambiguity—that is, the multiplicity of perception that is thematic in explicit expression, in communication.

In speaking of the sane person's protection against delirium or hallucination, Merleau-Ponty says of the structure of space: "Objects remain before him, keeping their distance . . . touching him only with respect." This is pure diachronic description as phenomenological reflection. Object confronts object in linear progression. Each object seeks its value by contiguity with its predecessor and its successor. The patient speaks: "Can't you hear my voices?" The doctor answers by remaining silent. The patient responds: "I am the only one who hears them then." The doctor communicates by continued silence. Doctor and patient have touched each other with respect. The structure of protection for the doctor is manifest. The synchronic moment of the doctor's sanity continues, he does not become an active participant in the pathological discourse, which is the patient's version of "sanity." The doctor's behavior is not a discourse in-sanity but with-sanity; the doctor (in Merleau-Ponty's phrase) becomes the " indirect voice of silence."

But what is the synchronic moment of the patient in communication? It is delirium and hallucination: "a shrinking in the space directly experienced"—that is, "Can't you hear my voices?" The voices possess me and I possess them, surely in hearing me you can hear them—this is the patient's claim for the immediacy of space (Natanson 1965). The patient's synchronic moment is embodied, "a rooting of things in her body" and "the overwhelming proximity of the object, the oneness of man and the world." The illusion of objectivity retains its structural integrity for the patient. The patient's pathology is diacritically marked by associations, ambivalence, autism, and altered affect, which are the repressions of everyday perception and objective thought. The very illusion of the pathological behavior as objective communication for the patient is an inauthentic structure of diachronic and synchronic being. The patient lives a discourse of subjectivity without body. The very pathology of the patient is, in Merleau-Ponty's sense, the existential creation of intersubjectivity in subjectivity by *abandoning* embodiment before other persons.

This process stands in direct comparison to belief and participation in communication as myth. The myth is structurally parallel to the objectivist illusion in pathology in that myth is the creation of intersubjectivity in subjectivity by the *invention* of embodiment before other persons and things,—that is, anthropomorphism. Levin (1979, p. 7) queries whether or not such a mythic experience "is *not* a symptom of *pathology* so much as it is a sudden perceptual *opening*, initiating a very wholesome, but also a very scary process of experiential deepening and expansion?" The answer is to be found in the second sense of structure that I want to discuss. This is to say, I would like to call attention to the multiplicity of perception that becomes phenomenologically thematic in expression, or what Merleau-Ponty (see chap. 1, above; Silverman 1979b) calls the hermeneutic of "good ambiguity."

Myth has its existence in communicative discourse or similar semiotic systems (Barthes 1972; see chap. 17, below). In a cryptic sense, we can view the generation of myths as pathology in reverse. In pathology, the person uses discourse and behavior to abandon embodiment, to create bad ambiguity, and to confine intersubjectivity in spatial subjectivity (Smith 1977). The reverse condition in mythology is the use of discourse and action (ritual) to invent embodiment (anthropomorphic beliefs), to create "good" ambiguity (where the actor shares responsibility with the gods, and thus not alone), and to confine subjectivity in temporal intersubjectivity (the union of person and persona—parallel to the pathological union of ego and alter ago). Myth allows discourse between the person and the unknown, be it natural or cosmic. "The myth holds the essence *within* the appearance; the mythical phenomenon is not a representation, but a genuine presence" (Merleau-Ponty 1962, p. 290).

Hence Merleau-Ponty is quite correct to allow that along with hallucination, myth "is a shrinking in the space directly experienced, a rooting of things in our body, the overwhelming proximity of the object, the oneness of man and the world." But as with pathology, the mythic experience is achieved at the expense of authentic being. The everyday perception or objective though which the myth *represents* is an objective illusion that represses the vitality of conscious experience as a phenomenology of communication. In short, pathology and myth are negative structural variations of the objectivist illusion. Pathology is a synchronic theme in which lived-experience for the patient is a diachronic monologue. Subjectivity is disembodied in a failure of communication as interpersonal perception and expression. And as reversibility of structure, myth is a diachronic theme in which lived-experience is the manufacture of synchronic discourse. Mythic subjectivity becomes the ritual embodiment of an invented dialogue containing the perceptions and expressions of personae, both natural and human.

What I characterize as therapeutic philosophy on the part of Levin is the assertion that mythology may be a healthy variation of pathology. Such a suggestion is especially enticing because of the structural affinity we just noted. Indeed, most of us can accept the therapeutic function of this or that form of mythology: some of us still buy American automobiles, some of us still go to church, and some of us still do attempt to teach first-year students at the university. With slightly more strain, we can even admit to the joys of some pathology: some of us still believe that only we hear the voice of truth and our certainty is confirmed by the silence of our doctor colleagues. Yet in the end, we shall object as does Merleau-Ponty—at least in my reading of him.

Although we recognize the structural affinity of pathology and myth, and their mutual creation in the passive repression of the everyday world of the natural attitude, we simultaneously perceive the intentionality of our behavior, especially in discursive communication. Philosophical consciousness is precisely the interrogation of the structural embodiment that we experience in transactions with others. Indeed, this conscious interrogation is the problematic of space:

> One can approach the space problem from at least two sides: either we do not reflect but just live among things, in which case we see space vaguely as

> the environment in which things are, or perhaps as a quality common to all things; or else we do reflect and grasp space by its roots to discover that spatial relations only exist and live through a subject who describes them; in that case, Merleau-Ponty says, we go from a "spatialized space" to a "spatializing space." In the former case, my body appears together with the things and their mutual concrete spatial relations as an irreducible multiplicity. In the latter case, however, I discover one single indivisible capacity which constitutes space. In the first case, we are concerned with physical space and its differently qualified regions; in the second, it is a question of the abstract homogeneous and isotropic geometrical space [Kockelmans 1970, pp. 281–82].

At this point, I hope that it is clear that I am arguing rather strongly for the fact that pathology and mythology constitute a *spatialized space* that in communication science is *parole parlée*. That is, in both the pathology of the patient and the mythology of the practicing believer "my body appears together with the things and their mutual concrete spatial relations as an irreducible multiplicity." For Merleau-Ponty the pathology is present in the patient; for Levin the mythology is prototypically present in the primitive society. In both illustrations, "we are concerned with physical space and its differently qualified regions." For the patient, physical space is subjectivity and the qualified regions exist as the intersubjectivity that is no longer embodied in others. For the primitive society, physical space is the anthropomorphic intersubjectivity of the rain forest and the qualified regions exist where embodiment is not possible.

By contrast, Merleau-Ponty's call for rediscovery through philosophical consciousness (see Lanigan 1972, p. 147) is a *spatializing space* that in communication science is *parole parlante*. It is speaking in which "I discover one single indivisible capacity which constitutes space." That capacity is the *radical cogito* manifest in the discourse of perception. Or to use Merleau-Ponty's words, the capability is the "gesture" of the body-subject. In discursive action, a person's gesture thematizes conscious experience as an "abstract homogeneous and isotropic geometrical space" that we denominate the *person*. In pathology the vicarious presence of association, ambivalence, autism, and altered affect are precisely the failure of gesture, of speech speaking. The patient is confined by concrete heterogeneous and differential arithmetic space. For the patient this space is synonymous with the unconscious and its morbid clinical incidents. The primitive society is likewise confined by concrete space. For such primitive peoples this space is synonymous with the artifactual preconscious and its institutional form in ritual memory. Likewise the failure of gesture as totem—ritual in this case also—brings the experiential presence of association, ambivalence, autism, and altered affect. In consequence, mythology and pathology both display a discourse practice (structure) that is a technical condition of "information." That is, both are a situation in which behavior results in a *context* that creates an acceptable range of *choices* (see chap. 14, below).

In either the pathological or mythological context, the person is (as Sartre argues) condemned to choose. As Merleau-Ponty describes the problematic, "It is essential to space that it continually is *already* constituted. One can therefore never understand it if one withdraws to a perception without a world." Thus, for "our primordial encounter with things, being is identical with being-situated" (Kockelmans 1970, p. 288). What is pathological or mythological here is the choice to locate the person by reference to the world.

In other words, the objectivist illusion of the world constituted in pathology and mythology is the positing of a spatializing space in an already constituted world, in a spatialized space. First, the positing is especially clear as a positivist phenomenalism in the discourse of everyday perception, which represses conscious experience. The sentences of the schizophrenic and the mythical story are always grammatically correct and recognizable as oral competence. What signals misadventure is the discursive performance, the gesture made. The performance is a "primordial encounter with things" and not the person's being-in-the-world. As Ellul (1975, p. 97) descriptively puts it, "myth is an anonymous discourse. No one is talking to anyone." Second, but in parallel fashion, the deceptive positing is clear in the appeal to "objective thought" that represses conscious experience. That is:

> Objective, geometrical space appears before us only when we thematize perceptual or lived space, without questioning its origin. Objective, geometrical space cannot be divorced from orientated or lived space, because it is merely an explication of them from a certain point of view [Kockelmans 1970, p. 288].

We are now in a position to suggest what Merleau-Ponty offers as an account of lived-space. In turn, this explication will permit a comparison with the interpretation that Levin and Koestenbaum offer. Merleau-Ponty says:

> How, then, can I who perceive, and who, *ipso facto*, assert myself as universal subject, perceive another who immediately deprives me of this universality? The central phenomenon, at the root of both my subjectivity and my transcendence towards others, consists in my being given to myself. *I am given*, that is, I find myself already situated and involved in a physical and social world—*I am given to myself*, which means that this situation is never hidden from me, it is never round about me as an alien necessity, and I am never in effect enclosed in it like an object in a box. My freedom, the fundamental power which I enjoy of being the subject of all my experiences, is not distinct from my insertion in the world [1962, p. 360; cf. Seamon 1979; Dillon 1978].

Several issues are resolved by Merleau-Ponty's explanation. First, he makes us sensitive to the operation of the phenomenological reduction of freedom, which carries with it an explication of lived spatializing. Again, a discourse example is helpful in illustrating the intentionality Merleau-Ponty describes. Here I refer to the technical concept of "communication." Communication is a discourse practice in which my speaking (*parole parlante*) is a *choice* that establishes a *context*. Recall that this formulation is the reverse of "information" in which context sets up a choice range. Communication, as a choice that grounds a context, is the horizon of freedom confirming that "I am given to myself" (Lanigan 1977, pp. 86ff.). It is only on this infrastructure of practice that freedom can manifest the informational, albeit functional, distinction of spatialized space, which is the physical world represented in *langue* and that of the social lived-world of spatializing space re-presented in *parole* (Jameson 1972).

And further, it is this infrastructure that is presupposed in the dysfunctions of pathology and mythology. In the dysfunctions I am surely in a situation hidden from me that is around me as an alien necessity and in effect encloses me as an object in a box. When I am no longer given to myself, I am no longer condemned to meaning. In-sanity becomes the transformation of non-sense; and in the structuralist fallacy, *langue* becomes the space of *parole*.

Although Levin (1979, p. 21) clearly does not advocate pathological behavior as a function of therapeutic philosophy, he does so for mythology. In fact, on the issue of sanity as a norm related to repression he suggests to us that "the functioning of the myth narratives and images directly corresponds to a dimension of our experienced embodiment which we have 'repressed,' and which therefore continues to haunt us with its crying need for release." Yet as Merleau-Ponty (1962, p. 294) warns, "If myths, dreams, and illusion are to be possible, the apparent and the real must remain ambiguous in the subject as in the object." If myth is therapeutic, it remains so at the expense of philosophic consciousness, which does not explore it and does not lend positive value to the ambiguity as a hermeneutic (Geertz 1973, pp. 88ff., 1983, p. 77; Morriston 1979). "That is to say that subjectivity is a flux, that it does not become static and does not know itself" (Merleau-Ponty 1962, p. 292). The same point applies to Koestenbaum's use of philosophic consciousness as therapeutic, as the phenomonalist practice of discourse as intervention.[3]

In short, Levin's account of sanity and myth, and Koestenbaum's

3. I am indebted to Professor Jnanabrata Bhattacharyya, director of the graduate program in the Department of Community Development at Southern Illinois University, for my understanding of *intervention* as a discursive practice of cultural and political domination.

approach to therapeutic practice, suggest to me that pathology is an objective illusion of the soul that should not be emulated. Yet, mythology for Levin and philosophy for Koestenbaum are an objective illusion of the heart that should be cherished in a vigorous therapeutic philosophy. I hope it is apparent that I disagree with these proposals. I disagree on two counts, which I stress in my analysis. First, when philosophy becomes therapeutic communication, it falls into a psychologism in the Cartesian tradition. The structure and content of conscious experience become a bad ambiguity that confines freedom and spatiality; choice and context become a binary equivocation instead of a phenomenological thematic grounded in the analogue of discourse. Second, when philosophy becomes therapeutic, it must rely on an objectivist illusion rather than on lived conscious experience. In pathology the objectivist illusion is contained in expression, and in mythology the illusion is enveloped in perception. Hence, pathology and mythology become functional because of their structural affinity with repression in the natural attitude.

Yet we cannot, to my mind, accept the proposition that the objectivist illusion in therapeutic philosophy can be a communication science application of philosophic consciousness. As Schrag (1980, p. 120) insightfully argues, "The meaning of myth is not the achievement of a representation mediated by an objectifying concept, but rather the *logos* incarnated in the experience of presence as the fulfilled moment of vision and action." Thus with Merleau-Ponty (1963a, p. 52), I prefer to conclude that in a rigorous phenomenology of communication "philosophy is not an illusion."

Chapter Six

Phenomenological Reflections on Habermas' Critical Theory of Communication

The years 1967 to 1969 are now a memory. Yet, memories shape desires as commitment. Persons commit themselves, as the French say, to *l'histoire*. Persons are the story of the moment that vehemently marks out a value choice that should be lived through in society. This social living through, this history, becomes for most a desire, a reminiscence. For a few, it is a memory. The memory is that consciousness and reflective capability by which we come to make personal choices of social consequence.

Our memory is critical of our actions: each person values society by participating in it. Indeed, this is the nature of government and the function of politics. But when action fades into habit, memory becomes an uncritical desire to be forgotten in the reminiscent familiarity of institutions or lost in fear. The years 1793 and 1794 are such a reminiscence. Only the student of political history has a memory that instantly pieces together the puzzle that was the infamous "Reign of Terror" by the Committee of Public Safety in the Paris Commune.

The political years 1967 to 1969 are a guaranteed memory, never to be lost to reminiscence. Rarely has such a brief moment of history been recorded so meticulously and analyzed so critically for its story. Two extraordinary examples are the critical case study analyses of the October 27, 1968, demonstration in London, England, against the Vietnam war (Halloran, Elliot, & Murdock 1970), and that of the "May Movement" by French students in Paris from November 1967 to June 1968 (Schnapp & Vidal-Naquet 1971).

The years 1967 to 1969 exist as a paradigm case in the evolution of a critical theory of political communication. They signal not a new reign of terror displaying the collision of theory and praxis, but a renaissance of humane discourse, a *Selbstbestsinnung* or critical self-awareness of the political meaning attached to social science research—the discovery of ideology as a level of meaning in research per se (Frankfurt Institute 1972). These years announce a rebirth of concern by European and Latin American scholars with the power of discourse in all modes of human life and the social responsibilities that attach to the exercise of that power. As Schnapp and Vidal-Naquet (1971, pp. 2, 49) suggest, *La Commune Etudiante*'s failed university strike demand for a return to the method of oral examination and the abolition of written examinations illustrates the critical theory perspective. That is, "the dream of a society that would be pure speech characterized the movement, but it was just that: a dream, since in reality 'pure speech' can only lead to 'pure action,' another dream of the movement." Thus Max Horkheimer, founder of the Frankfurt Institute for Social Research, reminds us:

> Men of good will want to draw conclusions for political action from the critical theory. Yet there is no fixed method for doing this; the only universal prescription is that one must have insight into one's own responsibility. Thoughtless and dogmatic application of the critical theory to practice in changed historical circumstances can only accelerate the very process which the theory aimed at denouncing. All those seriously involved in the critical theory, including Adorno, who developed it with me, are in agreement on this point [1972, p. v].

Memories shape commitment, but we must make our commitments critically.

WHAT IS CRITICAL THEORY?[4]

Following upon Horkheimer's remark about method and application, it is now apparent why it is necessary to begin this essay with an exercise in critical thought about a memorable event in political communication, the 1967–1969 epoch. Critical theory variously evokes denotations and connotations of a long tradition in German philosophy and sociology essentially located in a Marxist or neo-Marxist orietation, and historically referenced by the work of the Frankfurt Institute for Social Research

4. Portions of the analysis presented in this chapter are based on "Critical Theory as a Philosophy of Communication," a paper presented on May 30, 1977, at the International Congress on Communication Science sponsored by the International Communication Association, in West Berlin, Germany. It contains a short elaboration on a section from chap. 2, above, giving contextual clarity to the argument in the present chapter.

(Horkheimer 1972; Adorno et al. 1976; Jay 1973; Schroyer 1975). At the more recent end of this German tradition, the work by Jürgen Habermas (1970b; 1971a, b; 1973; 1975; 1979b), director of the Max-Planck-Institute at Starnberg, specifically focuses critical theory on the problem of communication, although this is not an exclusive direction in German social science (Merton & Gaston 1977). The result, over the long term, is a growing diversity of application (Rogers 1981). Originally a calculated attack on philosophic and scientific positivism, critical theory now has become a questioning of, and qualitative approach to, the study of communication in a world dominated by quantitative methodologies and the social perspective of an advanced industrial society modeled on the United States.

This new "second force" in critical theory shares the problematic determined by the older German "first force" school of thought whose advocates have been a majority in Germany and a minority in the United States. But this second force, which is often non-Marxist, owes its motivation to a number of grass-roots efforts—a political legacy of the 1967–1969 period—to move the academy into the community. I shall mention only the most important of these efforts, leaving the majority to citation.

In Europe, the second force effort began at a plenary session of the 1969 conference of the European Association of Experimental Psychology held in Belgium at the University of Louvain:

> On the one hand, there was genuine respect for much that has been achieved through the well-tried methods of clear-cut empirical hypotheses and their experimental testing. On the other hand, many felt that an unquestioned acceptance of the assumptions—social, scientific, and philosophical—underlying much of this research was a heavy price to pay for achieving a modicum of "scientific respectability" and even for making *some* gains in knowledge. It is possible that the "student revolution"—very much in evidence in the spring of 1969—had something to do with these conflicts [Israel & Tajfel 1972, p. 2].

The culmination of these and subsequent discussions was the publication of a now classic book edited by Joachim Isreal and Henri Tajfel, *The Context of Social Psychology: A Critical Assessment.*

Representative of a similar mood in Latin America was the publication of "Ideology and Social Sciences: A Communicational Approach" by Eliseo Verón (1971), then director of the Research Program on Social Communication at the Torcuato Di Tella Institute, Center for Social Research in Buenos Aires, Argentina. In this important article, Verón speaks in the voice of second force critical theory: "From the point of view of communication theory, ideology is a level of meaning, and this implies that it is a structural condition of production of messages within a human language system, including scientific communication" (p. 74). This critical judgment derives from the fact that "in science, the ideological level of meaning stems from all those options in the construction of scientific language that are not decidable in terms of the formal rules of scientific procedure. This field, as everyone knows, is very wide in the social sciences today" (p. 70).

At nearly the same time in Great Britain, a profoundly personal, yet parallel statement was issued by Trevor Patemen (1976) with the private (he refused complicity with commercial publishing houses) publication of *Language, Truth, and Politics: Towards a Radical Theory for Communication*:

> Of course, since I was a Ph.D. student in Philosophy, I was meant to get on with a conceptual rather than a substantive analysis, and the impossibility or emptiness of doing such a thing is one reason why this book exists and not a thesis shelved in the Library of the University of London. In any case, this book refocuses the problem of consciousness in a communicational perspective [p. 26].

Last, I should note that the once clear line existing between what I have called the first force, German, and the second force strain in critical theory is now becoming blurred. If I can characterize the overall movement or development of critical theory, it is to say that first force critical theory began with the Marxist problematic (that is, a theoretically defined problem) of social interaction and has developed a movement toward the problem of language (Apel 1967; 1972a, b; 1980; Habermas 1971b; 1976; McCarthy 1978; Dallmayr & McCarthy 1977). By contrast, second force critical theory began later in various countries besides Germany and often with a non-Marxist concern for the problem of language—in particular, the political nature of speech or language use—and moved to the problematics of society, especially those directly associated with the definition of situation within a speech community (Giglioli 1972; Sandywell et al. 1975; Smart 1976; Poster 1979; Fiske & Hartley 1978; Bisseret 1979; Blake 1979; Cotteret 1979; Grossberg 1978; Harms 1980; Jacobson 1980; Kress & Hodge 1979; Lemert 1979).

An especially good illustration of this second force orientation and of the empirical, qualitative method used by critical theorists is Mueller's study of the political sociology of language (1973; see Tsuda 1985). He begins his dialectic analysis with the data specifying the rewriting of standard German dictionaries and encyclopedias by the Nazis and subsequent modifications by the East Germans. This paradigm case is then used as a standard by which to generalize criteria inductively for comparative (dialectical) analysis with other data, such as linguistic stratification in social classes, and subsequent mass media appeals designed for maintaining these classes. Mueller's analysis is particularly useful for American political communication scholars, for he offers a very readable account of empirical research ranging over German and American mass media, voters, and political authority from a critical theory perspective.

At the risk of oversimplification, let me suggest that the empirical qualitative approach of critical theory, especially in its second force context, consists in the following process: (1) A paradigm case of empirical data is examined because it displays certain overt normative features. (2) A set of inductive generalizations is made from the paradigm case (that is, a theoretical exemplar is constructed). (3) The exemplar is used to locate and specify new data (often linguistic), which are, at least by first perception, value-free or "objective." (4) The ideological value inherent in the "objective" data is discovered and its actual value commitment exposed because of the exemplar.

Where the critical theory is informed by a Marxist perspective, we need to add a fifth step, which consists in (5) a demand for ideological correction of the "objective" situation by restoring decision-making power and control to the people whose actions constitute that situation. Such a demand usually rests on an analysis showing that the apparent "objective" situation exists as an institutional force that systematically frustrates an individual's ability to act otherwise. The extent to which the Marxist perspective is required by second force critical theorists has prompted in part the republication and translation of classic articles by first force authors (Adorno et al. 1976; Horkheimer 1972; Frankfurt Institute 1972) and new commentaries by their adherents and critics (R.J. Bernstein 1978; O'Neill 1976; Bologh 1979; Jung 1979).

In order to explicate the key issues with respect to the development of a critical theory perspective on political communication, I propose to divide the remainder of this chapter into three parts. The first section is a brief discussion of the HISTOMAT exemplar of Wulf D. Hund and Horst Holzer, which is a characteristic illustration of second force critical theory emergent in contemporary Germany. The second section discusses the communication model offered by Jürgen Habermas, largely because this model is the best effort by a first force critical theorist and typifies the Frankfurt School *theoretical* grounding. This theoretical position is to be distinguished from the technical, philosophical position articulated by Karl-Otto Apel (1980), which I shall note at relevant points of analysis. And third, I offer a critique of Habermas's model of universal pragmatics as a philosophy of political communication.

ELEMENTS OF A NEO-MARXIAN THEORY OF COMMUNICATION[5]

In recent years the work of German sociologists Wulf D. Hund (1980) and Horst Holzer (1973) began to attract increased international attention alongside the work by Habermas. Hund and Holzer are principally known for their writings on media theory and their orientation on historical-dialectical materialism (HISTOMAT). Their work is strongly rooted within the philosophical tradition of German social thought. It brings together the insights of critical theory and contemporary Marxist philosophy and can be called *neo-Marxian* in orientation.

This approach proceeds from the basic societal contradictions to be found in mass media production, distribution, and consumption. For example, it underscores, more emphatically than does critical theory, the antagonism of interests existing between capital and labor in media production. And it points to the commodity character of media products as an instrument of manipulation by mass communications. In addition, this approach assigns a fundamental role to the historical conditions of development and traces the emergence of mass communications back to the needs of the capitalistic model of production (Bisky 1976).

In this view, the antagonism between capital and labor manifests itself in the subjugation and dependence of media producers to media capital—that is, in the placement of the producers at the bureaucratic disposal of owners. The conditions of capitalist media production based on profit maximization considerations are seen as leading to increased concentration and monopolization. Thus, the commodity character of the media determines the selection of the content in accordance with the criteria of saleability and attractiveness to ensure profit maximization.

The indictment of *manipulation* is directed against those media products, such as sensationalist press reportage, that divert the attention of the mass audience from their objective interest and basic needs, from "the basic orientations rooted in specific fundamental conditions of the possible reproduction and self-constitution of the human species, namely *work* and *interaction*" (Habermas 1971a, p. 196). The accusation *in flagrante delicto* also encompasses the consumption of pure entertainment material for regenerative and recuperative purposes, as well as advertising that creates artificial needs and thereby produces delusions of a harmonious and homogeneous society.

5. This section was written originally by Dr. Rudolf L. Strobl independently of any knowledge of the other sections. With Strobl's permission, I have adapted and included this section to provide a concrete indication of a current model not generally known to researchers who lack fluency in German. For a more detailed discussion of this historical-dialectical materialist analysis of communication, see Strobl (1980), Coward & Ellis (1977), Mićunović (1979), and Grossberg (1979).

To recapitulate, this media theory can be described as an historically and dialectically determined analysis of mass communication, specifically in terms of the antagonism between capital and labor in media production. From this antagonism results the commodity character of media production and distribution, which is closely related to manipulation through mass communication consumption. Such an analysis calls for a proletarian-emancipatory alternate *publicality* (a neologism meaning the sphere where communications take place) utilizing the achievements of the bourgeois media under transformed structures of control.

Such a media theory aims essentially at the *democratic* transformation of prevailing conditions in the entire scope of mass communications. Whereas first force critical theory, which also has the same aims, tends to offer nothing more than abstract postulates and generalizations, neo-Marxian media theoreticians specify the aims of such a new media theory. In addition, they are proposing a long-term strategy for the *democratization of the mass media*, which has the following political goals:

1. changing the content of the mass media so that materialism and communication are not distorted as consumerism and persuasion (discussed below in the critique of Habermas), which has permeated deeply into the consciousness of employees and wage earners;
2. dismantling of the capitalist system and thereby the existing structures of mass communication and the subsequent creation of a political, proletarian *publicality* (Negt & Kluge 1972);
3. worker participation in all areas of mass media production (on the editorial, technical, and administrative levels); liberation of the workers in media production from subjugation and dependence on the providers of capital;
4. transferring media control from private owners to producers, expropriation of privately run media business, decentralization and demonopolization of media firms and their transformation into socialized institutions open to participation on the entire allocative and operational spectrum;
5. the formation of advertising and publicity cooperatives to distribute advertisements and publicity orders to all affiliated media on an equal basis and thereby to prevent concentration of communication powers; and
6. the political activization of the masses for communicative emancipation and the development of communicative competence—that is, action oriented toward reaching understanding (Habermas 1971a)—in the spontaneous creation of media programs through public articulation of objective societal needs and interests.

Hund and Holzer have been sharply critical of the traditional bourgeois mass communication research and its theories. According to them, the bourgeois communication research accepts mass media as tools of domination and the state of *speechlessness* in societal communication as given—that is, the lack of individual participation illustrated, for example, by the issue of "local access" in cable television licensing. They refer to it as administrative, directed, and bureaucratically enacted research: its findings and conclusions serve only those who are already dominating the existing order for the *consciousness industry*. Furthermore, it presumes the dualism of subject and object, and the divergence of *what is* from *what ought to be*. Bourgeois media theory is thus seen as a theory of domination.

Critical and neo-Marxian media theoreticians, on the other hand, focus on the mass media as instruments of liberation (Negt 1978; Negt & Kluge 1972). They see them as a means through which the objective and authentic interests of the masses can be articulated. Their communication research reflecting this perception centers on the social state of the media, culture, and the educational system in the context of conflicts between social strata, rather than within the media. These theoreticians reject the distinction between what is and what ought to be. Science is seen not as something separate from daily experience, but as a process that should contribute in form and substance to the proletarian context of life, which itself organizes the experiences of the masses in a specific way. The objective of critical and neo-Marxian communication research therefore is not the *distribution* of mass communications through mass media, but an absolute societal *communication* itself through the exchange of information about the objective interests and needs of the masses.

As a final point of emphasis, Hund and Holzer's philosophical orientation and thought based on *historical-dialectical materialism* (HISTOMAT) pertains to social research generally and to communication research specifically at the following three levels (Hahn 1968):

1. HISTOMAT contains, as a dialectic and materialistic philosophical theory of society, the basic solution of *epistemological* problems that we find in sociological research. These problems stem from certain peculiarities of this research and from social reality. This applies especially to the materialistic determination of the subject-object relationship.

2. HISTOMAT represents the basic solution of general *theoretical* questions that sociological research centers on and with which sociological research is connected through a number of special theoretical assertions. HISTOMAT offers the basic theoretical framework, terminology, and categories that also make possible the scientific analysis of single problems in an empirical way.

3. These two relationships are at the same time essential parts of the *methodological* function of HISTOMAT in relation to sociological research in terms of the use of certain logical procedures.

Habermas provides a theoretical discussion of these issues in part 2 of his *Knowledge and Human Interests* (1971a). Mićunović (1979) provides a specific illustration of them in his analysis, "Bureaucracy and Public Communication."

HABERMAS'S MODEL OF UNIVERSAL PRAGMATICS

In the latest essay describing universal pragmatics (Habermas 1979b), which extends the discussion of an earlier working position (Habermas 1971c [cf. 1984, 1:xxxix]; 1976), Habermas explains that the purpose of such a pragmatics is "to identify and reconstruct universal conditions of possible understanding (*Verständigung*)." As he further notes, such an analysis concerns the general presuppositions of communicative action, which is fundamental to working out the problem of *understanding*. What makes the model of universal pragmatics one of political communication is highlighted in his forthright declaration:

> Thus I start from the assumption (without undertaking to demonstrate it here) that other forms of social action—for example, conflict, competition, strategic action in general—are derivatives of action oriented to reaching understanding (*verständigungsorientiert*) [1979b, p. 1].

The axiological context for action Habermas outlines is thus inclusive of all the normal subtopics of axiology: politics, ethics, and morality (Habermas 1979a). In particular, we might characterize the universal pragmatics model as one of communicative ethics in which the standard constructs of communication theory are displayed: intention, punctuation, convention, and legitimation. It is a viewpoint Habermas (1979b, p. 2) confirms by stating: "I shall develop the thesis that anyone acting communicatively must, in performing any speech action, raise universal validity claims and suppose that they can be vindicated (or redeemed: *eingelöst*)."

INTENTION

Habermas (1970a) locates intention, the object of consciousness experience, within the hermeneutic theory of psychoanalysis. Explicitly he argues that psychoanalytic theory gives the researcher (1) a preconception of the structure of nondistorted ordinary communication; (2) an attribution of the systematic distortion of communication to the confusion of two developmental levels of symbols organization, the prelinguistic and linguistic; and (3) a theory of deviant socialization to explain the origin of deformation. The model of logic Freud provided in his analysis of thought, discourse, and behavior is widely recognized by European scholars but, Anglo-American researchers tend to discount Freud's work as empirically represented in its questionable contemporary use as a successful therapeutic procedure. In terms of Habermas's work in particular and European scholarship in general, it is well to recall that the Freudian heritage is the *logic model* (an exemplar) that is utilized to focus on new problems, issues, or data. The best detailed discussion of Freud in this context is that of Wilden (1980), wherein the Freudian semiotic model of condensation and displacement is specifically related to the theory constructs that constitute information theory and communication theory (cybernetics) and are exemplified in the technology of digital and analogue computers.

On this psychoanalytic base, Habermas builds a parallel set of theoretical propositions that indicate the meaning parameters in *normal communication*. First, in the case of nondeformed language games, there is a congruency of all three levels of communication as presented in the psychoanalytic model above. Second, normal communication conforms to intersubjectively recognized rules; it is public in this sense. Third, speakers are aware of the categorical difference between subject and object in normal speech. Fourth, normal communication provides a contextual situation in which an intersubjectivity of mutual understanding, which guarantees ego-identity, develops and is maintained in the relationship between individuals who acknowledge one another. Fifth:

> Normal speech is distinguished by the fact that the sense of substance and causality, of space and time, is differentiated according to whether these categories are applied to the objects within a world or to the linguistically constituted world itself, which allows for the mutuality of speaking subjects [1970a, p. 212].

Punctuation

The boundary limitation for the analysis of normal communication results from two postulates Habermas draws from his set of five propositions. He argues that psychoanalysis in the study of communication relies on a genetic connection beyond successive phases of human symbol organization. First, "the archaic symbol-organization, which resists the transformation of its contents into grammatically regulated communication, can only be disclosed on the basis of the data of speech pathology and by means of the analysis of dream material" (1970a, p. 212). Second, the symbol organization the psychoanalyst utilizes is a theoretical construct in that it genetically precedes language. In brief, Habermas goes on to suggest that such a theoretical construct presumes a theory of communicative competence modeled on Chomsky's model of linguistic competence/performance.

Habermas's theory of communicative competence is a combination of the problem as defined by psychoanalysis and the method of ordinary language analysis suggested by the conceptual analysts: Austin (1962), Grice (1967), and Searle (1967; 1969). In particular, Habermas (1979b) adopts Searle's general formulation of the speech act theory and applies it in the social context of communication (Sullivan 1978). That is, an interpersonal model of communication at the performance level is generalized to a model of social discourse (as a legitimation process) at the competence level. In this generalization of social levels from the individual to the mass, Habermas maintains the ideal speech situation as a construct—that is, Searle's model, where the interpersonal communication is always logical, literal, and contextually unambiguous. Let me simply indicate that there are serious problems in maintaining such an ideal in the analysis of empirical social research (Wellmer 1976).

Habermas offers the following set of theoretical propositions, which correspond at the social level to those that Searle (1967; 1969) presents for the interpersonal speech act. (1) The personal pronouns and their derivatives form a reference system between potential speakers. The identity of meanings, the foundation of all communication, is based on intersubjectively valid rules—at least two speakers understand the meaning of a symbol on the basis of reciprocal recognition. (2) The deictic expressions of space and time, as well as articles and demonstrative pronouns, form the reference system of possible denotations. (3) Forms of address (vocative), forms of social contact (greeting), of speech introduction and speech conclusion, indirect discourse, questions and answers, are performatory in that they are directed at the act of speaking as such. (4) The performatory speech acts form a system that finally enables us to mark the basic differentiations fundamental for any speech situation. Thus system relationships are formed between (a) being and appearance; (b) being and essence; and (c) fact and value—that is, what is and what ought to be.

Convention

The summary result that Habermas's model of communication achieves is a specification of the social levels of communication and the parallel validity claim that can be based on speech acts as rule-governed behavior with social import. By examining the formation and transformation of speech acts, Habermas (1976) arrives at two levels of communication. First is the *level of intersubjectivity*, at which the speaker and hearer, through illocutionary acts, bring about an interpersonal relationship that allows them to achieve mutual understanding. Second is the "level of objects in the world, or states of affair about which they would want to achieve a consensus in terms of the communicative role as laid down in the level of intersubjectivity" (p. 159).

In principle, therefore, every competent speaker has the responsibility of choosing among three modes of social communication (Habermas 1979b, p. 58): (1) communication to state a proposition that can be illustrated in the propositional attitude of a nonparticipating third person who hears a speech act. (2) Communication to stress an interpersonal relationship as such, as illustrated in the performative attitude of a participant conforming to the expectations of a second person. Or (3) communication to express an intention as such (that is, speakers present themselves before others). Each form of communication carries a claim to validity that is situationally recognized for its value (Hooft 1976).

LEGITIMATION

Habermas makes an explicit connection between communication and axiology, both in terms of how human communication leads to ethical judgments about persons and in terms of the social aesthetic (moral) values that dominate personal existence. Ultimately, his concern is with the special connection in communication by which personal ethics and social aesthetics form political norms of existence: social legitimation. Fiske and Hartley (1978) provide a useful empirical illustration of Habermas's view in their analysis of a British Broadcasting Corporation "News at Ten" program in which the main story is coverage of British troops in Northern Ireland. Their study provides a typical second force critical analysis in which the intended (by BBC programers) visual and oral information messages—a "social aesthetic" for Habermas—are structurally semiotic and thereby substantially perceived as norms of the "reality" of the situation, the "political norms of existence" for Habermas. In short, a political norm is offered as "information," thereby distorting the actual political situation and obviating viewers' opportunity to judge as individuals. Instead, mere viewing of the political norm message makes it legitimate information; this is social legitimation.

In careful propositional language, Habermas (1975) suggests that "only *communicative ethics* guarantees the generality of admissible norms and the autonomy of acting subjects solely through the discursive redeemability of the validity claims with which such norms appear" (p. 89). We should recall that communication is an action that deals with theoretical facts, values that have a pragmatic effect because they are formed in speech acts. In this context, Habermas advances three basic *pragmatic universals* (levels of understanding that emerge in human action), which are derived from the linguistic universals apparent in all speech communication.

First, "each specific language offers a reference system which permits a sufficiently reliable identification of something in the world about which one would want to make propositions." Second, "each specific language offers a *system* of personal pronouns and a system of speech acts with the aid of which we can bring about interpersonal relationships." And thirdly, "each particular language offers a *system of intentional expressions* for the self-presentation of subjectivity which, in spite of the degree of variation of its expression in particular languages, reflects the system of ego-delimitations" (p. 161).

For Habermas, then, social and political legitimation of personal and public action, whether technically instrumental or communicative, result in the formation of a communication ethic. That is, the rational society that manifests a universal pragmatics is a transformation of the communication community (*Kommunikationsgemeinschaft*) of those affected, who as participants in a practical discourse test the validity claims of norms and, to the extent that they accept them with reasons, arrive at the conviction that in the given circumstance the proposed norms are "right" (p. 105). A parallel argument in non-Marxist terms is made by Apel (1967; 1980).

In short, the critical theory model begins with an axiological pragmatics (legitimation) of speech communication based on the logical notion of ideal speech acts (convention). For Habermas, as a critical theorist, speech acts are part of the symbol formation process (punctuation) that derives its epistemological stages of development from the metaphysical approach of Freudian psychoanalysis and its theory of consciousness (intention). Thus, a theory of a rational society is an ideal generalized from a theory of normal communication in the rational person (Habermas 1979b, pp. 67–68). The resultant implications of the critical theory approach for political analysis and research as they relate to the traditional American view of empirical research are explored at length in the now classic essay by Reid and Yanarella (1974) entitled "Toward a Post-Modern Theory and American Political Science and Culture: Perspectives from Critical Marxism and Phenomenology."

A CRITIQUE OF HABERMAS AND CRITICAL THEORY

MARX AND PRACTICAL CONSCIOUSNESS

The concept and sometime slogan of "dialectical materialism" is, for all the caution of liberal politics in the West, intimately tied to the theory and practice of human communication. As Wellmer remarks:

> Only because Marx could rely on a revolutionary tradition, in which the intentions of achieving the freedom of the individual and personal happiness were already more or less clearly bound up with the idea of a public political arena constituted by citizens able to communicate with one another without coercion, and with the idea of *public* freedom and *public*

> happiness, was the young Marx's critique of Hegel able to become a criticism of the ideology of the bourgeois constitutional state of the advanced Western type [1971, p. 87].

The very concerns of "dialectical materialism" and "communication" are contemporary paradigms (Hickson & Jandt 1976) of what Habermas (1970a) calls *distorted communication*. As Marx suggests, "the chief defect of all previous materialism (including Feuerbach) is that things (*Gegenstand*) and reality, and the sensible world, are conceived only in the form of *objects (Objekt) of observation*, but not as *human sense activity*, not as *practical activity*, not subjectively" (Bottomore & Rubel 1963, p. 82; cf. Symthe 1977). Or as Apel (1972a, p. 3) asserts, "in my opinion, the chief question still is: whether it does or does not make a difference for the philosophy of science that in the human sciences, the *object* of science is also the *subject* of science, namely human society as a communication community." It is no surprise, then, that the technological consciousness of postindustrial democracy reifies, as a pragmatic of argumentation (Apel 1975, p. 247), the concepts of materialism and communication, thereby distorting them into *consumerism* and *persuasion*, respectively.

In the analysis that follows, I should like to illustrate the sense in which critical theory functions as a "militant philosophy" in the defense of communication as a human activity constituting the person as a subject in society. In addition, I should like to argue that critical theory as exemplified in the proposal by Habermas (1970b; 1971c; 1976; 1979b; 1984) for a "universal pragmatics" is grounded in the phenomenology of communication. Here I take the phenomenology of communication to be the subjectivity inherent in the existential speech act that makes consciousness a social product—that is, the constitution of the *Kommunikationsgemeinschaft*. Finally, my analysis attempts to raise the issue of the creation of values by positing a speech act phenomenology within the wider context of a universal pragmatics, which is a theme in the current research of Habermas (1979b, pp. 66–68; 1984a, b). In the development of these three themes, I hope to illustrate the appropriateness of Marx's contention:

> Language is as old as consciousness, language *is* practical consciousness, as it exists for other men, and thus as it first really exists for myself as well. Language, like consciousness, only arises from the need, the necessity of intercourse with other men. Where a relationship exists, it exists for me; the animal has no "*relations*" with anything, has no relations at all. For the animal, its relation to others does not exist as a relation. Consciousness is therefore from the very beginning a social product and remains so long as men exist at all [Bottomore & Rubel 1963, pp. 85–86].

In short, I wish to point out that the necessary dialectical materialism that communication creates is *not* consumerism grounded in persuasion. Rather, communication accounts for the dialectic in society by which individual persons constitute their consciousness of a lived-world (*Lebenswelt*) by the practical activity of speaking for themselves and others in the emancipatory process of identity, an authentic social existence. Interpersonal communication is thereby the legitimation of society as humanly lived (Lefebvre 1968, p. 66). As Merleau-Ponty (1964b, p. 130) suggests, "Marxism is not a philosophy of the subject, but it is just as far from a philosophy of the object: it is a philosophy of history (*l'histoire*)."

Militant Philosophy

"For the first time since Hegel militant philosophy is reflecting not on subjectivity but on intersubjectivity," says Merleau-Ponty (1964b, pp. 133–34) of Marx's insistence on the critique of the "objects of observation," which ignore the dialectic between the subject and the lived-world. At this point, we need to remind ourselves that human communication is itself an object of observation—a fundamental grounding. This is to say that metacommunication is a condition of human interaction in which communication is the methodology utilized to critique itself with attending implications for the description and explication of consciousness as bounded by society. In more familiar terms recalling the example of consumerism and persuasion, I am saying that a critical analysis of communication by a human communicator can lapse into reifying communication as language behavior (an object of consumption; the method of positivism) and into reifying the person as cognition (an object of persuasion; the method of ordinary language philosophy).

Habermas (1971b) correctly draws attention to the danger of reification by pointing out the appropriate social distinction between *purposive-rational action* (variously referred to as "instrumental") and *communicative action*. In this context, purposive-rational action is a condition of persuasion; that is, the state of affairs in which a preconceived metacommunication constitutes what communication is or can be—hence assigns a negative value to the emergence of an individual act in society. This negative value (consumerism) emerges in most cases as the *role* of the person in society as prescribed by society (metacommunication). By contrast, communicative action is a condition of emancipation (from the domination of persuasion), the state of affairs in which communication regulates what metacommunication is or can be—thereby assigning a positive value to the engagement of persons in individual acts (*parole*). The positive value is the generation of authentic existence (*parole parlante*) within the interpersonal boundaries (*langue*) of the social group (Habermas 1979b, p. 6).

At this point it is helpful to review the technical comparison Habermas draws between purposive-rational action and communicative action, because the distinction drawn illustrates what I have previously characterized as the "inductive" method of critical theory generally. In the former case;

> Instrumental action is governed by *technical rules* based on empirical knowledge. In every case they imply conditional predictions about observable events, physical or social. These predictions can prove correct or incorrect. The conduct of rational choice is governed by *strategies* based on analytic knowledge. They imply deductions from preference rules (value systems) and decision procedures; these propositions are either correctly or incorrectly deduced [1971b, pp.91—93].

In contrast, Habermas continues:

> By "interaction," on the other hand, I understand *communicative action*, symbolic interaction. It is governed by binding *consensual norms*, which define reciprocal expectations about behavior and which must be understood and recognized by at least two acting subjects. Social norms are enforced through sanctions. Their meaning is objectified in ordinary language communication. While the validity of technical rules and strategies depends on that of empirically true or analytically correct propositions, the validity of social norms is grounded only in the intersubjectivity of the mutual understanding of intentions and secured by the general recognition of obligations.

I have previously (Lanigan 1979a) made the argument that communication is by definition a speech act that succumbs to ambiguity when restricted to the status of an *action*. That is, interpersonal actions at any semiotic level are burdened by a good or bad ambiguity. Or, as Habermas (1979b, pp. 31–34) is forced to concede, the predictions of purposive-rational action prove correct or incorrect. Likewise, communicative actions are enforced or not by sanctions. In either case, the action is legitimized by the presence or absence of conative meaning (Habermas 1979b, p. 58). That is, a group expectation (social state of affairs) constitutes a negative value (it is a metacommunicative condition) of ambiguity—any result is held in question. Although Habermas contends that "learned rules of purposive-rational action supply us with *skills*, internalized norms with *personality structures*," we do not escape the metacommunication context. Our speech act may be the product of skill—for example, in the expression of an argument—or the act may reflect our personality structure, as in the perception of another's argument. Yet, the action is still Marx's object of observation in which the preconditions of communication (metacommunication) constitute inauthentically the human act. In short, ethical rhetoric (authentic discourse) is dominated by rhetorical ethics (inauthentic discourse; see chap, 1, above).

On reflection, then, it is apparent that critical theory is a militant philosophy in the problematic shift from an exclusive concern with subjectivity (bad ambiguity when counterposed to objectivity) to an inclusive concern with intersubjectivity (good ambiguity). Yet, the militancy of critical theory is subdued by the reification of practical activity as an object of analysis—which Marx warns against. Resolution of the problematic is, however, possible in the larger project of the philosophy of communication.

Phenomenology of Communication

Communication as a focus of phenomenological analysis is problematic when our analysis is limited to the "effects" of discourse at the interpersonal level. That is, the conception of communication as an action forces the analysis into a consideration of the causality of "meaning" (purposive-rational action) or "behavior" (communicative action). What is wanted, by contrast, is an account of the conditions for the *performance* (as production) of communication. Here the focus is on the *dialectic* of semantics, syntactics, and pragmatics in the sense of a semiotic phenomenology. In this context, semantics constitutes *capta*, or that which is taken to be the case (hypothesis). Syntactics accounts for *data*, or that which is given as being the case (hypostasis). And pragmatics is the realm of *acta*, or that which is done as the case (hermeneutic). The communication problematic advanced by Habermas is a digital logic that attempts to counterpose *capta* (communicative action) against *data* (purposive-rational action).

I am, therefore, in disagreement with the confirming interpretation that Wellmer (O'Neill 1976, pp. 248–49) ascribes to Habermas: "As epistemological categories, consequently, 'instrumental' and 'communicative' action represent the distinction between nomological and instrumental knowledge, on the one hand, and hermeneutic and reflective knowledge on the other. Correspondingly, they also reflect the methodological distinction between the 'natural sciences' and 'Geisteswissenschaften.'" This confusion is another instance of allowing familiar methodology to confuse the levels of communication and metacommunication—that is, the analogue distinction between a prereflective and reflective process (act) on the one hand and a preconscious and conscious act on the other. Although there is a categorical opposition between the prereflective/reflective and the preconscious/conscious that is binary in process, it is not a digital function in effect (as Habermas and Wellmer impute).

It is thus ironic that Habermas proceeds to argue for an "outer nature" (instrumental actions) and an "inner nature" (communicative actions):

> Linguistic communication has a double structure, for communication about propositional content may take place only with simultaneous metacommunication about interpersonal relations. This is an expression of the specifically human interlacing of cognitive performances and motives for action with linguistic intersubjectivity. Language functions as a kind of transformer; because psychic processes such as sensations, needs, and feelings are fitted into structures of linguistic intersubjectivity, inner episodes or experiences are transformed into intentional contents—that is, cognitions into statements, needs and feelings into normative expectations (precepts and values) [1975, p. 10; cf. 1979b, p. 41].

In this argument there is an equivocation generated in the following sequence of analysis. Nomological knowledge proceeds according to prescribed *rules* of reasoning, which in consequence become *tools* (instruments) for legitimate description (*explication*). Hermeneutic analysis describes the instrumental nature of legitimation and in consequence prescribes the reasoning that must be found in rules (legitimate *explanation*).

The equivocation occurs at two points in the argument. One is the concept of rules. Nomological knowledge relies on constitutive rules that entail regulative rules; explication entails (logically) explanation. In similar fashion, hermeneutic knowledge relies on the use of regulative rules that may be asserted as (but are not) constitutive; explanation can be made to explicate. In this sequence of events, we make the false assumption that rules define a state of consciousness ("inner nature"), rather than specify the relational process between the preconscious and the conscious. And we also incorrectly assume that rules indicate the emergence of the reflective from the prereflective as a static condition ("outer nature"). In point of fact, then, Habermas tends to make the instrumental-communicative action distinction rest on "action" as an object of observation, where observation is defined by rules conceived as normative conditions—that is, abstractions reified as perceptions (the form of the object of observation for Marx).

The second part of the equivocation concerns the concepts of nomological and hermeneutic judgment as they bear on the disjunction between the *Naturwissenschaften* and the *Geisteswissenschaften*. Where the process of observation is reified into the "state" of observation, we extend the ambiguity of rules (abstractions) utilized as conditions (perceived experience). It is widely assumed that this reification is legitimate in the physical sciences, for they are *data*-based, whereas the reification is illegitimate in the human sciences, for they are *capta*-based. As Habermas puts the issue,

> The cultural life context is formed on a level of intersubjectivity that is presupposed by the attitude of strictly empirical science but cannot be

> analyzed by it. If this is so, we are confronted by the question whether the cultural sciences in fact do not proceed within a different methodological framework and are not constituted by a different cognitive interest than the natural sciences comprehended by pragmaticism [1971a, pp. 140–41].

Of course, the point at issue is the nature and function of *acta*. (By identifying the problem as one of pragmatics, Habermas is entirely correct—even if we contest his conclusions.)

When we pay close attention to the place of action in the process of observation, we cannot dispose of the observer, the human agent. In this sense, the methodology of the natural and human sciences participates in the same process of legitimation. The dialectic is such that the natural scientist moves from the nomological to the hermeneutic as a process of legitimation, whereas the human scientist moves from the hermeneutic to the nomological as a process of value ascription. The point is that the dialectic process while directionally [descriptively] different [binary] is anological ['nature'] and not digital in consequence ['inner' or 'outer'] (Wilden, 1972; cf. 1980).

In short, the process of observation must be thrown over in preference to the observer, as Marx suggests. The practical activity of consciousness must be located in the person; we must focus on the *act* rather than the *action* (*data/capta*). In this sense, act is the name we can apply to the universal pragmatic that takes account of reified actions: nomological consciousness reified as *data* and hermeneutic consciousness reified as *capta*, where "reification" is rule-governed hypostasis (meaning) and hypothesis (behavior).

Before we take up the issue of pragmatics in the universal pragmatic, we need to discuss the ideal situation preconceived in the concept of "universal" as Habermas (1970b; 1979b, p. 29) derives it from the thesis of *communicative competence*.

SPEECH ACT PHENOMENOLOGY

The discussion of speech acts (Austin 1962; Searle 1967; 1969; Lanigan 1977) is a record of shifting perspective between the contexts of information theory (*data*) and communication theory (*capta*). Habermas locates this shifting argument within the "ideal" situation of language behavior by contrasting *linguistic competence* (according to Chomsky) with *communicative competence*. Although this move provides a certain amount of technical insight about human communication theory, I believe it is ultimately an unsatisfactory direction that falls victim to the very objection it is fleeing: "the idealization of pure communicative action would have to be reconstructed as the condition under which the authenticity of speaking and acting subjects can be imputed as well as verified" (Habermas 1973, p. 19).

According to Habermas:

> "Linguistic competence" is Chomsky's name for the mastery of an abstract system of rules, based on an innate language apparatus, regardless of how the latter is in fact used in actual speech. This competence is a monological capability; it is founded in the species-specific equipment of the solitary human organism. For such a capability to be a sufficient linguistic basis for speech, one would have to be able to reconstruct the communication process itself as a "monological" one. The information model of communication is suitable for this purpose [1970b, p. 361].

In contrast to the Chomsky theory of linguistic competence, which must assume an information theory model of human discourse (*langue* is reified as *langage*), Habermas argues that "on the contrary, in order to participate in normal discourse the speaker must have at his disposal, in addition to his linguistic competence, basic qualifications of speech and symbolic interaction (role-behavior), which we may call *communicative competence*. This communicative competence means the mastery of an ideal speech situation" (p. 367). Habermas (p. 369) further clarifies this thesis by suggesting that "communicative competence is defined by the ideal speaker's mastery of the dialogue-constitutive universals, irrespective of actual restrictions under empirical conditions." Thus, Habermas's proposal is the reification of *parole* as *langue* (which is assumed to be a reification of *langage* via linguistic competence).

The contribution Habermas makes to the ongoing analysis of speech acts is that he recognizes the *semiotic* requirement that communication be analyzed as the interaction of persons at the syntactic, semantic, and pragmatic levels. In this view, he advances beyond the work of Searle, who restricts his analysis to an information theory model grounded in a "monological" syntactics and developed as a "dialogical" semantics. However, Habermas accepts the same conditions of analysis Searle does by assuming the necessity of an ideal speaker in an ideal situation. This procedure repeats the mistake outlined above, in which rules are conceived as conditions of behavior and not inversely. "Ultimately, Habermas would want to argue, such communicative equality could only exist on the basis of real *social* equality. Here the theory of communication (aimed at truth) turns into political theory: the ideal speech situation becomes the ideal decision situation of Rousseau's *Social Contract*" (Pateman, 1976, p. 6).

In addition, the assumption of the "universal" perspective of the ideal speaker/situation does violence to the very concept of pragmatics. "Since most, if not all, signs have as their interpreters living organisms, it is a sufficiently accurate characterization of pragmatics to say that it deals with the biotic aspects of semiosis, that is, with all the psychological, biological, and sociological phenomena which occur in the functioning of signs" (Morris 1938, p. 30; see also Lanigan 1972). The lesson of Saussure that *parole*, *langue*, and *langage* are dialectically human communication is ignored by the technical approach Habermas takes.

I have argued in my *Speech Act Phenomenology* (1977) that a complete speech act analysis that includes a theory of communicative competence that *legitimizes* human interpersonal communication must be approached as a phenomenology of human interaction. In other words, an adequate account of communicative competence in a communication situation requires a "dialogical" consideration of pragmatics as the ground for syntactics and semantics. This is another version of the argument that *acta* (*parole*) must be the key for interpreting *data* (*langage*) and *capta* (*langue*). The social product of communication becomes the authenticity of a person speaking. Thus, the person legitimizes the act of communicating, rather than the false consciousness of the action defining the person—the mistake of positive behaviorism is thereby avoided.

It is necessary to point out that Habermas is quite aware of the difficulty attendant upon the notion of a "universal" in pragmatics as applied to speech acts. As he suggests:

> First, we would have to show that the structural change of world-views obeys an inner logic, such that the systematic variation of a basic pattern can be reconstructed. Over and above this, it would have to be possible to derive from the social evolution of world-views a universalistic morality based on the basic norms of speech and the ideas of the responsibly acting person developed in the model of pure communicative action. Then we could comprehend all divergent concepts of the person and the expressions of persons as modifications of the one universal idea of responsibility similar to those that guide us in relating to children [1971c, pp. 11–12; see also 1976; 1979b; 1984].

The consequences of this view of the idealization of the communication situation is in fact pragmatic to the extent that it allows Habermas to hypostatize levels of *choice* between various modes of communication. Choice is a fundamental concept here because it accounts for the "inner logic" that is possible among the pragmatic rules governing communication, such as social and cultural variation, psychological condition, and so on. In addition, this "levels" model of the communication act suggests the conditions under which the authenticity of communicating (morality) may be "imputed as well as verified."

There are four levels of choice between the different modes of communication. "On condition of free choice, every choice at a higher level eliminates choices at the next lower level." Habermas (1971c, p. 25) offers the schema presented in Figure 6 as an illustration of his model. As a matter of information, we should note that this working schema (and its

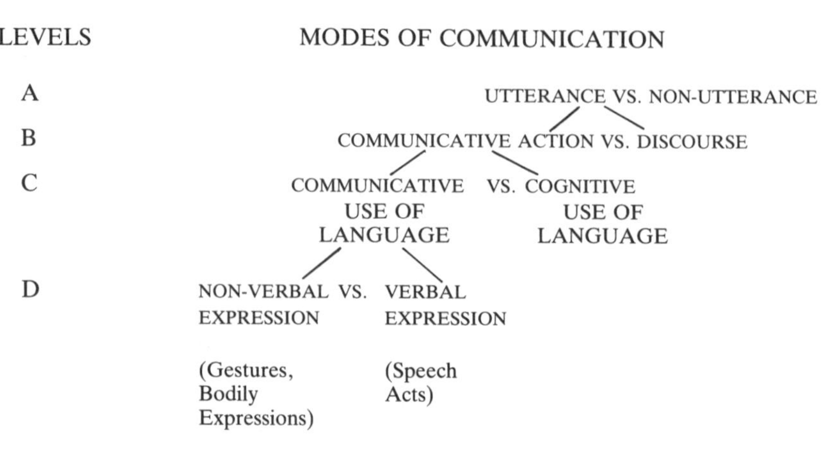

Figure 6. Choice levels in modal communication according to Habermas

variations [Habermas, 1979a, p. 196; 1979b, pp. 40, 209; 1984, 1:333, fig. 18]) of the modes of communication offered by Habermas already exists in large measure in the *Model of Sign Production* formulated by Eco (1976, p. 217). Eco divides the "physical labor" (empirical conditions) required to produce expressions into progressively higher levels of communication beginning with "recognition" advancing to "ostension" and then on to the level of "replica" and finally "invention." Eco's concern focuses on the production of "aesthetic texts" in which the hermeneutic of human sign production exemplifies as authentic social product in language—that is, signification in human code systems.

However, both Habermas and Eco take the restrictive view that dialogical communication in its pragmatic stance does not provide a basis for authentic choice where that choice is restricted to "freedom" in a social rather than personal sense. At the same time, they are unable to remove their analysis from the constrictions of the universal pragmatic that seems to be required for a transition from the problem of subjectivity to intersubjectivity in the analysis of communication as a *system*. Habermas concedes this point in his 1984 analysis (1:xxxix) by noting that the argument in the Gauss Lectures (1971c) "turned out to be mistaken." I believe this difficulty results in part from the failure to recognize the semiotic, rather than formal (Habermas 1979b, pp. 8–9), link between perception and expression (Lanigan 1979a). Perception is the social level that results from the infrastructure of expression, variously constituted by speech and communication acts (Lanigan 1979b). My position is illustrated in the schema in Figure 7 using the same general structure that Habermas presents.

LEVELS	MODES OF COMMUNICATION
A Perception:	THOUGHT VS. SILENCE
B Expression:	SYNCHRONIC LANGUAGE VS. DIACHRONIC LANGUAGE
C Speech:	RHETORICAL ACTS VS. MASTER SPEECH ACTS [Non-linguistic Acts]
D Communication:	SPEAKING VS. SPEECH ACTS

Figure 7. Choice levels in modal communication according to Lanigan

The perspective in this formulation is, of course, a specification of the dimensions of authentic choice as manifest in communication. As such, the social product of communication is produced by the *inclusion* of the choices at a lower level when the choice at a higher level is made. This position is clearly phenomenological in terms of social choice and existential in terms of personal choice. The arguments supporting this schema and analysis, which are technical and lengthy, have already been made elsewhere (Lanigan 1977). In short, I believe Habermas offers a successful parallel argument for social free choice in his discussion of social legitimation (which I will take up below) in his concept of *communicative ethics*, even though his analysis must still treat the person as an idealization in a like situation.

THE POLITICS OF SEMIOLOGY

Habermas (1975, p. 10) argues that "linguistic communication has a double structure, for communication about propositional content may take place only with simultaneous metacommunication about interpersonal relations. This is an expression of the specifically human interlacing of cognitive performance and motives for action with linguistic intersubjectivity." Speech acts then perform the function of a hermeneutic assessment for society. Speaking creates values; yet those values may not be overtly present to reflection on a social scale (What is a prudent act?), and the conscious values may be articulated but not known (What is an act in good faith?). In point of fact, the communication ethic is largely preconscious and prereflective:

> Only *communicative ethics* guarantees the generality of admissible norms and the autonomy of acting subjects solely through the discursive redeemability of the validity claims with which norms appear. That is, generality is

> guaranteed in that only norms that may claim generality are those on which everyone affected agrees (or would agree) without constraint if they enter into (or were to enter into) a process of discursive will-formation [Habermas 1975, p. 89].

In short, when communicators engage in communication acts that are both reflective and conscious (therefore *political*), they create values that morally link the subjective and the intersubjective. The semiotic connection of the personal and the interpersonal guarantees that the act joins, at one level, the preconscious and the reflective (expression). Yet again, the conscious and the reflective join (speech), as do the preconscious and prereflective (communication). Thus, the semiotic link that unites person and society is also the one that unites the modes of communication with pragmatic values. Recall Marx's assertion that "language *is* practical consciousness."

On the social level, Habermas (1979b, p. 49) provides an excellent statement of the political nature of semiotic analysis as the problem communicative action must address.

"It is a consequence of the fundamental contradiction of the capitalist system that, other factors being equal, either

- the economic system does not produce the requisite quantity of consumable decisions, or;
- the administrative system does not produce the requisite quantity of rational decisions, or;
- the legitimation system does not provide the requisite quantity of generalized motivations, or;
- the socio-cultural system does not generate the requisite quantity of action-motivating meaning."

The expression "the requisite quantity" refers to the extent, quality, and temporal dimension of the respective system performances (value, administrative decision, legitimation, and meaning).

It should not be difficult to see that in the phenomenological schema I present in Figure 7, Level A: "perception" is equivalent to Habermas's "socio-cultural system"; Level B: "expression," equal to "legitimation system"; Level C: "speech," equivalent to "administrative system"; and Level D: "communication," equal to "economic system." In making these ratios I want to assert the connection between authenticity of choice and language use/speech as a social product—that is, the Marxian thesis that "human sense activity" becomes a social product with personal value. Human communication is per se a political act (Cushman & Dietrich 1979).

To the extent that there is a system failure in a postindustrial capitalist society, there is a crisis of human identity. There is moral and political alienation and domination. The causality of this value interest in the person/society link is, as Habermas senses, contained in the *communication codes* that link the observation of action with the act of observing. The operative concept here is "code" where action, act, value, and interest are joint products of emancipation (Lanigan 1984). In this instance, "code" is the concept discovered by Merleau-Ponty that a primary characteristics of *human* communication is *parole parlante*: the speaking that is a speech act (communication ethic) and the speech act that is speaking (authentic communication):

> In the language of the Geisteswissenschaften we could say: The possibility that linguistic signs have meaning cannot be understood without presupposing a "meaning-intention" which expresses itself in the signs. In other words, not even the facts of science are facts for the unchanging "subject as such" (of "the language as such"), but they are constituted in a concrete and therefore historically determined human horizon of meanings [Apel 1967, p. 33].

In conclusion, let me suggest that the critical theory approach to a communication theory of society, initiated in the development of the speech act theory and the hermeneutic phenomenology of communication, represents a starting point in the analysis of the fundamental relationship between persons and societies. From Marx we gain an insight based on the nature of person and moral value. The fundamental grounding of emancipation from cunsumerism and persuasion as reified in social institutions is linked inseparably to the discovery of the communication community (*Kommunikationsgemeinschaft*) as a source of authenticity and interpersonal legitimation. Thus, "the greatness of Marxism lies not in its having treated economics as the principal or unique cause of history but in its treating cultural history and economic history as two abstract aspects of the same process" (Merleau-Ponty 1964b, p. 107).

[Section Two: EMPIRICAL RESEARCH]

Chapter Seven

Metajournalism

Merleau-Ponty on Signs, Emblems, and Appeals in the Poetry of Truth

Attica is a political memory. On September 13, 1981, we marked the tenth anniversary of a ten-minute period at the New York State Correctional Facility at Attica, New York, in which forty-three inmates and employees died, thirty-nine under gunfire by police and National Guard troops. In comparison with the Attica prison rebellion, there have been worse examples of property damage to a penal institution—for example, the $20 million worth of physical damage during the eight days of rioting at the state prison in McAlester, Oklahoma, in 1973. There have been worse examples of bloody mayhem, such as the riot at the maximum-security prison in Santa Fe, New Mexico, during 1980 in which thirty-three persons died. "Yet Attica remains the yardstick" (Anon. 1981).

But of what is Attica the measure? We should not be too hasty in perceiving Attica as a criterion only for penal disorders. We should consider the political characterization of Attica as a *rebellion* rather than a riot. The incidents at McAlester and Santa Fe are only riots. Attica is rebellion. As Foucault reminds us in his discussion of the American historical model for prisons, the Auburn, Massachusetts, prison of the nineteenth century: "The prison must be the microcosm of a perfect society in which individuals are isolated in their moral existence, but in which they come together in a strict hierarchical framework, with no lateral relation, communication being possible only in a vertical direction" (1979, p. 238). "The only way for prisoners to escape from this system of training is by collective action, political organization, rebellion" (Foucault 1974, p. 157).

Attica is a rebellion because Attica was open, organized, armed resistance to the power of authority on the Auburn model. Attica was overt rebellion against the penal institution and its vertical structure of communicative authority. And yet, Attica was a story about human beings, about individual lives suddenly and unexpectedly brought to their most existential moment. Attica was a covert rebellion of human dimension against the moral failure of the *idea* of the prison as a "perfect" society (Wicker 1975, p. 64; Foucault 1979, p. 305). This covert rebellion by prisoners was the demonstration of a political necessity in society—that is, the personal and social need for lateral communication. Communication among equals is the political demonstration of human society, of civility, and of morality. Thus, the Attica rebellion marked a social and political paradigm crisis in communality. Attica in the twentieth century stands as the anomaly for the historical Auburn model of the nineteenth century that yet endures.[6] Attica is a sign of Auburn. Attica is an emblem of failed civility. Attica is an appeal for a communicative ethic.[7]

The analysis that follows is my attempt to indicate the manner in which Merleau-Ponty offers us, through his semiotic phenomenology, a philosophic and theoretical account of human communication as coded in the genre of mass communication. This account in his essay "On News Items" ("Sur les faits divers") can be extended in Hjelmslevian function to Tom Wicker's *A Time to Die*. This book recounts Wicker's experience as an observer and reporter for the *New York Times* during the Attica rebellion.

I propose to develop the analysis of the Attica problematic and thematic in several parts. First, there is a brief discussion of metajournalism and its philosophic grounding in Merleau-Ponty's essay. Second, I suggest the phenomenological way in which Wicker's book is an illustration of Merleau-Ponty's semiotic metajournalism. Third, I offer some interpretations of metajournalism as a political code in constituting what Apel (1980, pp. 255ff.; 1981, pp. 28ff.) calls the *Kommunikationsgemeinschaft*.

MASS COMMUNICATION AS SEMIOTIC PHENOMENOLOGY

Merleau-Ponty begins his essay "On News Items" by recounting an incident he witnessed in the railway station in Genoa during Italy's Fascist period. A man jumps from the passenger platform in front of an oncom-

6. Foucault's analysis finds affirmation in Wicker's (1975, p. 7) comment that "the superindendent also was uneasy about 30 inmates who had taken part in an abortive riot at the Auburn Correctional Facility in 1970, and who had been transferred later to Attica."

7. I have in mind the critical theory view of communality that "only *communicative ethics* guarantees the generality of admissible norms and the autonomy of acting subjects solely through the discursive redeemability of the validity claims with which norms appear" (Habermas 1975, p. 89).

ing train. It is an act of suicide. A crowd of persons rush to witness the event and are harshly rebuffed by the police:

> This blood disturbed order; it had to be quickly wiped away, and the world restored to its reassuring aspect of an August evening in Genoa. All dizziness is akin. By seeing an unknown person die, these men could have learned to judge their life. They were defended against someone who had just disposed of his own. The taste for news items is the desire to see, and to see is to make out a whole world similar to our own in the wrinkle of a face [1964c, p. 311].

The facial grimace of the witness to self-inflicted death is a discourse of simultaneity. The nonverbal communication of the facial gesture is at once a sign, an emblem, and an appeal. The facial discourse as a sign contains a politically unacceptable signification. The gesture is a lateral communication of equality between the suicide victim and the witness. Each acts in opposition to established order. The act of personal freedom in suicide violates the social norm for order. And in the act of recognition, the witness admits the possibility of violation, itself a violation—but now one of political consequence. The recognition brings with itself the possibility of alternative norms—that is, lateral communication can codify a moral hierarchy competitive with that of vertical communication.

The blood of the suicide and the grimace of the witness are the same *signified*. They are an emblem of authority, a free use of the human body commanding political force. The *signifier* is, of course, the appeal to authority that is the expressive and communicative power contained as a communality in the shared actions of the suicide victim, the witness, and the rebuffing police officers. The signifier is what each person desires to see. "Seeing is that strange way of rendering ourselves present while keeping our distance and, without participating, transforming others into visible things" (Merleau-Ponty 1964c, p. 311).

The experience of the body coupled with the consciousness of choice powerfully codes the emblem in the appeal as a sign of political discourse. In his semiotic phenomenology, Merleau-Ponty specifies therefore the conscious experience that is a political discourse of authority in and for the individual person. But can this conscious experience be a product of the mass media? Does the text of mass communications signify a personal ethic with moral and political consequence, as Foucault and Merleau-Ponty hypothesize?

Affirmative answers to the questions posed have an American or European flavor under various nomenclatures such as new journalism, docufiction, investigative reportage, critical theory, political theater, developmental sociology, and so on. As Davies remarks:

> It is possible in this kind of communications analysis to deal serially with such issues as the rise of the novel, the influence of mechanization on art and architecture, the effect of print, or the impact of radio on a non-industrial society. It is even possible—in more absurd moments—to correlate "development" with the ideology of textbooks [1976, p. 60].

We are, in fact, confronted with two levels of interpretation when dealing with the match between the lived-world of other persons. First, we realize that there is a structural similarity between the events of our lives and those re-presented in the media. Both can have a serial presentation in the form of a linear causality of progression. That is, my memory of a self can be constructed in the same manner as my expectations for a character in reading a novel. Second, we realize that such a structural similarity is embodied. The conscious experience that is our style of living in a world of other persons is forever reversible as a semiotic. "This unity of the sensory experiences rests on their integration in a single life of which they thus become the visible witness and emblem" (Merleau-Ponty 1962, p. 319n). The system of Self-Other-World is an incarnate logic of intersubjectivity continually constituting expressions that are reversible with our original perceptions.

Eason (1977) offers us the neologism of *metajournalism* to describe a medium of the incarnate logic, the textual discourse, that a person lives in the conscious experience of mass communication in the Self-Other-World problematic. The term "metajournalism" specifies the semiotic character of the so-called new journalism movement in the United States during the late 1960s and early 1970s. As Eason notes:

> The New Journalism, that form of reporting associated with the narrative strategies of the novel and the short story, takes its energy from an image-conscious society in which traditional assumptions about manners and morals are breaking down. The writers find their stories in trends and events already transformed into spectacles by the mass media and use this image-world as a background for their interpretations. The central strategy of the New Journalism is to interpret public events as symbolic quests for significance by exploring the intentions, values, and assumptions of those affected by the events. Stories of political changes, the emergence of subcultures, space travel, murders, and executions all point to a common theme: the struggle for personal and group identity in a fragmenting society [1978, p. 1; see Nelson 1986]

Thus communal reality as a metajournalistic discourse presents both the truth of the existential choice in the *news item* as a semiotic artifact and the truth of the *novel* as another semiotic artifact within the phenomenological context of the possible as you and I can live it. Or as Merleau-Ponty (1964c, p. 313) expresses his semiotic phenomenology with respect to news items, "true little incidents are not life's debris but signs, emblems, and appeals. . . . Yet there is more and less in the novel than there is in true little incidents. It foreshadows momentary speech and gesture, and comments on them."

In these two genre perspectives—news item and novel—Merleau-Ponty indicates the poetry of truth hidden in the prose of discourse. This is to say, a person finds existential truths signified as emblems in the behavior of others, and signified as appeals in the narrative of mass communications. The two perspectives are not digital. We are not forced to choose one over the other in a futile Sartrian gesture of nothingness. Rather, the two views are the grasp (*Verständigung*) of analogues. The views are not merely functional analogues of one another, but analogues of the person. News items and novels are not just examples of the serial structure of information, but human values coded and embodied as poetic communication (Marcus 1974). News items as artifacts of consciousness; novels as artifacts of experience are both true to life because they are of life. In the phenomenology of the person, news items are emblems forming one boundary condition of interpersonal communication; novels are appeals forming the other boundary condition of social communication.

Foucault (1979, pp. 285–92; see Weiss 1978) demonstrates this concrete use of Merleau-Ponty's model of mass communication by showing its existence as a key factor in the emergent history of the prison. The truth of this interpersonally and socially bounded poetic communication, this conscious experience, is what each of us lives in the reading of a great author or in listening to a famed orator. We sense not a choice between the objective and the subjective, news item and novel, but the combining force of discourse that commands the analogy of Self with Other in their World. Or as Merleau-Ponty (1962, p. 79) describes it, we are conscious of being-in-the-world (*être-au-monde*). The metajournalistic discourse as an analogy of life is more true than the factual text. "The novel is truer, because it gives a totality, and because a lie can be created from details which are all true. The news item is truer because it wounds us and is not pretty to look at. They meet only in the greatest, who find, as has been said, the 'poetry of truth'" (Merleau-Ponty 1964c, p. 311).

TOM WICKER'S TIME

One of those "greatest," one of the authors who finds the poetry of truth, is Tom Wicker. The poetry of his prose is his metajournalistic book *A Time to Die* (1975). As the dust jacket of the volume declares to even the most casual reader: "*A Time to Die* is the gripping story of one of the most dramatic events in our time. It is simultaneously a unique venture in American self-examination." Wicker begins his story (pp. 4–5) with a forthright description of his about-to-be shattered bourgeois personal life. He is having lunch in the executive dining room of the National Geographic Society, "a few blocks from Lafayette Square and the White House." His lunch is interrupted by a telephone call: "'The most exciting thing,' his secretary said breathlessly, 'They want you to come to Attica.'" Wicker goes to the state prison in upstate New York. He goes as a reporter jerked out of his normal routine. He goes to get the facts of a riot. And he naively thinks, "And what was Attica or a prison riot to a political columnist?" He arrives and becomes more than a reporter. At the request of the inmates, he becomes an "observer." Yet he emerges as a "negotiator" thrust into a political situation where his own moral values contribute to his living or dying in the midst of the rebellion.

The text that records Wicker's conscious experience is both a novel and a news item; it is more true than either one. The metajournalistic text codes a semiotic phenomenology in which the discourse is a sign (a news item) whose analogue is an emblem (a novel) whose analogue, in turn, is an appeal—that is, the existential person who is Tom Wicker. For Wicker and for us, the produced text is the existential phenomenology of seeing that binds author and audience together in one semiotic movement of journalistic mass communication.

"He who sees believes himself invisible: for him his acts remain in the flattering entourage of his intentions, and he deprives others of his alibi, reducing them to a few words, a few gestures" (Merleau-Ponty 1964c, p. 311). Wicker's few words, his existential gestures of seeing, are not invisible to him or us. They are made all the more intense in his visible use of the third person to narrate the Attica story. The semiotic discourse of the third-person style allows us to see. Yet, the text also appeals to a second-person perspective, the reading audience. The text is thereby an emblem for the existential witness. We see Wicker as he sees himself. In both perspectives we are privy to the first-person narrator, which is discourse per se. Such discourse is a sign of the third-person form and the second-person content.

Wicker's discourse is a reversible dialectic, one characterized by suggesting the familiar movement of narration in terms of interlocking paradigmatic and syntagmatic shifts. At one level, the text is autobiographical and paradigmatic. There is Wicker the *New York Times* reporter and there is the substitutable Tom Wicker, "the youngest child of Delancy David Wicker, a railroad conductor of forbidding rectitude, and Esta Cameron Wicker, a woman of powerful personality from a proud Scotch family" (p. 11).

The paradigmatic substitution of Wicker the adult and Wicker the child become the measure of personal judgment. Wicker reexamines his lived-experience when his consciousness of life is threatened by the context of death as he voluntarily and repeatedly enters D-Yard where the prisoners at Attica hold his life in their hands. Wicker is, for example, again confronted and tested by the politics of race. He is a liberal white Southerner whose very existence invites inmate threats. As a child, he grows up in a family whose politics and moral views invite the challenge of white society in Hamlet, North Carolina. As an adult in D-Yard, he is part of the "political theater" in which he and the other "observers" represent the failure of white America to the mostly black and Puerto Rican inmates of Attica (pp. 39, 76).

At a second level, the text is historical and syntagmatic. The discourse of the book is an account in fifteen chapters of six days—it takes six days to move from the broken bolt on a hallway door to inmate rebellion to the death of forty-three persons. Yet, these six days are simultaneously the *durée* of the forty-five years of Wicker's life. From September 8 until September 13, 1971, Wicker relives all that he holds sacred about himself, other human beings, and the world that matters to both.

Picture yourself as Wicker did on September 12, 1971, when negotiations are at a standstill, when the New York state police and National Guard are poised to attack the rebelling inmates, when the inmates are close to executing their hostages. Picture Wicker when the inmates demand that he come alone to talk yet one more time. Listen to Wicker's description of existential crisis:

> That could mean his life, either as an executed hostage or as an accident victim of a general attack when the troopers finally did come over the wall. There was no moral or any other kind of law or situation that forced him to return to D-Yard in such circumstances, particularly when it was not clear that anything would be achieved by it. He had faithfully done everything asked of him already; surely that was enough.
>
> On the other hand . . . he knew . . . he must either finally meet his own expectations for himself or abandon them and his idea of who and what he was [p. 211].

As Merleau-Ponty (1964c, p. 313) instructs us, and as Wicker witnesses in his metajournalistic writing, "The novel gives the context. The news item on the contrary strikes us because it is a life's invasion of those who were unaware of it. The news item calls things by their name; the novel names them only through what the characters perceive." Indeed, Wicker's *A Time to Die* is for us the novel made news item and for Wicker the news item made novel—with all the good ambiguity that these rhetorical combinations entail. The metajournalistic genre is, thus, not the paradox of news item and novel. Nor is it the confusion of factual reporting with editorial-page comment. It is not the corruption of prose by fiction. Metajournalism is, in Merleau-Ponty's phrase, the *poetry of truth*. It is the positive ambiguity of discourse that authenticates the communality of the person.

THE COMMUNALITY OF COMMUNICATION

Attica is a personal memory for Wicker. But I began my analysis by stating that Attica is also a political memory (see Chap. 6). In this apparent opposition there is a positive ambiguity. We sense the paradigmatic and syntagmatic movements of the Attica events. We see their parallel to the reversibility of moments in Wicker's life. We understand the method of metajournalism wherein news item and novel are blended together in a unique genre of discourse. There is a lived-experience, a consciousness of the communality of communication. "In what situations and by virtue of what criteria may one participant in a communicative exchange, claim for himself an emancipated consciousness, and consider himself, therefore, to be authorized to act as a social therapist?" (Apel 1980, p. 285). Or restated in its classic Platonic version, How does one morally and politically distinguish among the discourse of the philosopher, the sophist, and the statesman? (see chap. 17 below). Is Wicker, or perhaps we should say, is the persona of the text *A Time to Die*, the conscious experience of an observer, a reporter, or a negotiator? How does Wicker the moralist, the communicator, and the politician at Attica make a choice, knowing that, as Merleau-Ponty (1962, p. xix) suggests, in choosing a role to live he is "condemned to meaning"?

There are two responses to this interrogation. One is a consideration of the human body in its social role as a sign. Such a sign contains synergistically the elements of death and life. The probability for death is an overt emblem of the life being judged, by Wicker and others. Life is his appeal to be absolved from judgment and its possibility. Indeed, Foucault reminds us:

> The judges of normality are present everywhere. We are in the society of the teacher-judge, the doctor-judge, the educator-judge, the social worker–judge; it is on them that the universal reign of the normative is based; and each individual, wherever he may find himsef, subjects to it his body, his gestures, his behavior, his aptitudes, his achievements [1979, p. 304].

We are not surprised, then, as Wicker explains his feelings after the first round of negotiations with the Attica inmates: "death was not what Tom Wicker was at Attica to abet. He had realized that in the moment he turned away from the hostages. *Nobody gets killed*. That was his goal, but the trooper's guns dealt in death" (p. 56). We are then witness to Brother Juan, an inmate, who pleads: "We need your help, this is no joke. . . . This could turn into another My Lai, right here" (p. 94). We are with Wicker when Brother Flip says to the negotiators: "We are advocating communications and understanding." It is a peroration that itself concludes with the unexpected, but existential, truth of the moment. Brother Flip makes a claim for immediacy: "I want to thank all of you beautiful people for coming here. Stand with us now . . . walk with us . . . die with us, if necessary" (pp. 96–98). The startling, but quiet, impact of an invitation to die by choice is bounded by the inmate who goes berserk by charging the negotiators, waving a sword and screaming, "Everybody gonna die . . . gonna die!" (p. 106).

There is an eloquence of the situation in which Wicker the negotiator becomes the victim through the agency of this bodily presence. The gesture of physical presence, having his body in jeopardy—this is his catharsis. In one syncretic movement, Wicker is neither moralist nor reporter. Wicker, who enters Attica as an emblem of his own bourgeois morality in order to appeal as an observer to the inmates, exists as an observing human being. He is the bodily appeal to the inmates and their hostages; he is an emblem personifying the message "Nobody gets killed."

Yet we find hidden in this existential problematic a phenomenological, albeit political, thematic—the exercise of *power*. The challenge to and use of power by Wicker in a moral and reportage sense carries with it the infrastructure of power politics. The consciousness of power is the "politics of experience" in R.D. Laing's (1967, pp. 25, 30–32) sense; it is the politics of the body. Foucault captures this thematic in his *Discipline and Punish: The Birth of the Prison*, when he reviews the problematic of contemporary prison revolts:

> In fact, they were revolts, at the level of the body, against the very body of the prison. What was at issue was not whether the prison environment was too harsh or too aseptic, too primitive or too efficient, but its very materiality as an instrument and vector of power; it is this whole technology of power over the body that the technology of the "soul"—that of educationalists, psychologists, and psychiatrists—fails either to conceal or to compensate, for the simple reason that it is one of its tools [1979, p. 30].

Thus we have from Foucault the positive ambiguity of the "body" as a discourse of the institutionalized person and the social (i.e., personalized) institution. This ambiguity of the institution as the social norm is one level of politics: the *Lebenswelt* versus the *Weltanschauung*. Politics on this level is a condemnation to meaning, a condemnation coterminus with human experience. To be physically situated is to be politically committed; this is one form of the poetry of truth at Attica.

A second response to the interrogation posed above—How does Wicker cope with commitment?—can be made at the level of consciousness. This level is also a political thematic. Human consciousness has its parallel semiotic structure with the body. Consciousness too is a sign whose emblem and appeal evoke a political consequence.

If we take two selected examples of discourse that thematically mark the Attica rebellion, we can judge the sense in which the discourse is an accurate measure of the politics of consciousness. The examples I have in mind are familiar to us. One belongs to Wicker. It is the discourse of semiotic appeal: "nobody gets killed." The other illustration belongs to the frenzied anonymous inmate. It is the discourse of a semiotic emblem: "somebody gonna die." In these two texts we have the explicit dimension of a philosophic proposition (i.e., the primacy of the *Lebenswelt*) whose empirical test is the death of forty-three human beings and the life of one, Tom Wicker.

Using the standard Hjelmslevian (1961; see Barthes 1968) model for analysis, we can separate a signifier and signified at the level of connotation and denotation for each proposition. On an initial semantic determination we can locate the denotative level with its constituent signifier and signified. For example, let us examine the connotation of "nobody" (Figure 8). As a signifier this term has two digital or analogue signified possibilities. The term can signify "inmates" (the example used in Figure 8) or "observers" or "negotiators" or "hostages." Also, "nobody" can signify only "inmates" or only one of the other terms cited. In consequence, the connotative level contains an essential denotative ambiguity—that is, several signifier-signified combinations are possible. First, for example, the signifier term can be deconstructed into its valence terms: "no" and "body." Here the signifier "no" is combined with the signified "body" as the denotation supporting the connotative signifier "nobody." Secondly, we can leave the denotative signifier "no" constant and vary the signified by the paradigmatic substitution of "inmate" (Figure 9).

This second interpretation is in fact Wicker's initial impression of the situation at Attica. The denotation consisting of "no" "inmate" has its analogue at the level of connotation. Here we make the paradigmatic substitution of "no" and "inmate" for "nobody" (Figure 10). Thus, we have a semantic specification of the essential characteristics of inmates (and hostages). They are nobody—they have no bodies—they get killed—they do not exist. Any action taken against them has no content (signified); it is neither right nor wrong, it just happens. We have an explication of the killing of forty-three inmates and hostages by the police. Consciousness becomes the politics of experience. We have an understanding of the terrible torture and mayhem inflicted on the surviving inmates by the prison guards and state police troopers. We have the exercise of absolute political power, the conscious power of life and death. We have the politics of Norbert Woods, supervising official at Attica, "We warned 'em. . . . We *told* 'em" (Wicker 1975, p. 287).

Before looking at the syntagmatic relationship between "nobody" and "gets killed," we should examine the opposition of "nobody" and its valence counterpart "somebody"—that is, the negative and positive

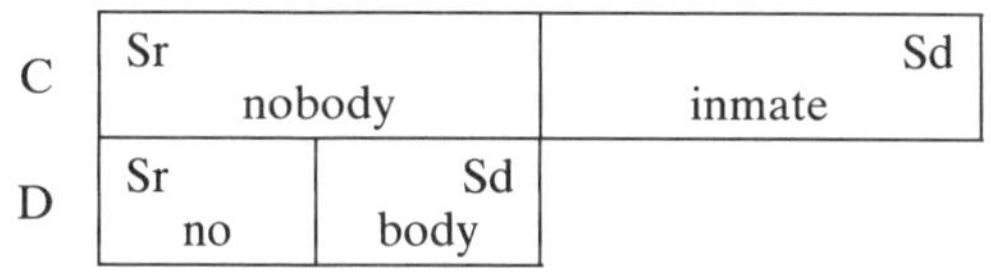

<table>
<tr><td>C</td><td colspan="2">Sr
nobody</td><td>Sd
inmate</td></tr>
<tr><td>D</td><td>Sr
no</td><td>Sd
body</td><td></td></tr>
</table>

Figure 8. Connotation (C) and denotation (D) of the signifier (Sr) and the signified (Sd) for the negative signification 'nobody.'

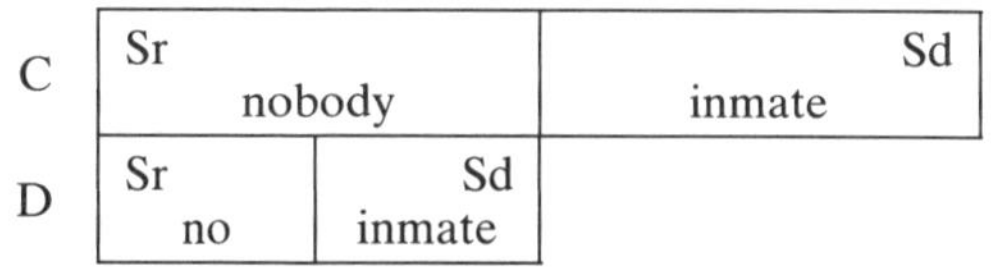

<table>
<tr><td>C</td><td colspan="2">Sr
nobody</td><td>Sd
inmate</td></tr>
<tr><td>D</td><td>Sr
no</td><td>Sd
inmate</td><td></td></tr>
</table>

Figure 9. Paradigmatic substitution of 'inmate' for 'body.'

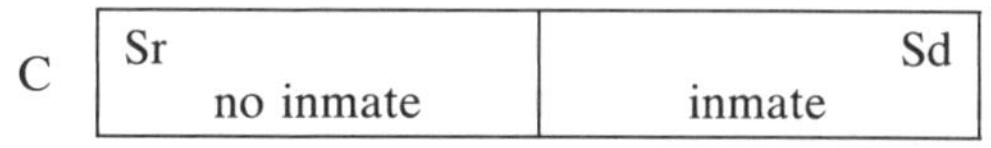

<table>
<tr><td>C</td><td>Sr
no inmate</td><td>Sd
inmate</td></tr>
</table>

Figure 10. Paradigmatic substitution of the denotation for the connotative signifier.

signifiers. The same deconstruction used in Figure 8 for the term "nobody" applied exactly to the term "somebody" (Figure 11). The positive valence of "some" connected with "body" explicates the sense of identity and existence the inmates (and hostages) felt: the hostages because they have inmate protectors who keep them alive, and the inmates because they are exercising political authority over their own lives. The police are not in control of the facility, the inmates are. In an explicit denotative signifier-signified that connotes "somebody" (Figure 12), Wicker (1975, pp. 55–56) recalls a speech made by Brother Herb to his fellow inmates in D-Yard: "That was a hell of a speech you made, Brother Herb. Mind if I ask your full name? Brother Herb looked at him haughtily. 'I am Attica,' he said, and moved with dignity into the crowd." The Reverend Jesse Jackson has immortalized this semiotic device (Figure 13) in the rallying call of the Chicago-based PUSH group: *"I am some body!"* (Pace et al. 1974).

In short, the negative ambiguity of "nobody" reflects the death of the individual and its institutional form, which is the death of society: the prison. In comparison, the positive ambiguity of "somebody" reflects the life of the individual and its institutional form, which is the life of society: politics—that is, a body politic literally re-presented in a body of persons (a group) that can exert pressure as a social force (see chap. 9 below).

C	Sr somebody		Sd inmate
D	Sr some	Sd body	

Figure 11. Connotation and denotation for the positive signification 'somebody.'

C	Sr somebody		Sd Attica
D	Sr I	Sd am	

Figure 12. Connotation and denotation for the ontological signification 'Attica.'

C	Sr some		Sd body
D	Sr I	Sd am	

Figure 13. Connotation and denotation for the ontological signification 'body,' i.e., 'person.'

The proposition "nobody gets killed" stands at the connotative level as a syntagmatic whole uniting the signifier "nobody" to the signified "gets killed" (Figure 14). Recalling the previous analysis of the denotation for "nobody," a syntagamatic substitution can be made of "no" "body" for "nobody." Thus, the connotative signified "gets killed" receives the same denotative signification and "nobody" refers syntagamatically to "hostages" and "inmates" (Figure 15). The explication clearly indicates the conscious equivalence of "gets killed" with "hostages" and "inmates."

It is no minor point that the semantic features of the proposition "nobody gets killed" reflect Wicker's preconscious understanding. The discursive proposition has the implication of objectivity in its third-person construction; it stresses a passive verb voice. The valence of the proposition is negative. The proposition is a sign of death. Its signifier is an emblem of death: nobody is a dead body. Its signified is an appeal to death: getting killed is Attica.

The proposition "somebody gonna die" also stands at the connotative level as a syntagmatic whole consisting of the signifier "somebody" and the signified "gonna die." Taking the signifier "somebody" at the conno-

C	Sr nobody		Sd gets killed	
D	Sr no	Sd body		

Figure 14. Connotation and denotation for the negative signification 'gets killed.'

C	Sr inmate		Sd gets killed	
D	Sr no	Sd body		

Figure 15. Connotation and denotation for the positive signification 'gets killed.'

C	Sr somebody		Sd gonna die	
D	Sr some	Sd body		

Figure 16. Connotation and denotation for the positive signification 'gonna die.'

C	Sr somebody		Sd gonna die	
D	Sr neg.	Sd power	Sr assault	Sd D-Yard

Figure 17. Paradigmatic and syntagmatic substitutions signifying the ontology of power, i.e., the 'body' as political signification [neg. = negotiators, et. al.].

tative level, an initial supporting denotative signifier is "some" and its signified is "body" (Figure 16). With appropriate paradigmatic substitution, "some" becomes the "negotiators" (a term that includes variously the prison officials, the guards, the state police, National Guard troops, and negotiators per se) and "body" becomes "power" or "authority." Again by comparison, the signified part of the proposition, "gonna die," at the connotative level carries a denotative infrastructure (Figure 17). This infrastructure consists of the signifier "assault" and the signified "D-Yard." Does the "D" undercode "die" or "death" in D-Yard? The fact that the inmates dug protective trenches in the yard and that many are killed in them adds semantic force to the interpretation of "D-Yard" as a chosen site of death, as a cemetery.

But there are other semantic features of the whole proposition "somebody gonna die." That is, the proposition has the implication of subjectivity in an implied first- or second-person construction. It implies an active verb voice. The valence of the proposition is positive. The proposition is a sign of life. Its signifier is an emblem of life; somebody is a live body. Its signified is an appeal to life; going to die leaves time to live. As Herman Badillo, a corrections official, comments during the ill-planned hasty assault on D-Yard: "There's always time to die. . . . I don't know what the rush was" (Wicker 1975, p. 286).

In these two propositions, "nobody gets killed" and "somebody gonna die," we have an illustration of the communality of communication, the *Kommunikationsgemeinschaft*. The first proposition reflects the felt and shared conscious experience of the *Gemeinschaft*, those who felt a bond with them, the negotiators. As Wicker (p. 295) describes his own conscious experience, "'No body gets killed.' That had been his aim. That had been his promise to himself, never spoken to anyone else. That was what he had set out to achieve, with his gifts and his standing and the trust men placed in him."

Just as poignant, the proposition "somebody gonna die" reflects the *Gemeinschaft* (i.e., the anonymity of society's action) in the exchange of conscious experience lived by those who were about to do the killing, the prison guards, the National Guard, the state police, the prison officials, and governor of the state of New York, Nelson Rockefeller, whose participation was his refusal to communicate, to negotiate, to recognize somebody at Attica (Wicker 1975, pp. 200, 208). There were, after all, more votes outside the walls of Attica than inside (see chap. 9, below).

We face, in conclusion, the semiotic fact that discursive action is political. The communality achieved in mass communication is a normative process that is reflexively semiotic in nature and function, both creating and destroying human realities. Recall that I posed a question for metajournalism as exemplified in Wicker's *A Time to Die*: "In what situations and by virtue of what criteria may one participant in a communicative exchange claim for himself an emancipated consciousness and consider himself, therefore, to be authorized as a social therapist?" (Apel 1980, p. 288). Wicker gives us an answer in his text, which turns out to be the existential communality he achieves in the examination of his own life. It is a political situation where his very living communicates his morality. Apel summarizes this thematic:

> Everyone must take upon himself a non-groundable—or not completely groundable—"moral" decision of faith. There exists, however, even in this

> situation of the solitary decision apparently no better ethical regulative than to realize the possible critique of the ideal communication community in one's own reflexive self-understanding. I believe that this is the principle of potential moral self-transcendence. [p. 288]

One technique for illustrating this theme of moral self-transcendence is political metajournalism, like that of Tom Wicker. This genre of mass communication is, simply, a paradigm of the poetry of truth.

Chapter Eight

Guess at the Words

How to Phenomenologically Research the Hermeneutic Experience of Language and Logic

Communicology is the theory and practice of human communication. As such it partakes in the methodologies of both philosophy and science as research operations. It is in this sense that this chapter is about communicology. What I propose to do is to report the results of empirical research, but research that is phenomenological in its method and hermeneutic in its subject matter. Having said this much, I need to immediately suggest that I shall soon argue that such positivist exclusions as eidetic and empirical, experiential and experimental, or qualitative and quantitative, are dysfunctional in doing human research. Although I think that this summary judgment is generally true for the practice of both philosophy and science, it seems to me to be particularly true for communicology.

By way of illustrating my argument, I want to first review in a general way the problematic of the *hermeneutic experience* as a *subject matter* for research in communicology and the way in which that subject matter is eidetically the philosophic problem of parts and wholes. Second, I briefly discuss the distinction between information theory and communication theory as they relate to the eidetic nature of the problematic. Last, I report the empirical thematics that derive from the problematic. This is to say, I illustrate how the eidetic problematic of parts and whole in information theory compares with that of communication theory in an empirical message that is, indeed, thematic as a *phenomenology of method* and as the meaning of a hermeneutic of experience. My goal, in short, is to respond to Roman Jakobson's observation:

> The comparison of incomplete and explicit messages, the fascinating problem of fragmentary propositions, challengingly outlined in Charles Peirce's persual of "blanks" and in the semiotic studies of Frege and Husserl, strange as it may seem, have found no response among linguists. The artificial treatment of messages without reference to the superposed context once more exemplifies the illicit conversion of a mere part into a seemingly self-sufficient whole [1971a, 2:282].

In meeting this challenge, I shall be following in most respects the thesis adopted by Husserl as he opens Investigation III of the *Logical Investigations*. There he says rather concisely:

> But one needs here a supplementary distinction between the *phenomenological* moments of unity, which give unity to the experience or parts of experience (the real phenomenological data), and the *objective* moments of unity, which belong *to the intentional objects and parts of objects, which in general* transcend the experiential sphere [1970, 2:442].

With this overview in mind, I now should like to turn to a short review of the hermeneutic experience in the context of communicology as a human science perspective.

THE HERMENEUTIC EXPERIENCE

The historical characteristics of the hermeneutic experience emerge in some ten propositions as Palmer (1969, pp. 242–46) closes his book *Hermeneutics*.

1. *The hermeneutic experience is intrinsically historical.* Every human experience is historically located as an event, a situation, that is lived through. Our conscious experience is reflexively an experience of consciousness; I come to know what I am as a person by understanding how I am situated among other persons in a commonly shared world. Here we can recall the communicological classification of Schutz (1967) in which the historical world of intersubjectivity consists of *consociates*, persons who share temporal and spatial experience—the here and now; *contemporaries*, persons living in my time, but located elsewhere; *predecessors*, those persons who preceded me in time and location; and last, *successors*, those persons whose history will commence after my death, but with whom my discourse will be present (see chap. 16 below).

2. *The hermeneutic experience is intrinsically linguistic.* The language system is not some arbitrary tool by which to manipulate ciphers; language is not a mere statistic. The articulation of language is a complex personal gesture in which unique sounds as vowels, consonants, and

silences in their unique eidetic structure form a human medium of communication (Schutz, 1973, 1:287–356). The experience of expression is reversible with the consciousness of perception; language (*langue*) is the empirical record of that eidetic phenomenon (*parole*) (see chap. 15 below).

3. *The hermeneutic experience is dialectical.* Understanding is not a simple causality to be located and reified in a single judgment. Consciousness as an eidetic fact is always a synergism with experience as an empirical fact. As Merleau-Ponty (1962) so forcefully argues in his *Phenomenology of Perception*, we do not live in Descartes' world where I am forced to choose constantly between what "I think" and what "I feel." Rather, we live as human beings where the dialectic of mind and body is a constant state of capability pregnant with ability; I live in a process of conscious experience in which "I can" exist with others in a lived-world of mutual history and discourse (see chap. 7 above).

4. *The hermeneutic experience is ontological.* Both understanding and language are the agency (*geste*) by which we live and come to know the reality of ourselves and others in a shared world. Reality is not an ontological construct in either the tradition of Plato's idealism or in the shadow of Aristotle's realism. Reality is a constitution of human conscious experience through the communicative medium of language and related semiotic systems.

5. *The hermeneutic experience is an event—a "language event."* As Michel Foucault (1972; see Lanigan 1984) suggests in his *The Archaeology of Knowledge*, discourse is always an event in which the gesture of writing or the articulation of sound "opens up to itself a residual existence in the field of memory" and yet it is "subject to repetition, transformation, and reactivation" (p. 28). Last, the event of communication suggests the modality of any one speech act or statement by locating the contextual modality of the acts that precede and follow it.

6. *The hermeneutic experience is "objective."* Following on the points already made in the first five propositions, I agree with Palmer (1969, p. 244) when he asserts that "the ground of objectivity lies not in the subjectivity of a speaker, but in the reality which comes to expression in and through language. It is in this objectivity that the hermeneutical experience must find its ground." This is in fact what Husserl has in mind during his analysis of parts and wholes.

7. *The hermeneutic experience is led by the text.* The text provides a dialogical structure in which the reader or listener is invited to explore the dimensions of understanding. As an initial stage of the dialogical process, a person in the modality of conscious experience comes to the text as a modality of experienced consciousness. Hence, the text is a communicative event of capability. I discover in the text a message—that is, my own possibility for understanding over and above the misleading causality that

mere analysis would generate. The monologue of the text allows me to discover human dialogue.

8. *The hermeneutic experience understands what is said in the light of the present.* The process of interpretation requires a direct application to the present situation. Rather than a mere taxonomical project, interpretation requires an explication that makes objective what is both eidetic and empirical in the text as message. The location of the text is a specification of its synchronic and diachronic moment and its paradigmatic and syntagmatic structure—that is, the text has an ontological status and a historical signification in the understanding of the human auditor. The text is always a message in lived experience.

9. *The hermeneutic experience is a disclosure of truth.* As Palmer (1969, p. 245) suggests, "Truth is grounded in negativity; this is the reason that the discovery of truth proceeds best within a dialectic in which the power of negativity can operate." Truth is a moment of understanding, an aesthetic moment, in which the text as an expressive event is manifest to perception. Truth is not, therefore, merely eidetic or empirical, but both, and synergistically so. As Foucault's work suggests, there is a hermeneutic primacy to the Law of Noncontradiction.

10. *Aesthetic must be swallowed up in hermeneutics.* In other words, aesthetics and the process of valuing perception must be dialectically united with expression as the explication of understanding. Perception and expression are a reversible modality of conscious experience that is overtly manifest in the media of communication—that is, in being a human Being (*Dasein*).

Given this propositional description of the hermeneutic experience with particular reference to human communication, we are now in a position to examine the eidetic problematic created by taking communication per se as the subject matter of a hermeneutic experience. The paradox of parts and wholes is immediately apparent as we realize that the human experience of communication is a presentation containing a re-presentation at several levels of analysis and synthesis. There are two resolutions to this paradox: one is information theory as the answer of positivism, the other is communication theory as the answer of phenomenology.

EIDETIC PROBLEMATIC

In the discussion that follows, I am summarizing an extended discussion of the interrelationship between information theory and communication theory that appeared some years ago (Lanigan, 1979b; see Jakobson, 1971b; see chap. 14 below).

Let us look at information theory first. This theory solves the paradox of parts and wholes, choice and context, presentation and re-presentation, within a "superposed context" (to recall Jakobson's phrase). Information theory hypostatizes a context in which choices are made; in other words, a whole is assumed in which parts are selected or a presentation is assumed to control all subsequent re-presentations. "Information" becomes the "reduction of uncertainty" in which a probability of choice is constructed. Each choice made has information value—that is, it tells you whether you have made an efficient selection or merely confirmed what you already knew (which is redundancy). Information theory thereby prescribes a *context of choice*, but no choice per se. We may speak metaphorically and say that each "choice" narrows the "context," but this type of thinking is illicit. The holistic notion of context turns out not to be the object with which we start, but the goal with which we seek to end, but cannot. We reduce our uncertainty about the context, yet we never in fact locate the context. This is why the information theorist is forced to talk about "information" as a post hoc selection, rather than the "meaning," which is the located context per se.

Communication theory is in an opposite stance inasmuch as "meaning" is the key ingredient for analysis. The communicologist hypothesizes that a choice always leads to a context. "Communication" becomes the "constitution of certainty" in this view. Each choice made has meaning value—that is, it tells you what your choice is by immediate combinatory association with all the possible choices not made. Communication theory thereby prescribes a *choice of context*. Unlike the digital logic of information theory in which all choices are either/or selections, the analogue logic of communication theory entails all choices as both/and selections by combination. The paradox of parts and wholes is resolved by understanding that a synergistic effect occurs with an analogue logic wherein parts constitute wholes and those wholes are simultaneously parts of other wholes in a field of possibility, as Husserl argues.

What we have so far is a discussion of information and communication theories as answers to the paradox of parts and wholes when considered at one level of analysis. Such a limitation is usually sufficient when dealing with machines, for example, that are by definition self-restricted as one-level entities. However, when we are dealing with human beings, whose communication systems operate simultaneously at several levels and via memory may invoke a temporal dimension that reverses valences and substitutes systems, the linear application in one dimension of information theory and/or communication theory becomes completely inadequate for dealing with a person's hermeneutic experience.

The answer to the multidimensional problem lies in viewing communication theory as a construction principle per se—that is, as a formal version of the hermeneutic experience (Lanigan, 1979b). This is to suggest that the hermeneutic experience can be represented by communication theory where that theory *both* entails itself *and* information theory in any given description of human communication. In simple terms, I am suggesting that communication theory as a choice of context entails both another choice of context (communication theory) and a context of choice (information theory). In previous research (Lanigan, 1979b; 1982a; 1983a), I demonstrated the eidetic ground for this analysis. In other empirical research (1979a; 1982b; 1983b), I show a similar result and this chapter is a continuation of that empirical series of projects.

EMPIRICAL THEMATICS

We are now in a theoretical position to examine the research project I call "Guess at the Words." Research issues between information theory and communication theory are immediately clear when we examine an empirical example of language and its meta-representative function as a message in human communication. The example has to do with the standard concern in linguistic communicology with the fact that all human languages have a tone system roughly describable as composed of "vowels" and "consonants," which provides a binary system of contrast (disjunction) if viewed as an example of information theory or a binary system of comparison (conjunction) if viewed as an example of communication theory. This also is the basis of C. S. Peirce's (1931–35/1958, 4.537) distinction among *tone, type*, and *token*.

The linkage of vowels and consonants, thus, offers an ideal research situation. On the one hand, it is a situation that can be analyzed simultaneously for its eidetic structure and content as well as its empirical qualities. And the difficult conditions of dealing with representations of representation *in a hermeneutic experience* can be empirically specified in a way that maintains the richness of that human awareness of conscious experience.

I take as my initial phenomenological description of the problematic the account given by Yuen Ren Chao (1970), which is a prototype analysis of the information theory point of view. In discussing vowels and consonants, he offers two empirical illustrations of "information" as the reduction of uncertainty:

> There are ways of distinguishing vowels unambiguously, but they are not used in normal writing, which is intelligible without full syllabic representation, just as *ngl*sh w*d [sic w**ld] b* *nt*ll*g*bl [sic *nt*ll*g*bl*] wh*n sp*lt w*th n*th*ng b*t c*ns*n*nts [1970, p. 106].

Later on in his analysis, Chao offers the follow-up illustration:

> All items in a list of symbols do not have the same information value, since they do not occur with the same *frequency*. Since there are fewer vowels than consonants and vowels occur more frequently than consonants, each of the latter gives much more information than the former; hence it is much easier to g**ss *t th* w*rds wr*tt*n w*th**t v*w*ls than to *ue** a* **e *o*** **i**e* *i**ou* *o**o*a*** (cf. p. 106) [1970, p. 205].

It is interesting to note that the artist who composed the cover illustration for Chao's book phenomenologically reduced and interpreted his examples in a precise hermeneutic experience:

g**ss *t th* w*rds
*ue** a* **e *o***
wr*tt*n w*th**t
ie* *i**ou*
v*w*ls
*o**o*a*** [Book Cover Illustration, Chao 1970]

When I first saw this book cover illustration of the message, I immediately recognized that the artist had reduced the information theory example to a complete expression of the hermeneutic experience of language, which is a meaning in human communication—that is, the artist renders an empirical example of the eidetic condition of parts and wholes in communication. The cover illustration instantiates the eidetic rule that communication theory entails both communication theory and information theory. The eidetic is made empirical as the hermeneutic experience, and it is done phenomenologically.

In order to confirm my analysis of what the artist had done, I designed a simple empirical experiment that requires respondents to reconstitute the hermeneutic experience of a message written in the English language. I constructed a research protocol (see Figure 18) that asks respondents to constitute the message encoded in the "cover illustration" example. Having so constituted all or part of the message, the research protocol then asks for a brief description of how the respondent proceeded to interpret (translate) the encoding and decoding.

We need to recall that Chao's example (p. 205) contains two sequenced sentences that would normally read: "Guess at the words written without vowels. Guess at the words written without consonants." It is important to *not* use this version of the encoded message, because it obscures (by suggesting a single context of choice—namely, the sentence) the relationship between vowel and consonant, word and sentence, sentence and message, and thereby appears to confirm an information theory descrip-

NAME________________________ DATE ______ FIRST LANGUAGE_____
AGE __________ HOME COUNTRY ________________ SEX ___________

Instructions:

The message given below is culturally encoded.

In the blank space provided, write out a complete translation.

G**SS *T TH* W*RDS

*UE** A* **E *O***

WR*TT*N W*TH**T

IE* *I**OU*

V*W*LS

*O**O*A***

Translation:

____
____
____
____
____
____

Now that you are finished with the translation, explain in a few sentences what the key elements of the code are, that is, HOW were you able to translate?

Figure 18. Research test protocol

tion as adequate when it is not. By using the message format of the artist's illustration in the test protocol, the *meaning* levels of vowel/consonant, word/sentence, sentence/meaning are preserved as possible choices of context, any of which will entail both other choices of context and contexts of choice as a synergism.

Another point to keep in mind about the test protocol is that it asks respondents to constitute meaning, not reduce uncertainty. Here, the ten propositions of the hermeneutic experience are relevant. Respondents will be successful with the test protocol insofar as they intuit that eidetic and empirical phenomena will combine to create understanding. As Husserl summarizes the issues:

> A thing or piece of a thing can be presented by itself—this means it would be what it is even if everything outside it were annihilated. If we form a presentation of it, we are not necessarily referred to something else, included in which, or attached to which, or associated with which, it has being, or on whose mercy it depends, as it were, for its existence. We can imagine it as existing by itself alone, and beyond it nothing else. If it is intuitively presented, a context, a whole including it, may nonetheless be presented with it, must inevitably be so presented [1970, 2:445].

In a more precise version that readily illustrates the thesis of communication theory, Husserls argues:

> One sees further that the form-contents of higher level necessarily form a whole with the whole descending series of forms of lower level, and in such combination always represent *complex forms to the ultimately foundational elements*. In the sphere of complex sensuous shapes, particularly visual and auditory ones, this can be readily illustrated, whereas the general fact can be seen *a priori* from concepts [1970, 2:479–80].

In short, Husserl gives us a concise description of the phenomenological research function we can anticipate in the research protocol provided by the artist's illustration of the vowel/consonant differentiation in the English language (see Figure 18).

The research protocol was given to fifty persons in all. I devised two test groups from the point of view of the propositional description of the hermeneutic experience. One test group consisted of faculty and graduate students in the Department of Speech Communication at Southern Illinois University. The protocols were administered in July 1983 with no other instructions than those given on the protocol (see Figure 18). Respondents were asked to return the protocol sometime during the following two weeks; most returned the completed protocols in a day or two, a few within a week. The protocol asked for certain types of demographic data intended as additional descriptive information about the persons. The goal was to have a maximum range of types of persons, so a rough balance between males and females was sought and, in addition, a wide range of ages. Because I had a hypothetical concern that the native speakers of English would not be able to intuit the differentiation between the logical syntax of English (an information theory model) as written and the hermeneutic logic of their own institution (a communication theory model), I included persons whose first language was not English to see if a contrast emerged. None did emerge in either group.

I presumed that the department respondents would provide more successful (phenomenological description) and better expressed (phenomenological interpretation) protocol responses because of their communication training, and I also expected the second test group to be

TABLE 1

DEMOGRAPHICS FOR TEST GROUPS

Group	*Respondents*	*Sex*	*Age Range**	*First Language*
GSD**	20	M = 11 F = 9	19 – 27	English = 13 Other = 7
DEPT***	30	M = 19 F = 11	21 – 60	English = 24 Other = 6

* Years
** General Studies Area D; students in a first year course: Interpersonal Communication.
*** Department of Speech Communication; SIU-C faculty and graduate students.

successful, but to a lesser degree. The general studies respondents were thirty undergraduate students in an interpersonal communication class at Southern Illinois University. Their protocols were administered in August 1983. The group had the same demographic characteristics as the first group, but the age range was smaller (see Table 1).

The comparative results from the two groups of respondents are presented in Tables 2 through 9. Given these results as empirical evidence of various levels of hermeneutic experience, we can analyze each one in terms of its illustration of information theory and communication theory, and their respective interpretative levels. As an initial orientation to the interpretation of test results, it will be useful to indicate how each group of responses fits into the selection of possible logics between information theory and communication theory. As illustrated in Figure 19, the research protocol message is a complete semiotic system that operates on essentially three levels. Level one is the connotative semiotic in the standard Hjelmslev (1961; see Eco 1976; Wilden 1980) system and here is represented by the inscription presence of LETTERS representing VOWELS and/or CONSONANTS. Level two, which is entailed by level one, is the denotative semiotic represented by the inscription of STARS and/or absence as visual/inscribed SPACES, all of which is inscription presence by CIPHERS. Level three is that of the metasemiotic, the process relationship (hermeneutic) that allows the first two levels to operate as eidetic and/or empirical instantiations. The hermeneutic experiences of the respondents are illustrated in Tables 2–9.

Table 2 records the response constituted by those who understood the research protocol message in terms of information theory. They perceived the fact that the context was fixed as a SYSTEM and within it they could (1) choose either vowels or consonants as letters to match the

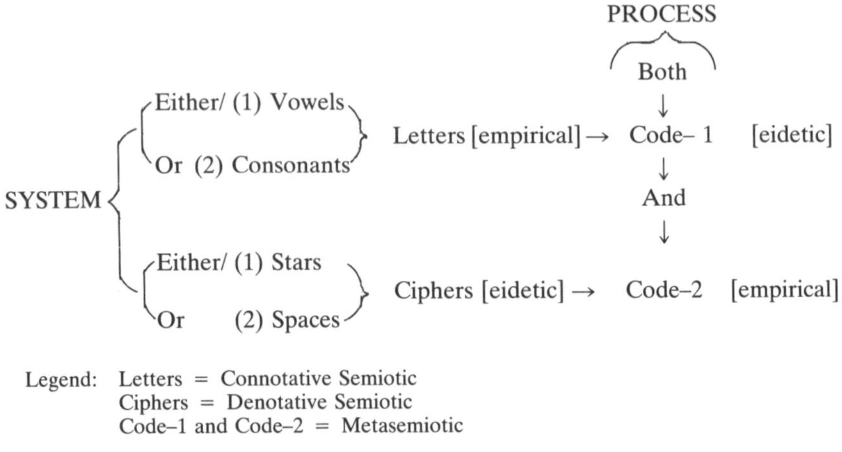

Figure 19. Communication theory entailments: Letters and ciphers.

TABLE 2

MESSAGE TYPE ALPHA

GUESS AT THE WORDS
GUESS AT THE WORDS
WRITTEN WITHOUT
WRITTEN WITHOUT
VOWELS

GSD = 9 [1 = overwrite]
DEPT = 3

TABLE 3

MESSAGE TYPE BETA

GUESS AT THE WORDS
GUESS AT THE WORDS
WRITTEN WITHOUT
WRITTEN WITHOUT
VOWELS
CONSONANTS

GSD = 5
DEPT = 25 [1 = overwrite]

letters given, (2) treat stars and spaces as the presence or absence of letters, and (3) could see stars only as spaces. Figure 20 maps this process on a formally defined Hjelmslevian grid. Table 3 records the same process, except that this group was able to see that vowels *and consonants* are arbitrary representations via stars for spaces in the semiotic system. What is presumed by all respondents in Tables 2 and 3 is that the system is the context; hence there is no eidetic provision for the fact that letters re-present that which is absent (e.g., experience of level differentiation). We may consider Tables 4 and 5 as variations of Table 3 and its explanation. Similarly, Tables 6 and 7 are variations on Table 2.

TABLE 4

MESSAGE TYPE GAMMA

GUESS AT THE WORDS WRITTEN WITHOUT VOWELS CONSONANTS
GSD = 1 DEPT = 0

TABLE 5

MESSAGE TYPE DELTA

GUESS AT THE WORDS WRITTEN WITHOUT VOWELS
GSD = 1 DEPT = 0

TABLE 6

MESSAGE TYPE EPSILON

GUESS AT THE WORDS WRITTEN WITHOUT
GSD = 1 DEPT = 0

TABLE 7

MESSAGE TYPE ZETA

[various word fragments]
GSD = 3 DEPT = 0

TABLE 8

MESSAGE TYPE ETA

GUESS AT THE WORDS WRITTEN WITHOUT VOWELS AND CONSONANTS
GSD = 0 DEPT = 1

TABLE 9

MESSAGE TYPE THETA

GUESS AT THE WORDS WRITTEN WITHOUT VOWELS GUESS AT THE WORDS WRITTEN WITHOUT CONSONANTS
GSD = 0 DEPT = 2

Table 9 records the response of persons using a communication theory perspective. They perceive the fact that their choices constitute a context (phenomenological description), which itself entails choosing another context (phenomenological reduction) and within that context a person can make discrete choices (phenomenological interpretation). They perceive the fact that choice is a PROCESS containing various systems as a context where (1) vowels and consonants are letters displaying their differentiation by combination with the letters given, (2) stars and spaces combine as ciphers of the presence and absence of letters *and* breaks between groups of letters (words), and (3) vowels designate spaces that

	Connotative Semiotic			
[DESCRIPTION] Analysis; Synthesis	Sr VOWEL [or CONSONANT]		Sd [LETTER]	
	Denotative Semiotic			
[REDUCTION] Definition: Articulation; Partition	Sr STAR	Sd VOWEL [or CONSONANT]	Sr [CIPHER]	Sd [LETTER]
	Form (Constant)	Substance (Variable)	Substance (Variable)	Form (Constant)
		Metasemiotic		
[INTERPRETATION] Syncretism; Resolution		Sr:Sd SPACE	Sr:Sd [LETTER] (absent)	
		Sr Purport	Sd Purport	

LEGEND: (1) VERTICAL CONNECTIONS = Process (Paradigmatic)/Relational Hierarchy; Relation (Both/And Function)
(2) HORIZONTAL CONNECTIONS = System (Syntagmatic)/Correlational Hierarchy; Correlation (Either/Or Function)
(3) Sr = Signifier Functive
(4) Sd = Signified Functive
(5) All terms are Hjelmselv's (1961) definitions.

SEMIOTIC PHENOMENOLOGY WORKSHEET

Figure 20. Semiotic entailments of information theory

are present (can be empirically instantiated in some way in the system) as opposed to those that are absent and cannot be realized (see Figure 21). These respondents intuit that the essence of the hermeneutic experience in the research protocol message is that (1) vowels and consonants as a combinatory set (connotative semiotic) entail (2) stars and spaces as a combinatory set (denotative semiotic), which in turn entails (3) the combinatory set of letters and ciphers (metasemiotic) that as a process is the *meaning* of the message. In brief, the meaning of the message is that differentiation is shown by combination. Less precisely, we can say that contrast is best understood as comparison or that combination allows selection.

Table 8 represents an interesting proof of the hermeneutic experience as grounded in communication theory by *extending* appropriately the message with the inclusion of the word "and" to mark the combination rule and by the elimination of repeated sentence elements (redundancy is eliminated). One combinatory sentence is produced (unity is predicated). The message becomes the meaning. Department respondents used several phrases to describe the successful constitution of the meaning when they moved beyond the digital (either/or) choices *in context* to the analogue (both/and) choices *of context*. For example, choice of context was described as finding the "content of the message," "context of the message," "the continuous sentence," and the fact that the message was "contextualized by meaning, not lexically."

One general studies respondent described the completion of the test according to Table 3 as "duplication, alternation, contrast." Had the respondent been able to apply this description to the constitution of the message, rather than its deconstruction, the result would have been appropriately Table 9, not Table 3. This is to say, the respondent experienced "duplication, alternation, contrast" as a digital logic rather than as an analogue, combinatory logic. The respondent was not able to convert "information" into "meaning." This fact in itself illustrates readily enough Husserl's contention:

> In the sphere of the phenomenological events of the "stream of consciousness," a law of essence paradigmatically illustrates the non-independence just mentioned, the law, namely, that each actual, fulfilled conscious-present necessarily and continuously passes over into one that *has* just existed, so that our present conscious state makes continuous demands on our conscious future [1970, 2:461].

Or as Holenstein summarizes, "The meaning is by no means objectively conscious in the act of signifying. It can however at any time be rendered objective and plain by a retroflective regard" (1975, p. 70).

Although the theory of information may pretend to the objectivity of

	Connotative Semiotic			
[DESCRIPTION] Analysis; Synthesis	Sr VOWELS [LETTERS]		Sd CONSONANTS [LETTERS]	
	Denotative Semiotic			
[REDUCTION] Definition: Articulation; Partition	Sr STARS [CIPHERS]	Sd SPACES [CIPHERS]	Sr STARS [CIPHERS]	Sd SPACES [CIPHERS]
	Form (Constant)	Substance (Variable)	Substance (Variable)	Form (Constant)
		Metasemiotic		
[INTERPRETATION] Syncretism; Resolution		Sr:Sd VOWELS	Sr:Sd SPACES (present)	
		Sr Purport	Sd Purport	

LEGEND:
(1) VERTICAL CONNECTIONS = Process (Paradigmatic)/Relational Hierarchy: Relation (Both/And Function)
(2) HORIZONTAL CONNECTIONS = System (Syntagmatic)/Correlational Hierarchy: Correlation (Either/Or Function)
(3) Sr = Signifier Functive
(4) Sd = Signified Functive
(5) All terms are Hjelmslev's (1961) definitions.

SEMIOTIC PHENOMENOLOGY WORKSHEET

Figure 21. Semiotic entailments of communication theory

meaning in communication by its specification of "information," it is, as Merleau-Ponty would say, an "objective illusion" (see chap. 5 above). It is in the view of communication theory that we can take Holenstein's retroflective regard in the stream of consciousness and discover meaning in human communication. We have just surveyed an empirical experiment that demonstrates this fact. Yet it is *empirical* only because its retroflective regard is *eidetic*; it is *experimental* only because its retroflective regard is *experiential*; it is a describable *quality* only because its retroflective regard is *quantifiable* as an explication. Indeed, communication theory is hermeneutic only to the degree that it entails information theory and makes of it a meaningful human stream of consciousness, rather than a rule for experience.

In short, the empirical research project that I call "Guess at the Words" gives way to an eidetic understanding of the experience of differentiation as synergistic because it is a communication used to examine the essence of a particular communication. It is a part that is retroflective on the whole.

Recalling the ten propositions with which I opened this chapter, we can now see the sense in which the information theorists of positive science ask us to take human communication as a conscious experience that is *either* historical, *or* linguistic, *or* dialectical, *or* ontological, *or* an event, *or* "objective," *or* led by the text, *or* understood in the present, *or* a disclosure of truth, *or* a mere aesthetic in contrast to science. This is the digital logic of exclusion in which the first exclusion is the awareness of human meaning as lived.

Against these ten propositions so construed, Husserl offers us one "universal proposition" when he argues as a contemporary communication theorist would:

> *"Pieces" are essentially mediate or remote parts of a whole whose "pieces" they are, if combinatory forms unite them with other "pieces" into wholes which in their turn constitute wholes of higher order by way of novel forms* [1970, 2:483].

Put more concisely, he says simply, "*unity is in fact a categorical predicate*" (1970, 2:478). We need only add that in the human science of communicology, as we see in the experiment "Guess at the Words," such a unity is conscious experience as lived. Human communication is in fact a novel form of meaning.

Chapter Nine

Urban Crisis

The Phenomenology of Social Polarization and Communication

The phenomena of "urban tension"—or more properly "urban crises"—are distinguishable by several characteristics, not the least important of which is *polarization*. Polarization is a behavior stimulated by one of two social practices: isolation or confrontation. Within the urban problematic, polarization creates a lived perspective of reality based on value divisions that characterize one individual as "good, right, lawful, rational," and the like, whereas his or her neighbor becomes "evil, wrong, unlawful, irrational," and so on. Such value orientations have a logical progression that ultimately has to rely on a *power* concept of self-assertion for self-preservation (Foucault 1965; 1979). In a word, *violence* becomes the ethic of polarization.

There is a viable alternative to this ethic of destruction and death. Such an alternative is suggested by the problem itself—namely, the need for relevant, meaningful communication. It should be a communication operable within the contexts that also breed isolation and confrontation (see chap. 1 above). At present, communication exists but it is seldom relevant or meaningful, because it does not function within the crisis environment where isolation and confrontation compete (Habermas 1984, 1:244). That is, communication per se has come from outside the crisis situation; a relevant and meaningful process of communication should originate (in the phenomenological sense of being created) within the situational tensions (Hunter 1963).

POLARIZATION

Isolational Polarization

The phenomenon of isolation is best viewed from two perspectives: (1) the isolation of the in-group versus the isolation of the out-group; and (2) the isolation of an elite leadership within the in-group by virtue of the external conflict existent between the in-group and the out-group (Olmsted 1959; Worth 1964). The first variety of isolational polarization within the urban environment is exemplified in the growth and development of the Black Muslim movement. Under the dissident, and eventually estranged, leadership of Malcolm X, the militancy of the Black Muslims reached what may be called the *crisis level* of isolational polarization. The followers of Malcolm X preferred to be left alone and were willing to kill those who would interfere with their desire for privacy.

It is important to note that this xenophobic attitude is *not* what is commonly known as "fanaticism." Fanatics are those who believe in their own creed to the extent that they wish to eliminate its opposite (Russell 1967). This is to say, the eradication of the polar opposite ideology (or its spokesperson) is more important than the promotion of one's own program (or leader). The isolational polarization of in-groups like the Black Muslims ("Muslim" literally means "one who submits") is akin to the ideology of the "new left" or "far right" as they exist in twentieth-century American politics.

Behavior reflecting isolational polarization is common among the urban dwellers of the inner city. The usual storefront organizations that provide a structural base for this process of polarization are typically initiated and staffed by blacks, although there are groups composed of Puerto Ricans, Mexican-Americans (Chicanos), and "poor whites" (Hillbillies: Appalachian whites). In each case, however, the group is racially isolated (Vise 1967; Bureau of the Census 1969). There are few permanent working coalitions between racially different groups and each in-group isolates itself, believing that strength and power as a racial unit are gained whereby the group can *protect itself* from opposing "forces." *Protection* or *defense* is a critical concept in this situation because it draws the line between the fanatics who are *not* open to communication with their opposite number and the isolationists who are open to dialogue.

Urban individuals with the traits of isolational polarization see their environment as oppressive for a variety of social, economic, and political reasons. They experience these situational factors as the *institutions* of "other" persons not living in their neighborhood—the "Establishment," in other words. Past experience and daily living leads them to believe—often with adequate justification—that they as individuals cannot communicate with the institutions. They come into contact with other persons who represent the anonymous oppressive forces in the urban life-world (the white caseworker, the white "ghetto merchant," the white police, and others). Inner-city residents find, to their dismay, that they are not dealing with other human beings but with a personified extension of an institution or power structure.

There is no inherent evil or wrong in an institution, but its administration is another matter. For example, "law and order" is an institution that operates in American society. Certain transgressions against society are punished—sometimes. Within urban centers the institution of "law and order" comes to represent an "evil," an "enemy," because it is administered as such. To wit: a study prepared for the President's advisory commission on crime found in an examination of police procedures in Chicago, Boston, and Washington that 27 percent of the police forces committed offenses normally considered felonies or misdemeanors. Minor shakedowns for meals, drinks, and small favors were too numerous to be accurately included in the study (Advisory Commission 1968, pp. 204–96). Such actions are almost universally against minority groups within the inner city.

Thus, it is common for individuals to band together within the inner city and form urban organizations that emerge as vanguards for the protection of their members. Typical organizations are the Black Panther Party, the Latin Americans' Defense Organization (a Chicago-based group of Mexican-Americans), the Brown Berets, and operation Crescent (a militant white group in Chicago). In varying degrees, all these organizations represent groups of urban residents functioning on a paramilitary basis or striving to create an operational elite to function for neighborhood protection.

These groups become isolated within the larger community surrounding their "neighborhood," be it a city block, a school district, or an entire community. At a minimum there is a physical threat of enclosure by outsiders, not to mention the intimidation of stereotypic or psychological enclosure. Communication beyond the neighborhood locale is often terminated by the very creation of the in-group although, ironically, the underlying purpose for organizing the neighborhood is usually to communicate its problems to the outside world.

My analysis is illustrated by Pinderhughes, a black psychiatrist, who likens the Black Panther movement to the problem of independence in an "adolescent-parent" situation. That is, whites are viewed as "parents" who restrict the "adolescents," the blacks, in their social roles. A solution becomes possible when the parent perceives the situation as the adolescent perceives it; then communication can take place (Grotjah 1968, pp. 15–16). The most specific examples that bears out the Pinderhughes hypothesis is the militant black organization in Los Angeles called US.

"US is Black People; whites would be THEM" (*Time*, July 19, 1968, p. 20). Communication with US members is progressing slowly, and it has eroded some of the isolational polarization (see *Psychology Today*, March 1970, pp. 40–53).

A second perspective of isolational polarization is the appearance of an elite leadership whose power is generated by progressively focusing on the degree and kind of difference between the in-group and the out-group. The isolation of an elite is accomplished by expanding the membership limits of the in-group to create more contrast between the elite (which becomes the in-group paradigm) and the out-group. The obvious secondary effect is to allow, by degrees, a specification of "in-ness" that the in-group faction (or a leader thereof) can claim. For example, the speeches of Stokely Carmichael after the summer of 1968 used the polarized terms "white" and "colored." The more explicit bifurcation of "white" and "black" was abandoned in an attempt to expand the membership limits of the in-group (See *New Republic*, August 24, 1968, p. 18). "Colored" extends beyond "blacks" to encompass "brown" persons—Mexican-Americans and Latin Americans who also are polarized by "whites" (in jargon terms: Chicano versus Anglo). The functional result of this strategem was to concentrate leadership in the elite that claims the highest degree of in-group qualification. That is, the "blacks" are *more* "colored" than the "browns," hence an elite claim to leadership *by nature*.

Such isolational polarization is the result of the technique of negative definition by kind and then by degree. What is not "white" is "colored"; what is not "black" but is not "white" is "brown," and so on. The criterion of judgment is always some natural characteristic. In the urban environment the criterion is skin color or occasionally language characteristics as a secondary cue if the skin code is ambiguous. (This urban phenomenon is more typical of Mexican-American in-groups and white in-groups that isolate on ethnic or economic levels. Nonetheless, the language characteristic is closely linked to "suspected" racial characteristics in a stereotypic process.) This natural criterion is a very important tool. Undoubtedly it can and does function within an in-group when it becomes necessary to isolate one in-group faction from another faction. In a leadership question the natural criterion will operate nicely when "black" must be separated from "brown" or "yellow" or whatever.

Isolational polarization, which creates the negatively defined *elite*, is the most dangerous because the channels of communication are based on physical factors of race that are immutable. By physical fiat, one group is not interested in discourse with the other group. Unfortunately, thinking with the color of one's skin comes tragically close to thinking with one's blood, a phenomenon that Adolf Hitler exploited. Yet this tendency on the part of the urban citizen creates a polarization reaction from the "whites" who choose to assert their own form of *elite* grouping.

The best hypothetical example is probably the white city official who engages in isolational polarization by creating an elite that is a category bigger than its opposite (a tyranny-of-the-majority scheme). That is, a municipal leader can talk about "outsiders" (persons who do not live on *your* block or *mine*) or the "communist conspiracy" (persons who cannot be recognized readily, as *we* can) as responsible for some problem in the city. It was not the work of any of *his* residents or "our people." He creates an "elite" by negative definition: everyone not a resident is an "outsider." Values are also attached by negative definition: residents are lawful, outsiders are unlawful, and the like. Communication becomes difficult, if not impossible, because the value dichotomy is like the race polarity, and the dichotomy is simply not visible to communication once it is fixed in a situation.

Confrontation Polarization

Put simply, confrontational polarization is the opposite of isolational polarization. There are two varieties of confrontational polarization: (1) the confrontation of the out-group by the in-group to force uncommitted persons to choose within the polarity, and (2) the internal confrontation of factions within the in-group that results in a traditional "elitism."

The first variety of confrontational polarization operates in a situation where opposing groups have the characteristics of the "fanatic." Each group (considering itself the in-group) is more concerned with stopping its opponent (the out-group by negative definition) than with self-protection. Unlike isolational polarization, which is defensive, confrontational polarization is *offensive* in tactic. The underlying assumption for this offensive theory of action is that the majority of persons (the public at large) belong to an uncommitted middle that will be moved by a minority willing to commit itself to the point of overt action. This is the credo of the "new left" in particular and is not far removed from the philosophy of the "far right" in the United States. Both political factions depend on an identity of direct involvement where they organize specifically to "fight" or "stop" one another from overwhelming the "silent majority."

The new left is probably represented best in the actions of the Students for a Democratic Society in their role as an in-group. Through various projects they attempted to define the social, economic, and political problems of America as the oppression of "rightist" elements. Thus, the polarization of in-group/out-group was engaged. The SDS attempted to work with oppressed Americans—blacks and "poor" whites mostly—by organizing them to take direct action against the "institutions" of the "power structure." Thus, confrontational polarization became the application of organized in-group action against the power structure or its symbols (usually the police) characteristic of the out-group. For the SDS the so-called power structure was a product of unacceptable "rightist" thinking whose destruction was more critical than the existence of the SDS itself. The personification of this ideology was the role of the Chicago Seven in the courtroom. Their disruption and attempted destruction of the trial procedure (a symbol of the out-group) was more important than saving themselves from jail.

But why the use of *force* (organized action) to confront an opponent? The SDS would argue that the power structure is literally that—a structure that systematically operates by applying force in various sectors to enforce its will. The power may be political, as in the traditional Chicago machine enforcement of "ghetto" politics according to its will (Wilson 1965). Or the power may be economic, where redevelopment programs such as those of the Department of Housing and Urban Development are used to frustrate living conditions by destroying more living space than they create for given low-income groups in the inner city. HUD programs have been used maliciously by local politicians in a systematic process of leveling whole city blocks in the inner city—blocks that "coincidentally" housed newly opened storefront offices for protest organizations. Or the use of force may be social, where ethnic prejudice is used as a form of de facto segregation. In each of these cases, power is used against inner-city residents under the guise of helping to relieve their situation.

The SDS worked to create an opposing power base, believing that power must be met with power. The ideological presumption is that a confrontation of power blocs will force the uncommitted middle to rally to the "just" side—theirs! At a minimum, confrontational polarization finally forces a division of "friends" and "enemies" by identifying respective political commitments within the "silent majority."

On the other side of the political question, far right in-groups attempt to utilize the existing power structure to maintain the status quo as they perceive it. Obviously, force is considered the necessary tool in an area that does not conform, whether it be an entire black community or a rent-strike in one building. Just as the new left works, so does the far right. Stopping the other group is critical to the point of committing one's own group to the struggle even if it risks self-destruction. "Better Dead Than Red."

Confrontation polarization for in-groups and out-groups represents a martyr psychosis. The most striking confirmation of this analysis was the occasional assaults of Minutemen (a far right militant group) on pacifist Quaker groups. In a very tragic sense both sides were victims of their own philosophies. It is not surprising, then, to find that the use of any means up to and including violence (or silence, which can be just as deadly) is advocated and used. For the new left the means may involve burning buildings or the like, whereas far right groups would use the more sophisticated (often silent) approach of detention camps through law enforcement (i.e., having a U.S. attorney general who would enforce the provisions of Title II of the Internal Security Act of 1950—presumably constitutional under the precedents of the Nisei internment by the Department of the Army in World War II).

"Elitism" is the second facet of confrontational polarization. When one in-group, such as the new left, sets itself against an out-group, such as the far right, there must be a plan of action for the confrontation to be an in-group success. This requirement generally evolves into the creation of a policy that, of course, generates an in-group faction of ideology-makers to lead the in-group organization. For example, the SDS at one convention was torn apart by conflicting in-group factions attempting to gain control of the organization so that the SDS as a whole would reflect one particular ideology.

This is to say, there was one faction at the convention arguing for anarchy as a power method. Another faction wanted a Peking-oriented ideology. The "old guard" was attempting to maintain a status-quo-plus-improvements approach (*New Republic*, June 29, 1968, pp. 12–13; Glassman 1969). In each faction, "elitism" is considered a necessary element in organizing and initiating the in-group's power function, which is the vehicle to create polarization by confrontation. The successful creation of an elite makes communication within the organization very difficult, and policy commitments as an organization become impossible. The result of an elitist power struggle is a disorganized movement with an ambiguous policy. There is a generalized desire for confronting the out-group, but factions cannot overcome the leadership problems brought on by elitist maneuvers. The situation is then intensified, usually by the creation of a secondary elite (a personality contest) as a reaction to the primary elite (a membership faction of the in-group).

A similar analysis of a far right in-group would likely reveal the same characteristics as the far left: multiple factions, no united national organization or ruling coalition, reliance on force to achieve goals, the desire for polarizing confrontation within the in-group and with the out-group, and an ultimate faith in the success of the "just" cause.

The confrontations of in-groups and out-groups on the political right and left leave little room for communication. Both sides believe that an inevitable dialectic will take place. They believe a confrontation can dissolve their opponent into their ranks or literally exterminate those who do not assimilate. Both sides are convinced they will win the engagement because they are right, whether morally, politically, socially, or economically. Their ideologies are couched in one-dimensional terms of *kind* where the compromise of *degree* is not admitted. Both sides act as though force is the ultimate instrument to secure the good, the right, the honorable—as they define it. Such total commitments allow either chaos or dictatorship, life or death.

COMMUNICATION

Isolation Communication

Where isolational polarization threatens to create a problem, "isolational" communication (self-identity as an equal competitor) can be used to produce a viable alternative to destructive polarization. The same situational elements that create isolational polarization can be redirected to make communication a by-product of isolation behavior. The specific procedures are those of the phenomenological approach to the discipline of communicology. The individual can be instructed in the theory and technique of *egocentric speech* as it occurs in a dialogue situation of synergic perception and expression. The basic concept is that the polarization of individuals can be used as the "content" base from which to build a positive structure of self-identity and commitment, rather than the negative structure of defensive isolation from others (Kwant 1969). Egocentric discourse can be the dialectical tool used in community organizations to make the members competitors (not combatants) with the out-groups perceived to be the polarized "enemy."

A notable example of egocentric dialogue in the political sphere was the creation of "balanced" delegations to the national conventions of the American political parties. These are not the products of isolational polarization, as was the Mississippi Freedom Party that was essentially the black substitution for the regular white Democratic Party delegation from the state of Mississippi. Rather, the new challenging delegations at the 1968 conventions were competitors with, not combatants against, the "power structure." These delegations were functional alternatives in a dialectically structured power situation that allowed the challenging participants to identify with the competitive process by their commitment to it.

Within the economic sphere, egocentric dialogue has brought about the proposal for an urban bank system that would provide the financial base that the inner cities need to compete with, not isolate from, the suburbian economy. The community bank concept was first proposed by militant leaders in several black communities and then was taken up by the 1968 presidential candidates. The dialogue appeared to be successful with the creation of the Council of Urban Affairs that would handle such economic proposals (*Time*, December 20, 1968, p. 16).

A third area of egocentric dialogue of "isolational" communication is within the social setting of the inner city, specifically in education. Here the model of egocentric dialogue is exemplified by Harlem Prep. In the fall of 1967 the Urban League established Harlem Prep in a National Guard Armory on the Harlem River in New York City. The school concentrated on fundamentals, and the literature and history of black

America. Classes were informal and open within a seminarlike format. The use of the Socratic method created a sense of competitive identity in the students. All twenty-seven of the original graduates of Harlem Prep were admitted to colleges and universities such as Vassar and Berkeley (*Newsweek*, July 8, 1968, p. 46).

The application of positive techniques to create a sense of *interlocking identity and competition* provides a basis for communication within a dialogue context that otherwise would result in varying forms of isolational polarization, if left to an uninterrupted negative progression. Where an effort is made to create isolated forms of communication to make communication possible in the outside world, the basis of isolational polarization is eschewed. Egocentric dialogue is a new and experimental technique in the urban crisis, but it is an alternative to a negative escalation into power camps. Indeed, "the dialectic of racism and power can be transcended only by refusal to respond to the rhetoric of Black Power as if it were a call to battle" (Burgess 1968, p. 131).

Confrontational Communication

Confrontational communication as a structural action must be derived from a base similar to the one used in confrontational polarization. The egocentric function of dialogue for individuals must be enlarged to a level of *group interaction*. The in-group operation in the examples cited above is an example of confrontational (or egocentric) group communication. Group dialogue identifies one in-group within the community at large by committing the in-group to interactive relationships—true dialogue—with the community. In each of the previously cited examples individuals with a sense of identity and purpose united to compete as a unit in a situation where the *collectivity* of the in-group required recognition and dialogue as a basis from which *individuals* could emerge.

Negative and disruptive confrontation (without dialogue) occurs, not as the result of an individual polarized by conflict, but because the individual is caught up in the crowd phenomenon of an in-group being confronted by or confronting an out-group. Confrontation communication can avoid this problem by transferring the lesson of personal egocentric dialogue within a single group context to the context of group versus group. Thus, group action—like individual interaction—could contribute in a positive manner to a dialogue where commitment by in-groups allows each group to develop a purposeful identify from its interaction with the other group. This group identity becomes a group entity that continually undergoes revision and adjustment for growth and development, but not at the expense of its dialectical partner.

The dialogue approach of both isolational and confrontational communication can be susceptible to the charge that it really amounts to "acquiescing to the power structure," or "playing the white man's game," or the like. Such an interpretation frequently overlooks two fundamental points about the process of communication as egocentric dialogue: (1) the effectiveness of "isolational" communication depends upon the individual's creation of an identity with a past heritage and culture, and (2) the utility of confrontational communication depends upon the competitive power of individuals who offer a united front and a workable alternative to the existing system. This second point does not amount to the destruction of the opposition, but to its reform. In both cases, the product is positive and constructive, and in both instances the human agents are "their own person." To such advantages there is only the bleak alternative of destructive and negative polarization, usually administered by an elite of some type *for* the individual.

The choice itself between polarization and communication is an *individual* choice. Polarization offers life to the more powerful combatant; egocentric speech offers life to all who choose to speak. "That we have delayed in choosing or, by delaying, may be making the wrong choice, does not sentence us to separatism or despair. But we must choose. We will choose. Indeed, we are now choosing" (Advisory Commission 1968, p. 408).

COMMUNICATION AS CHOICE

Polarization is a social phenomenon with positive characteristics demonstrated in a reductive tendency toward isolation. Polarization has a negative manifestation as an attempt to confront the opposing force by creating a power-based offensive posture. When the group polarization is positive in nature, it exhibits an "elite" leadership characteristic of inclusiveness. Where the polarization is negative, the growth of "elitism" provides an exclusive nature to the group.

Communication also functions dialectically in an isolational and confrontational context. Communication as "isolational" concentrates on providing an egocentric aspect to personal speech and interpersonal relationships. Speech as dialogue can be expanded to a collective level to provide a group with a competitive base of power; this is confrontational communication.

In short, communication can be a viable alternative to silence or violent polarization, if it is chosen. That choice has been made in some areas, and not in others. Yet, in a very real sense the choice is always being made, for inaction is the choice of not choosing. "We are willing, frequently, to let our silence count as consent on a good many issues which we think are either too trivial or too delicate to push the point" (Worth 1964, p. 33).

Chapter Ten

Life History Interviews

A Teaching and Research Model for Semiotic Phenomenology

The Federal Writers Project was abolished in 1939 by the United States Congress. The project was a victim of the now infamous House Un-American Activities Committee chaired by Senator Joseph McCarthy. A unique undertaking of the Works Progress Administration (WPA), the project functioned during 1938 and 1939, the last years of the Great Depression. While Adolf Hitler was telling the German people what its condition was, Franklin Roosevelt was quietly sending some sixty-five hundred unemployed writers out to ask the American people what its life was like. These writers conducted interviews and transcribed more than ten thousand personal narratives. These life-history narratives are, in fact, personal accounts of significant life-events that signify the very lived-world of ordinary persons whose discourse reduces society and culture to its communicated essence. The phenomenology of the existential narrative records human conscious experience.

As these persons express their life experiences, as they tell their story, we perceive a discursive process of consciousness that explicates the experience of personal, social, and cultural reality (Kamler 1983). In short, the narration of the life-event instantiates the existential value and phenomenological meaning of society, of the lived-world of others. The eidetic and empirical moments form a dialectic of expression and perception in which the life-event is the life-history. Discourse forms a *l'histoire* in which personal consciousness is social experience (Lanigan 1982a; 1984; Johnson et al. 1982).

Both the unique data of life-events and the methodology for analyzing such data are the focus of my concern (Bogdan & Biklen 1982). My interest in the data stems from an undergraduate course I teach, "Communication and Social Process." Its purpose is to teach students how human communication functions as a social institution, both in the semiotic sense of social formation and in the phenomenological sense of personal identity as a transformation in society. In this course I am concerned with the fact that despite the enormous amount of information generated under the banner of the "social sciences" in the last fifty years, there is precious little understanding of what individual persons in society think, do, and believe as confirmed from their own lips to their own satisfaction (Nelson 1986). In short, the social world as displayed in survey research is largely an unacknowledged fiction in the context of human conscious experience. Persons are treated as anything but the *society* they live.

As part of this ideological failure, my second concern is methodology. With an undergraduate class, I want to discuss research methods in a rigorous way. Yet I also want students to become proficient with a method that personally allows each one of them to experience the conduct of research as a social event. In my attempts to formulate the undergraduate class plan in conjunction with ongoing graduate student research projects, it became obvious that although graduate students are frequently told about research and given something like replication exercises, they also seldom have the actual research experience while still taking course work. In short, I determined that what a teacher only tells graduate students or only does with undergraduates might well be converted into what and how students at both levels might do to learn a research method devoted to life-event data gathering and analysis.

The remainder of this chapter is a display of the very dialectic of teaching and research that entails the data and analytic method of life-event investigation in the *human sciences*. First, I discuss the life-event investigation as a pedagogical focus in the classroom. Second, I shall take up the theoretical orientation of such research—its ideological stance, if you will.

TEACHING LIFE-EVENTS METHODOLOGY

After a silence of nearly fifty years, Ann Banks (1980) presented the life histories of eighty persons who were interviewed as respondents by some forty-one members of the Federal Writers Project. I used Banks's book *First-Person America* as a data source for my class. On the one hand, it gave us access to uncatalogued materials available only at the Library of

Congress. On the other hand, it is a book that acknowledges its own lack of theory and the post hoc nature of its methodology. The life-events of interviewed persons are vicariously grouped under the designations Old Times, Immigrant Lives, The Yards, Industrial Lore, Monumental Stone, Rank and File, Tobacco People, Women on Work, Troupers and Pitchmen, The Jazz Language, and Testifying.

There is an anti-intellectual notion that life histories speak for themselves—which of course they do not. Rather than suggest ideological naivety, we should note with some caution at this point that Banks's work is considered standard scholarship in the area of "oral history" employed as a methodology. For example, Thompson's classic work *The Voice of the Past: Oral History* (1978) specifies the key ingredient of such research to be the establishment of a correlation, in Hjelmslev's (1969) sense, between the official record and the personal narrative. This either/or approach to "facts" and "true reality" is just what Banks attempts in a long introduction to her book. Yet what I want to point out (and it is a key point in the classroom experience) is that the Banks book is merely data collection and post hoc theory as an artifact of the editorial process. We can and need to move onto theoretically informed analysis where "correlation" as an either/or logic is not a conflation of the law of identity.

The eighty narratives in the book have a semiotic structure that can be phenomenologically reduced—a fact that is preconsciously signaled by Banks's groupings of narratives and the very selection of eighty accounts from the ten thousand available. The narrative life-events have a phenomenological meaning that can be explicated as an interpretation of the data—a fact prereflectively signaled by Banks's concern to reinterview informants and interview writers in order to learn what the experience meant (not to learn if the original narratives were "accurate" by comparing them with other records—which standard oral history methodology requires!). We should also note that a National Public Radio production (1980) based on the Banks book, which aired under the title "First-Person America: Voices from the Thirties," also filled in the theoretical void by interviewing, not Banks; but several of the original WPA interviewers to get their theoretical assessment of what they did and why, especially with regard to the discovery of social orientations in the United States of America.

Returning to the classroom experience, the first step is to learn the communicative distinction between inscribed life-events and oral accounts of life-events made explicit in the National Public Radio production as opposed to the book edited by Banks. Students were first asked to *write* an autobiographical essay—that is, an account of a life-event, a story about themselves that remained in their memory as a critical communication event. Their recollections were universally about a single event in which they had a personal investment of social learning that instantiated a moral/social value. Some were positive memories, some were negative, some had been expressed before, some were confessional, but all were communication events lived through as existential moments. These written protocols were shared among the class members so that every person had both an autobiographical essay and one from each other person in the class. A standard semiotic phenomenological analysis was written up for each essay. Figure 22 is a sample of the protocol used for analysis (cf. Figure 2). (See Lanigan [1979a; 1982a; 1984] and especially Watson & Watson-Franke [1985] for an overview of semiotic phenomenological theory and praxis that is referred to here.)

In such an analysis, students are asked to follow the three-step method of description, reduction, and interpretation. The description in this case is the autobiographical essay. The reduction consists of abstracting words and phrases that function as existential signifiers—that is, as *revelatory phrases*. Such significations are *revelatory* in that they signify the lived-meaning of the discourse as a life-event. One way of describing such signifiers is that they are the words and phrases of the person, words that nominate what the discourse is about as a conscious experience. The reduction typically specifies an affective, cognitive, or conative boundary for conscious experience. Intentionality emerges as a communicative focus on one of the Jakobsonian functions of discourse—that is, the emotive, conative, referential, poetic, phatic, or metalinguistic (Holenstein 1976).

The third step of analysis involving phenomenological interpretation (hermeneutic) requires two procedures. First, the list of revelatory phrases obtained from the reduction step is critically examined and one or two selected as the signified in the discourse. Second, a particular signified is then used as the key part of a hermeneutic proposition—that is, a statement, written by the analyst, that gives the meaning implicit in the explicit discourse. Often such a proposition does not need to be constructed, but rather upon reexamination of the text a complete sentence can be located and used as the paradigm. In other words, a seemingly unimportant statement (sentence) can be (is) the preconscious, prereflective meaning used by the respondent. Confirmation is often readily at hand with such respondent reactions as "that's what I meant, but I didn't know I said it" or the reaction to the analyst's proposition, "that's what I was trying to say." In either case, both the respondent and the interviewer discover the sense in which the *phrase* is indeed *revelatory* of lived-meaning.

Having learned the analytic method of phenomenology using a written document, the class then proceeds to do similar analyses of each of the eighty written narratives in the Banks book. We have two objectives. First, does the display of natural attitude ("words speak for themselves")

Semiotic Phenomenology Analysis Worksheet

1. DESCRIPTION: Thematizing Capta as Signs.
{Specify the Respondent's Protocol for Discourse; What is the thematic context?}

2. REDUCTION: Abstracting Capta as Signifiers.
{Specify the Respondent's Revelatory Phrases; What is the problematic Focus of the text?}

3A. INTERPRETATION-GENERAL ESSENCE: Explicating Capta as Signified. {Specify the Respondent's Key Revelatory Phrase; What is the Locus of the text?}

3B. INTERPRETATION-ESSENCE: Stating the Respondent's Hermeneutic Proposition. {Analyst's protocol ascription of Respondent's reduced description; What is the existential meaning communicated?}

Figure 22. Semiotic phenomenology analysis worksheet

in the editorial groupings (the chapters) in the Banks book have any signification per se? Is there a semiotic system at work that expresses a social function of the persons interviewed? Is there a phenomenological system at work that expresses their personal nature? Secondly, does our analysis indicate an essence of a conscious human experience that we all share, that all the informants also share? Does the explication of the life-event specify an existential meaning ("words are persons speaking"), a conscious experience that is just as much a part of society today as it was in the past?

The second stage of the classroom learning experience is to move from mediated communication where a written document is a communication filter (a contrary logic form—i.e., the logic of the language) to the oral environment (the oral expression system or logic of the speaker). In this move, from orality to inscription and inscription to orality, the semiotic logic of inscription present in any literate use of *langue* is bypassed. It is in this sense that oral communication as *parole* (speaking) becomes a direct (unmediated) source of meaning. Such meaning is a direct expression rather than perceived meaning; note that inscription reverses the dialectic of communication. When I write a message, I inscribe a perception—I become the other in place of my self. By contrast, the practice of utterance in its oral form creates a message as an expression. The message is thereby a presentation (oral; human) rather than a representation (inscribed; artifact).

As an initial oral project in the class, students are assigned to conduct oral interviews, using audio–tape recorders, relative to the social perception of obesity. This project was coordinated with ongoing research by a doctoral student (Spitzack 1984; cf. Ablamowicz 1984; Nelson 1986). The *topical interview protocol* (which is *not* a questionnaire) used in this phase of the class experience is reproduced as Figure 23. Students interviewed persons to obtain life-event narratives about body-image and body perception in order to determine if obesity in American society is a communicated social meaning and the sense that it signified. Once again, the semiotic phenomenological procedure is followed. The audio-taped narrative is the capta/data of description. Reductions are made indicating the revelatory phrases, and interpretations are drawn or constructed from the respondent's key revelatory phrase. The process is then repeated using each student's interpretation as a captum/datum. These interpretations are then reduced and a final hermeneutic proposition generated. The research result, a generated definition, is thereby a specification of the meaning of obesity as communication by all the informants. Here we have the communicated process of reference, ascription, and predication, not the location of a referent.

The research result in methodological terms is important, especially in the sense that we should not slip back into a positivistic hypostatization. This is to say, the research procedure is about communication and the social process by doing it, and systematically researching what they were doing. The final classroom experience is a conscious experience that entails both a reflexive and intentional activity that is a life-event per se, that is, an actual life-history interview (see Figure 24 for the topical protocol used).

Interview Opening

I'm doing research on communication topics in my communication class. One of the topics we're interested in is how people talk about cultural perceptions of the human body. I'm interested in getting some descriptions of your own bodily experience in American culture. I have about ten topics I want you to talk about. At most, it'll take 45 minutes. Do you have any concerns before we begin?

Topical Protocol {use Topics in any order in spontaneous oral questions}

1. AMERICAN STANDARDS FOR "PROPER" WEIGHT.
2. MALE/FEMALE DIFFERENCES IN WEIGHT PROPRIETY (= PROPER *IMAGE*).
3. CULTURAL WEIGHT STANDARDS IN RELATION TO OWN EXPERIENCE.
4. CURRENT IMAGE OF BODY.
5. RESPONDENT'S CRITERIA USED TO ASSESS OWN AND OTHER'S BODY.
6. HOW BODY CHANGES ARE MADE.
7. BEHAVIORAL CHANGES ACCOMPANYING BODY CHANGES–CHANGES IN PHYSICAL APPEARANCE.
8. RELATIONAL CHANGES WITH BODY CHANGES (INTERACTION CHANGES).

Hypothetical Questions (use when the Respondent doesn't seem to be able to answer or go on)

1. IMAGINE YOURSELF AS YOU GO THROUGH AN AVERAGE DAY. HOW DOES YOUR RELATIONSHIP WITH YOUR BODY CHANGE IN VARIOUS SETTINGS?
2. LET'S SAY YOU'RE FEELING VERY POSITIVE ABOUT YOUR BODY. WHAT KIND OF THINGS WOULD YOU DO?
   (PROBES: ACTIVITIES, ATTITUDES, PERSONALITY)
3. IF A STRANGER SAW YOU ON THE STREET TODAY, HOW WOULD S/HE DESCRIBE YOUR BODY?
4. WHEN YOU SEE OTHER PEOPLE, WHAT DO YOU NOTICE FIRST ABOUT THEIR BODIES?

Interview Closing

These are all the questions I have. Thank you very much for your time and interest. I'd like to assure you that everything we've talked about today is confidential and your name won't be used. I would like to ask specifically, however, if you have any objections to this tape being used for my research? (response) Is there anything you'd like to add at this point? (response) (standing) Thanks again.

Figure 23. Interview protocol: dissertation on obesity

Interview Opening

I'm doing research on communication topics in my communication class. One of the things we are interested in learning more about is how people view their own lives. We like to get people to tell stories about themselves that suggest something interesting or important in their lives. Most people find it is a lot of fun to just talk and in the process create a short biographical account of their lives. I'll mention several topics that should help you talk about your life. At most, it will take about 45 minutes. Do you have any concerns before we begin?

Topical Protocol {use topics in any order in spontaneous oral questions}

1. CHILDHOOD OR TEENAGE EVENT THAT YOU RECALL WITH HAPPINESS/ SADNESS.
2. YOUR BEST FRIEND WHEN YOU WERE GROWING UP.
3. WHAT YOU DO TO HAVE FUN.
4. WHAT WORK AND OCCUPATION MEAN.
5. THE EMBARRASSING THING YOU WOULD LIKE TO FORGET.
6. THE THING OTHER PEOPLE ALWAYS REMEMBER ABOUT YOU.
7. THE PERSONAL VALUES YOU HAVE; WHAT IS IMPORTANT IN YOUR LIFE.
8. WHAT YOUR FUTURE WILL BE.
9. WHAT OTHER PEOPLE MEAN TO YOU.
10. HOW THE REAL WORLD INFLUENCES YOUR LIFE.
11. WHAT A "GOOD DAY" IS LIKE.
12. THE PERSON YOU WISH YOU WERE.
13. THE STORY YOUR PARENTS LIKE TO TELL ABOUT YOU.
14. WHAT THE FILM VERSION OF YOUR LIFE WOULD BE LIKE.
15. WHAT YOU ARE THINKING ABOUT RIGHT NOW BECAUSE WE ARE TALKING ABOUT YOUR PAST.

Interview Closing

I think our time is about up. Thanks for your time and help. I want to assure you that everything we talked about today is for my own use and I will not use your name if you prefer. Do you mind if I use your name in my research report? (If respondent says "YES"–say: Your comments will be confidential then. I won't use your name.) Is there anything you would like to say at this point? (response) (standing) Thanks again!

Figure 24. Interview protocol: life-history research

THE THEORY OF LIFE-EVENT RESEARCH

I should now like to turn away from the classroom as a site of instructional research and discuss the place of life-event theory in general as a human science application of method (see Anderson 1987). The sense of the current situation is hinted at in my remarks about the Banks book and the standard oral history book by Paul Thompson (1978).

There is an established tradition with life-events data in the communicative sense of action in society. This tradition is marked in the discipline of sociology by the work of the "symbolic interactionists" at the University of Chicago and by the phenomenological applications of Alfred Schutz (see chap. 16). In one perspective—namely, that of the working group on life-history method of the International Sociological Association—the symbolic interactionist tradition has come full circle and we are now in the situation of taking up the questions of life-event data and methodology after decades of benign neglect in the discipline of sociology. In this respect, we can read with insight the reports of current research in Daniel Bertaux's *Biography and Society: The Life History Approach in the Social Sciences* (1981). We also have the third edition of *Symbolic Interaction* by Manis and Meltzer (1978), which records the origin and development of the life-event research in the broad sense with which I am concerned, in particular the encompassing phenomenological basis of symbolic data and the semiotic nature of interaction among human beings. Here—the theoretical reflection that Manis and Meltzer offer—is a place to ground the data found in books like that of Banks.

I think I can best illustrate my point by citing the seven theoretical propositions that Manis and Meltzer articulate for life-events research. And these propositions can then be summarized in two ways. First, I cite the *reductions* that Manis and Meltzer offer. Second, I abstract from Banks's introduction to her book those revelatory phrases that are an *interpretation* of the reduction that Manis and Meltzer cite. In short, I shall conduct part of a brief phenomenology of the semiotic system that is symbolic interaction—a life-event. Of course, a complete understanding of this somewhat pedagogical analysis requires a reading of the cited texts (the "description" step in phenomenological method) under discussion here.

The first Manis and Meltzer proposition states: "Distinctively human behavior and interaction are carried on through the medium of symbols and their meaning" (Manis & Meltzer 1978, pp. 6–9). The reduction that Manis and Meltzer offer is: "the meaning component in human conduct" (1978, p. 5). Banks gives us the appropriate revelatory phrase as an interpretation; in the narratives we find "perspectives and sensibilities" (1980, p. xx).

The second proposition is: "The individual becomes humanized through interaction with other persons." Reduced this means "the social source of humanness." For Banks this is the narrative as a "liberating and exhilarating experience" (1980, p. xix).

The third proposition is: "Human society is most usefully conceived as consisting of people in interaction." The reduction is "society as process." The Banks interpretation is society as "mosaic" (1980, pp. xv–xvi).

The fourth proposition is: "Human beings are active in shaping their own behavior." The reduction is "the voluntaristic component in human conduct." The Banks interpretation is the "natural association of ideas and memories" (1980, p. xv).

The fifth proposition is: "Consciousness, or thinking, involves interactions with oneself." The reduction is "a dialectical conception of mind." Banks's interpretation is that the narratives are "knowing-advice" (1980, p. xii).

The sixth proposition is: "Human beings construct their behavior in the course of its execution." The reduction is "the constructive, emergent nature of human conduct." The Banks interpretation is narrative that is "practice" (1980, p. xx).

The final, seventh, proposition is: "An understanding of human conduct requires study of the actor's covert behavior." The reduction is "the necessity of sympathetic introspection." The Banks interpretation is the discovery of "process" (1980, p. xvi).

By way of a very brief conclusion, let me suggest that the place of life-events research and teaching as a model for semiotic phenomenology is to be found within the process of communication itself. A fundamental requirement for using the life-events approach to human science research is to realize that communication as an empirical phenomenon is solely dependent upon its eidetic status (Holenstein 1976). This is to say, the unique relationship that is coded in the life-event is the fact that the life perspective defines the event (see chaps. 5 and 7). As Michel Foucault so eloquently summarizes, "a statement is always an event that neither the language (*langue*) nor the meaning can quite exhaust" (1972, p. 28).

Part Three:

Semiology

[SECTION ONE: EIDETIC RESEARCH]

Chapter Eleven

Structuralism and the Human Science Context of Phenomenology and Semiology

Structuralism is a revolutionary approach to research. Like most revolutionary candidates in the social and human sciences, its novelty is matched by an ambiguity of program and a vicarious purpose. It should be no surprise, then, to read in one distinguished survey of the subject that contemporary structuralism is "one of the newest and most exciting schools of thought that is currently sweeping over the Western world" (Rossi 1982, p. ix)—and yet that "there is no structuralist sociology" (Lemert & Nielsen 1982, p. 327). These counterposed comments are the telltale sign of philosophical thinking moving into the business of theory construction in the human sciences (Blackwell 1976). Yet it is the human sciences like anthropology, communicology, linguistics, and sociology that made the philosophical problematic viable (Paci 1969).

As an analytic approach to discussing "structuralism," I propose to avoid the usual historicism that turns to the philological occurrence of the concept. My concern is with the paradigm candidate "French structuralism" as it emerges today in the context of phenomenology and semiology. This "structuralist" movement of thought is not sweeping the Western world, yet it has a track record of empirical research in various human science disciplines and a philosophical base (Lanigan 1972; 1979b; 1982a).

French structuralism is neither a disciplinary lacuna—for example, Is French structural linguistics different from an American version?—nor is it a methodological *gestalt*—for example, Is structuralism a theory or merely a procedure? French structuralism is, like its chief rivals French phenomenology and semiology, a philosophical claim about the ontology and epistemology of science (Runciman 1973). But it is a limited thesis. French structuralism is a claim for the immediacy of social practice as science, especially where scientific procedure applies its practices to the *institutions* of human conscious experience (Lemert 1981). For example, practice is the institutions we call language, communication, society, and the person (Leach 1976). Such institutions are the problematics of contemporary disciplines in human science—disciplines marked by their philosophical orientation (Rossi 1982; Lanigan 1984).

Three topics constitute my analysis in this chapter. First, there is a description of the philosophical orientations that account for French structuralism as a problematic. A "problematic" is a problematical context within which an issue, or set of issues, functions as a criterion for analysis and judgment of the problem per se. Such a criterion usually meets the theory construction requirement of being a necessary condition, especially where "truth condition" logics are inapplicable to the human behavior being analyzed. Second, I focus on the preference for society and social norms that structuralism displays in the practice of its philosophical orientations. Third, there is the interpretation of judgment (eidetic science) and practice (empirical science) that constitutes a thematic for structuralism.

A "thematic" is the use of a criterion, derived from a problematic, that meets the theory construction requirements of being a sufficient condition description or explication of the original problem under investigation (see, e.g., chap. 6 above). Here the sufficient condition nominates a solution to the problem or suggests a typology of possible solutions within which a possible necessary condition solution can be found as also sufficient. In traditional theory construction language, the "context of discovery" in the problematic leads to the "context of justification" in the thematic as a hypothesis or an abductive logic (Rule + Result = Case), and not conversely as either a deductive (Rule + Case = Result) or inductive (Case + Result = Rule) hypostatization (Eco 1976, Peirce 1931–35, 1958, 2.623).

PHILOSOPHICAL ORIENTATION

Descombes (1980) offers one of the most comprehensive accounts of contemporary French philosophy available, yet he does not have a chapter on "structuralism" in his book. The discussion of structuralism is there, but within the progressive context of French phenomenology and French semiology. The philosophical theory of signs (*sémiologie*) is the grounding for the concept of structure. Hence Descombes describes the progressive philosophical maturation of the human sciences in the French context. Note that it is the French paradigm of structuralism that occupies our concern, because it is the one with which the human sciences debate is sustained in the United States specifically and in Europe generally (Lemert 1979).

Descombes notes that there are three structuralisms. He names them respectively *structural analysis*, *semiology*, the "the critique of both phenomenology and *semiology*" (p. 81). Descombes discounts "structural analysis," by which he means a structuralist anthropology and linguistics with historical roots in Russian formalism, as having little or no bearing on the contemporary French scene. By comparison, "semiology" challenges phenomenology as the proper account of "meaning" in the human sciences and philosophy. However, structuralism in its current status is *critique*. It is the critique that forecasts a counterposition to both phenomenology and semiology.

We discover with Descombes that structuralism is a critique of both ontology and epistemology. Ontology is critiqued in the attack on phenomenology, where phenomenology is a philosophical position that argues for the primacy of the *person* as the source of all normative judgment (eidetic science is *human*) and normal practice (empirical science is *social*). Epistemology is critiqued by structuralism in the attack on semiology, where semiology (or semiotics—this latter term being the Anglo-American preferred name) is a parallel philosophical position that argues for *culture* (the primacy of human institutions) as the source of normative judgments (eidetic science is *individual*) and normal practice (empirical science is *conventional*).

In short, structuralism as critique is axiological in the traditional sense of philosophy. The critique is meant to be a criterion of judgment (the problematic) and practice (the thematic), which posits or constitutes the context of both judgment and practice. Creative axiology as *structural critique* becomes the functional equivalent of theory construction in the human sciences (Barthes 1968). In turn, ontology is thereby normed as an inferential product, and epistemology is normed likewise as an inferential process.

How this critical method argument of structural critique carries forward requires some discussion of Descombes' first version of structuralism—that is, the *structural analysis*—which he obviates. We cannot accept his dismissal of linguistic (Hjelmslev 1961) and anthropological (Levi-Strauss 1969; Leach 1976) structuralism so quickly, precisely because the structural analysis at issue has a philosophical grounding.

At issue is the early work of Jakobson (1971) with the linguistic structure of narrative in Russian folktales, and then with distinctive features in comparative linguistics and communicology. Holenstein (1976) shows that as a student of Edmund Husserl, the founder of phenomenology, Jakobson's "structural analysis" is already a *phenomenological structuralism*. Thus, Jakobson's theory of communication is phenomenological by placing the human source of the social as an ontological condition of epistemology.

The axiology of the human sciences is plain: eidetic distinction is prior to empirical feature in the most human of social institutions, articulate discourse (Hjelmslev 1961; Benveniste 1971a). This argument is generally referred to as the "primacy of the speaking subject." But for reasons of philosophical accuracy, we should amend that reference to the *primacy of the person speaking* as the origin of meaning (Merleau-Ponty 1962).

Descombes' second version of structuralism, *semiology*, is the response to Jakobson's phenomenological structuralism. The concept and practice of "meaning" is at issue. Following the Jakobson tradition of communicology, semiology takes the linguistic model of structure in language (Saussure 1966) and generalizes it to all social institutions as the code of individual practice (Eco 1976). Phenomenology is turned on its head; the empirical distinction becomes the eidetic feature. Yet the empirical distinction as a convention of practice has its source in the individual eidetic judgment. The code may dominate the source of practice, but the primacy of meaning still rests with the person as an individual practitioner. The ontological position of the phenomenologist is set aside to accommodate the epistemological practice of the semiotician.

Again the axiology is manifest. Empirical distinction is prior to eidetic feature in the most conventional of individual performances, discourse that articulates reality. Although popularly indexed as the "death of the subject," this argument also is restated best by the positive formulation: culture constitutes meaning; there are no significations by social individuals (Leach 1976; Lemert 1979).

What, then, is the philosophical ground of structuralism conceived as structural critique? As Hawkes (1977, pp. 17–18) argues, "This new concept, that the world is made up of relationships rather than things, constitutes the first principle of that way of thinking which can properly be called 'structuralist.'" By way of defining the relationships he has in mind, Hawkes cites Jean Piaget: the structuralist relationships are (1) wholeness, (2) transformation, and (3) self-regulation. These elements are of course derived from the critique of phenomenology and semiology with their contingent structural procedures.

In the case of structural relationships in phenomenology (Lanigan 1976), the "wholeness" of phenomenological description requires an explicit depiction of phenomena, their essence as relational structure and content. Procedures of suspended prejudice (*epoché*) provide scientific neutrality as a context of discovery. "Transformation" is parallel to phenomenological reduction—that is, the specification of general essence by reason of necessary and sufficient (not truth) conditions. Here the procedure of imaginative free variation draws, for example, on transformative moves akin to the linguistic model of Saussure (1966). Linear series of items, syntagmatic chains, are context for linear hierarchies, paradigmatic items, set in orthogonal position as a process boundary. The two dimensions account for a third, combinary structure, just as in the spatial analogy width and height account for the structure called "depth" in perception or "articulation" in expression (see Fig. 5).

Last as a procedure is phenomenological interpretation. Because description creates wholeness and reduction is a transformation of the phenomenon, self-regulation is a parallel procedure to phenomenological interpretation. Such interpretation is the *reflexive* inference about the description and reduction that is both a signification (the original depiction) and a meaning (the depiction as accurate description)—that is, reflexivity.

In comparison with phenomenology, the structural relationships in semiology as structural critique also follow a set of procedures parallel to wholeness, transformation, and self-regulation (Lanigan 1972; 1982b). Recall that for Saussure a "sign" is defined as the differential (paradigmatic function) and mutual (syntagmatic function) entailment of a signifier (expression form) and a signified (perception form). In such a schema, the sign functions as a transformation procedure in which the self-regulation of units (i.e., signifiers) constitutes the units per se (i.e., signifieds) as a condition of wholeness. A simple linguistic illustration is our usual grammatical understanding of a noun (a transformation concept) that allows us to understand both the function as the "subject" of a sentence (signifier: the noun's expressive condition) and the function as the "object" in a sentence (the noun's perceptive condition as a referent: a signified).

In short, the philosophical ground of structuralism is a theoretical commitment to relationships, rather than categories, as the source of meaning in phenomena. Such relationships are manifest by methodological procedures that reflect wholeness, transformation, and self-regulation. The theory and method derive their metaphysical status by opposition to the ontology represented in either phenomenology or semiology. This is to say that structuralism in its contemporary version as the "critique model" opposes the ontological claim of phenomenology that human values are grounded in the conscious experience of persons. Likewise, the critique model denies the claim of semiology for an ontology of social values grounded in the experience of consciousness as manifest in the normative practices of everyday life.

SOCIAL NORM AS PERSONAL PERFORMANCE

The concept of practice is a key idea in the critique model of French structuralism. Within the problematic of the "economy of logic," Bourdieu distinguishes the "universe of discourse" and the "universe of practice" (1972, p. 110). These ideas have many operational schemata in the work of authors like Bourdieu, but those schemata that Eco (1976) formalizes under two interconnected headings are the most systematic—namely, (1) the Theory of Codes and (2) the Theory of Sign-Production. In terms already familiar to our analysis, a practice can be viewed as a social example of self-regulation. A code can be conceived as a transformation (representation of a presentation), and a theory of sign-production functions as wholeness—that is, as process completion or signification (sign-production).

In such a table of equivalences, structuralism places an ontological emphasis on society and its institutions. Human values are collective in society; society has a worldview, a *Weltanschauung*, that is limited in a hierarchical fashion by the cultural preferences and practices of a given era, a *Zietgeist*. In a word, *culture* is the normative criterion for structuralist thought, method, and research.

Structuralism is interested in all the institutions of society, but the universe of discourse or language as the practice of the speech community (*langue*) is the exemplar. To be specific, Lyons (1977, pp. 231–323) suggests that the structuralist argues "that every language is a unique relational structure, or system, and that the units which we identify . . . derive both their essence and their existence from their relationships with other units in the same language-system." We require a certain amount of caution at this point in distinguishing the names of sociolinguistic (communicological) categories.

In the context of French linguistics, *discourse* divides into three normative categories of human expression and perception: *parole*, *langue*, and *langage*. *Parole* is the act of speaking and signifies the discursive practice of an individual person. Such discourse is the empirical and eidetic record of a *Lebenswelt*. *Langue* is the speech act (combined lexicon and diction) of preference in a given social group. In most speech communities, the sense of connotation or denotation in signification involves a parallel norming of group affiliation as between peers (*Gemeinschaft*) or nonpeers (*Gesellschaft*). *Langage* is the "language-system" or "sign-system" in ideal form; the constitutive rules (*Weltanschauung*) for discourse embodied in a so-called natural, which is to say cultural, language. Perhaps it is also helpful to note that the *parole*, *langue*, and *langage* distinction functions in a combinatory manner much like the medieval trivium where rhetoric, grammar, and logic were categories of discourse practice (Overfield 1984; Ferruolo 1985).

With these basic categories of discourse in place, we can now make an oversimplified, but very useful, distinction among structuralism, phenomenology, and semiology. Structuralism makes the theoretical claim that *discourse as practice* requires only *langue* or its functional equivalent in a nonlinguistic system of enactment, such as learning, cultural preference, or similar normative behaviors that are self-reflexive. *Parole* (the empirical practice of empirical subjects) and *langage* (the empirical practice of eidetic subjects) are fictions for the conservative structuralist. They are fictions that hide reality from persons who do not perceive that their speech is merely the display of the language (*langue*) into which they were born and that the logico-grammatical rules (*langage*) of that language are abstractions for that same learned-language. Bourdieu (1977, p. 72) names this phenomenon the *habitus* that consists in "systems of durable, transposable *dispositions*," which are not an adherence to rules in any knowing sense. In other words, learning and habit promote the false belief that there are speaking subjects and eternal meanings.

As historical referents for this developing movement, let me note in passing that structuralism often is marked as the attack on the conception of a speaking subject, and poststructuralism is the additional attack on the notion that meaning can be ontological.

Semiology makes a claim similar to that of structuralism with the added ingredient of *langage*. This is to say, there is *langue* defined in "discourse as practice," but there is also the analytic discovery of eidetic elements. These eidetic elements are discovered in *practice as discourse*—that is, in *langage*. The practice abstracted from the discourse is Bourdieu's "universe of practice," the theoretical grounding of a logic that is literally realized, made empirical and real, by use. For a "theory of signification" as *langue*, there is a "theory of codes" as *langage*. In brief, grammar is born of logic. *Parole*, as the rhetoric of the person, the speaking subject, is a fiction for the semiotician. *Parole* is discounted as theoretical hypothesis without utility in the human sciences.

Phenomenology, particularly with the Merleau-Ponty heritage, is a claim for all three communicological elements: *parole*, *langue*, and *langage*. The ontological base of discourse is *parole* in the person, but it is a *parole parlante* or *langage* that has a reflexive counterpart in *parole parlée* or *langue*. *Langage* is a "speech speaking" in which "speech" as *langage* is the embodied ground of discourse, the human personal *discourse of* practice: *parole*. In addition, *langage* is a "speech spoken" in that "speech" as *langage* reflects the human personal *practice of* discourse: *langue*.

In traditional discursive terms, the phenomenologist grounds rhetoric (*parole*) and grammar (*langue*) in logic (*langage*), but phenomenology is always reflexive—it is the logic of the phenomenon. The phenomenon at issue is discourse, so the concern is the incarnate logic of rhetoric and the incarnate logic of grammar. For the phenomenologist, discourse is embodied in the person. There is no other ontological grounding for expression and perception (Merleau-Ponty 1962).

Given these comparative features of structuralism, semiology, and phenomenology, my analysis can turn now to the interpretation of judgment (theory construction as eidetic science) and practice (theory construction as empirical science), which are thematic for structuralism as a human science methodology.

JUDGMENT IN PRACTICE, NOT DISCOURSE

So far, the practical investigation of structuralism is advancing in a structuralist fashion. My analysis progressively explores the practice of structuralism by comparison and contrast with other theoretical practices—namely, semiology and phenomenology. And it does so with a careful examination of the model of discourse that is said to account for all forms of practice like discourse. The question to be posed now is: Can the linguistics model, discourse, be left behind? Can the "practice of practice" inform the ontological position of structuralism as a theory and method in the human sciences or not?

Because we are dealing with practice and not discourse, we presumably are avoiding the logical paradoxes of a formalist logic model of language as suggested by Russell and Whitehead (Lanigan 1972). How this structuralist thesis of practice can be argued requires a return to the distinction between Theory of Codes and Theory of Signification suggested by Eco (1976).

Following Hjelmslev (1961) a code can be defined as a rule that governs other rules—that is, a relationship among or for relationships. This is not a situation in which a rule governs itself, hence a rule is not the base condition for its own application as a metarule. A code, by definition, thereby avoids the logical paradoxes inherent in purely formal deductive systems. In this context, structuralists usually define a system-code as a *structure* where the name "system-code" stands for relationships (a system) held together by another relationship (a code). As Eco (1976, p. 38) suggests, a structure is "a system (i) in which every value is established by positions and differences and (ii) which appears only when different phenomena are mutually compared with reference to the same system of relations."

It should be easy to detect the methodological assumptions built into the idea of a structure as a theory of codes. Some phenomenon is required for purposes of value reference (signification or meaning), a phenomenon that is both an eidetic and empirical presentation of wholeness, transformability, and self-regulation. Inasmuch as the semiotic paradigm candidate was *langue* (the discourse of the speech community), and the phenomenological paradigm was *parole* (the discourse of the person), the structuralist candidate is *culture*. But the conception of eidetic exemplar of culture must always be a *specific*, *concrete* culture, otherwise the practice or empirical exemplar of *society* as a fixed temporal and spatial phenomenon would not be a signification. Recall Eco's specification for system *values*. They are established by positions and differences with reference to the same system of relationships. In short, a system value is a differentiation by combination. This value is produced by an analogue logic in which the differentiation is a relationship (a presentation), one that defines the condition under which other relationships (re-presentations) can be constituted.

To illustrate the theoretical issue, then, a performance is a representation (e.g., obeying a traffic signal), in society, that acts as a practice or presentation (e.g., the social value called "obedience"). The performance as practice is a structure; likewise the practice as performance is a structure. To exemplify the latter point, obedience is legitimized as a social value when there is no one else to observe the performance—for example, stopping your automobile at the red traffic light even though there is no supporting or opposing traffic, and especially when there are no witnesses at all!

Unlike a system of discourse or *langue*, fixed by exclusively *social* usage, the structuralist argues that the systems of a culture offer a value stability that is functionally fixed (even though cultures evolve over time and situation). Hence, a structuralist argues that the fundamental systems of culture—that is, language (*langage*), kinship, and commerce—are all indexed to the same cultural value(s). Culture on this view is an eidetic science that governs empirical systems. Each system is in fact a system-code where the code is a representation of the presentation of culture. Such a reflexive logic is best illustrated methodologically. For example, language, kinship, and commerce, when individually defined according to system values, all have the same *eidetic characteristics*, such as (1) exchange, (2) temporal and spatial dislocation, (3) social use, and so on. As a simultaneous condition, the various systems as a concrete example of the system-code or structures all display the same *empirical characteristics*, such as (1) locus of identity (failure of exchange), (2) temporal and spatial location, (3) nonsocial use (deviance), and the like.

In short, structuralism takes advantage of culture for methodological use in the human sciences, just as the physical sciences utilize nature. Culture, just as nature, is a relationship that governs other relationships by ensuring that the relationship (i.e., structure) always accounts for the wholeness, transformation, and self-regulation of all other relationships based upon it. This is one reason why the structuralist doctrine of method is used in both the physical and human sciences, why one is frequently a model for the other (Eco 1976; Jakobson 1971).

The Theory of Sign-Production is Eco's (1976) name for the more general issues of structure as *human communication*. This is to say, the meaning and understanding of codes and system-codes is at some stage dependent upon an embodied structure. This is the ontological problem per se. I have already suggested that this problem is settled in principle by structuralism in the hypothesis that the embodied structure is exemplified by practice in *society*. By close comparison, the semiotic thesis is that the embodiment is a performance in *culture*. Recall, also, that the phenomenological position is more concrete, arguing that embodied structure occurs in the *person*, the consciousness of experience as lived reflexively by an individual human being.

The basic difference in these positions can be methodologically suggested as follows. (1) Structuralists view the process of communication as a *practice* in which a human *group* is the channel of communication for any given medium (language, kinship, commerce, etc.). Individual performance is representation of practice; performance is a relationship that is a signification (Hawkes 1979). (2) Semioticians view the process of communication as a *performance* in which a *person* is the medium of communication (speaker/listener, peer/nonpeer, subject/object, etc.) for *culture* as the channel of communication—observed most explicitly in cross-cultural research where there are obvious, numerous channels at work. Group practice is a representation of performance; practice is a relationship that signifies (Saussure 1966; Eco 1976). (3) Phenomenologists argue that the process of communication, meaning, is a presentation of performance in which the *person* is the channel of communication for given practices of representation (speaking, interacting, sharing, etc.) that are the media of communication. Performance is the practice of human being; performance is the meaning of practice (Merleau-Ponty 1962; Descombes 1980).

Although I have made very effort to provide a brief analytic discussion of the key features in structuralism as contextualized by both semiology and phenomenology, it would be dangerous not to acknowledge certain limitations. Contemporary research in the human sciences, especially in communicology and psychology, inherits *methodological techniques* and a common *Geistewissenschaften* humanistic interest from each of the three schools of thought (Descombes 1980). Because these schools represent a certain historical and disciplinary evolution, they share as many similarities as dissimilarities. Some I mentioned previously, others I did not. I noted *phenomenological structuralism* (Holenstein 1976), but there is also a *phenomenological semiotics* (Eco 1976, pp. 157, 167, 205, 250), *herme-*

neutic semiology (Silverman 1979a), and *semiotic phenomenology* (Lanigan 1982a, b; 1985), among others.

In short, the movement in intellectual history that we call *Structuralism* is now an American phenomenon some twenty-five years after its birth and maturity in France. We know and use the theory along with its contextual theories, semiology and phenomenology, but we are just beginning to appreciate the research results that appear in such journals as *Semiotica*, *Journal of Phenomenological Psychology*, *Communication*, *Research in Phenomenology*, *Semiotext(e)* and others. As these journals record, the first step in useful empirical research is the eidetic research that constitutes a theory. The theory of structuralism was the start of a first step in the human sciences; semiology and phenomenology are the conclusion of that step. These three theories are, thus, the chronicle of contemporary ontology as a movement from *habitus* to understanding in the theory and praxis of human science.

Chapter Twelve

The Foundations of Semiotic Phenomenology

Phenomenology is both a school of thought in the philosophy of science and subsequently a research procedure in the human arts and sciences (Kockelmans and Kisiel 1970; Natanson 1973; Strasser 1974; Lanigan 1979). Phenomenology is the rigorous examination of conscious experience, especially as manifest in human communication and action.

There is both an American and a European tradition for phenomenology, beginning in the early twentieth century with Charles Sanders Peirce, in the United States, and with Edmund Husserl, in Germany. As Spiegelberg (1956) notes, there is evidence suggesting that Pierce knew Husserl's work in part, but the reverse was not true. Yet, there are biographical and philosophical indications that Peirce and Husserl represent one of those fascinating historical coincidences of parallel research. Both were schooled as a logician and mathematician; both sought to establish philosophy as a rigorous science. Both were systemic thinkers reacting against introspective psychologism. And both were firmly committed to a systematic examination of phenomena as consciously given in experience.

Although phenomenology accounts for a large and influential group of scholars and researchers (Spiegelberg 1982), there are four who directly concern themselves with semiology. These semiotic phenomenologists are Husserl, Peirce, Alfred Schutz, and Maurice Merleau-Ponty. Their contributions can be illustrated in synoptic form by outlining the elements of phenomenological method and its exemplification with respect to a theory of sign-production in human communication that each adopted in his philosophy.

Before discussing Husserl's work, however, brief mention should be made of the German philosophical tradition that precedes him and Peirce (Apel 1981). Hegel (1967) introduced "*phenomenology*" as a systematic term in his *Phenomenology of Mind*. This work is devoted to a discussion of the triadic concepts of "subjective mind," "Objective mind," and "absolute mind." Subjective mind refers to the emergence of consciousness in a person's psychological and anthropological constitution; objective mind is the signification of consciousness in sociological and political experience. Absolute mind signifies consciousness as manifest in the system of judgments forming art, religion, and philosophy.

Following Hegel, and preceding Husserl as his teacher, Brentano (1874) investigated objects of mental phenomena, which he categorized generally as (1) ideas, (2) judgments, and (3) the phenomenon of "love and hate" that contains emotions and volitions. Of particular concern to Brentano (1981) was his nonpropositional or modal theory of judgments. The unity of consciousness in this context defines the object of judgment as the same object of the idea that the judgment presupposes.

HUSSERL'S TRANSCENDENTAL PHENOMENOLOGY

Phenomenology in Husserl's treatment (1970; 1962; 1950) is not systematic in the sense of a schemata of procedural steps. It is systemic in the suggestion of several investigative reflections or *reductions* that constitute a philosophical method. Koestenbaum (1967) and Ihde (1977) discuss the variety and range of reductions developed by Husserl, which can be summarized as three procedures.

First is the *descriptive reduction*, which is a focus on phenomena as directly given in experience. Husserl gives this procedure the name *epoché*, which means a "bracketing" of experience. In precise words, the *epoché* establishes the parenthetical boundaries that allow us to focus on a phenomenon and suspend our presuppositions about it, especially those scientific and philosophical hypostatizations that confuse our judgment of experience as lived. The *epoché* permits the correction of our "natural attitude" about phenomena. Husserl's *epoché* illustrates his famous methodological dictum: "Back to the things themselves!"

Second, the *phenomenological reduction* is an intuiting of the general essence that is to be found in phenomena. Husserl argues that the technique of "imaginative free variation" is the ground for phenomenological reflection, which follows upon the descriptive reduction. Such variation consists of alternately including and excluding the characteristic elements making up the description. The analytic product is a constitution and explication of the general essence of a phenomenon—that is, a *core* of immanent foregrounding and a *horizon* of transcendent backgrounding. The specified phenomenon, or *noema*, is the actual object of experience available to the perceiver (*Ego*) as consciously engaged in awareness.

The third reflection is the *eidetic reduction*, which Husserl often refers to by the simple name "intentionality." As a phenomenological requirement, intentionality is an equal analytic and descriptive focus on phenomena in terms of their structure in consciousness, or *noesis*. Thus, the eidetic relationship is a reciprocal and simultaneous concern with the noetic intending act (e.g., the perceiving or expressing) and the noematic content (e.g., the perceived or expressed). Intentionality is the "consciousness of . . ." that constitutes phenomena. Husserl's phenomenology is transcendental in the sense that the goal of analysis is the *eidos*, or pure intentional structure of ego, which cannot be empirical. This idealistic view is now largely abandoned or modified, due primarily to the influence of Merleau-Ponty and Roman Ingarden.

Although one of Husserl's best students in the sense of accepting the tenets of the phenomenological method, Ingarden rejected transcendental idealism in favor of realism. Among his major contributions to the construction and application of phenomenological procedures is the discussion of the literary work of art (with extrapolations to music and painting) as constituted by intentional acts (Ingarden 1973; 1964–66). Thus, Ingarden's work is an important illustration and elaboration of Husserl's phenomenology as it bears on the problematics of expression (Falk 1981).

Husserl's semiology (see 1950, vol. 12, *Zur Logik der Zeichen (Semiotik)*, pp. 340–73, 524–30), as discussed primarily in "Investigation I "(Expression and Meaning") of the *Logische Untersuchungen* (1900–01; trans. 1970), is a consequence of his phenomenology. In his study of signs, he argues for the discovery that language is not constituted as a phenomenon of consciousness.

One of the more essential features of Husserl's phenomenology is therefore the distinction made between *meaning* (*Bedeutung*) and *manifestation* (*Kundgabe*). It is a distinction that directly derives from the conception of the sign as a semantic *indication*. Both meaning and manifestation as products of speech are tied to indication, which is the indexical, objective genitive force of language (Orth 1973). Meaning is signification as indication. That is to say in the use of language there are statements, which are a "system of habitual signs" (Husserl 1969). The indicative force of statements suggests that meaning is an expressed *judgment*. Manifestation, by contrast, is affective and emerges as expressed volition. Manifestation points back to the speaker in the process of expression. As Husserl reminds us, "all expressions in communicative speech function as indications" (1900–01; 1970, p. 277).

For Husserl, meaning and manifestation are mutually exclusive functions. Yet they are in mutual dependence as phenomena. Meaning leads to manifestation. The act of speaking is an intentional act of meaning where the meaning is embodied in speaking and in language as spoken. Husserl (1969) contends that signs are embodied and that the semiotic movement is what constitutes meaning as a communicative experience. The active process of expression makes this embodiment (an intentional act) known as a habitual system (a meaning intention). But this very fact of habituation establishes the conclusion that language is not constituted by consciousness. Language is merely constituted by *praxis*.

Thus, Husserl, in the communicative process, distinguishes between the *meaningful sign* and the *mere sign*, between the *verbal sign* and the "sign stripped of meaning," and between *indicating meaning* and *meaning indicated*. In short, speech as oral discourse indicates and is thereby subjective genitive, whereas language signifies and is objective genitive.

SCHUTZ'S DESCRIPTIVE PHENOMENOLOGY

Schutz (1973) develops his phenomenology in response to the problematic nature of intersubjective understanding (see chap. 16 below). He openly acknowledges his incorporation of Husserl's semiology of indication in the examination of interpersonal communication. But Schutz reconstructs the index thesis to apply to the dynamic intersubjectivity that occurs in speech communication viewed as *encounter* (Eckartsberg 1965). Husserl merely suggests that his remarks about speakers might be applied in like manner to auditors, but Schutz decisively marks out the listener from the speaker in the semiotic process of communication. Stated in a more positive sense, Schutz realizes that the roles of speaker and listener are embodied in the person as a communicator—that is, a person who is simultaneously and synergistically a speaker and listener in one embodiment. Such a person is explicitly conscious of speaking and listening as the habituated experience of self in a world of others. Therefore, Schutz (1967) suggests that intersubjective understanding is grounded in communication acts based upon signs that constitute first, *artifacts* capable of interpretation, secondly, *meaning* derived from a sign system, and thirdly the *indication* of past experience.

For the speaker the three sign functions combine into an *expressive scheme:* the scheme is the indication of the communicator's own meaning. It is the subjective and occasional meaning displayed in speech acts. Thus, speaking becomes an act of choice in which artifacts are created for interpretation. These artifacts provide for an interpreted meaning derived from the system in which they occur. The speaker's meaning becomes the coincidence of the past in the present. That is, the sign as artifact expresses a "subjective meaning" not dependent on interpretation (see Figure 32).

The listener, on the other hand, is caught up in an *interpretive scheme*. Within this scheme the perceiving communicator encounters artifacts born of past experience. The artifacts are perceived as repeatable signs functioning in a known semiotic system of communication. Here the indication as a present condition of consciousness directly refers to past experience. The sign as artifact is precisely signification by a communicative act. As Schutz explains, the listener is overwhelmed with the understanding that "I can do it again." That is to say, the sign has "objective meaning" that is systematic, hence predictable and controllable.

In summary, Schutz explains that phenomenologically the use of signs is a basis of understanding through interpersonal communication. The intersubjective function blends the speaker and listener into interlocking conscious views of an artifact, which is *understanding* as a phenomenon per se—that is, an experience that is lived. Thus, language in this view can come to constitute consciousness as situated in communication acts. Schutz discovers that either speech or language can constitute consciousness in the worlds of associates, contemporaries, predecessors, and successors (see chap. 16 below).

PEIRCE'S PHANEROSCOPY

Like Husserl, Peirce (1931–35, 1958, 1.280) never gave any systematic account of his phenomenology. Yet the direct link between phenomenology as an epistemology and ontological categories of Firstness, Secondness, and Thirdness does provide a systemic view of phenomena as Peirce's Doctrine of Categories (Savan 1952; Brinkley 1960). As Freeman (1934, p. 21) notes, "the method of the phenomenology consists in dissecting out the categories by analyzing experience into its fundamental elements."

Before offering a brief definition of the ontological categories, it may be useful to reduce Peirce's very technical semiology (1931–35; 1958; 1953) to those aspects of phenomenology that he found necessary for analysis. Peirce used a *logic of relatives* in order to work out the possible types of relationships and signs that can be found in phenomena. The relatives are *monads*, *dyads*, and *triads*.

Reversing their order for ease of understanding, a triad is a relationship between three elements where meaning is impossible without all three constituents; a dyad is a relationship between two constituents in which both elements are necessary; and a monad is nonrelative, for it consists of only one element and as such is considered apart from any relationship to another thing or subject. The corresponding *signs* are the *symbol* (triad), the *index* (dyad), and the *icon* (monad). Using his view of logic as a normative science, Peirce proposed to study signs in these three classifications by what he called, respectively, *formal* or *speculative grammar* (formal conditions of the truth of the symbols having meaning—i.e., the iconic); *formal logic* (formal conditions of the truth of the symbols—i.e., the indexical); and *formal rhetoric* (formal conditions of the force of symbols, or their power of appealing to the mind—i.e., the symbolic).

From an ontological point of view, the monad becomes the category of firstness, the dyad becomes the category of secondness, and the triad becomes the category of thirdness. In brief, firstness is existence without dependence upon any other subject or object. Secondness is the condition of being relative to, responsive to, or in reaction to, something else. Thirdness is a relationship of mediation in which a first and second element are related one to the other.

Peirce's dedication to keeping his ontology closely related to experience led him to develop his belief in phenomenology as a method of analysis, but it also led to his abandonment of "phenomenology" in favor of the new name "phaneroscopy." Ironically, the primary reason seems to be the discovery of the categories. Phenomenology as a method allowed their discovery, but it also required that the limitation to three categories not be fixed as an ontological requirement. As Freeman (1934, p. 28) remarks, "Thus, the limitation of the number of categories to three and only three appears to be too great a task for the phenomenology; and, in my opinion, no thorough-going phenomenologist would ever have undertaken such a limitation."

MERLEAU-PONTY'S EXISTENTIAL PHENOMENOLOGY

Merleau-Ponty (1970, p. 25) comments that the task of the communicator is "to produce a system of signs whose internal articulation reproduces the contours of experience." His statement foreshadows the way in which phenomenology functions most completely as an infrastructure of semiotic communication. For Merleau-Ponty (1962; 1964a, b, c; 1968) the phenomenological method consists in three procedures that are at once systematic and systemic. That is, each step follows upon the other in a dialectic progression from description to reduction to interpretation, and yet each step is a part of the others in a systemic completeness of reflexive intentionality.

The first step in the analysis is *phenomenological description*, which for Merleau-Ponty is a focus upon experience (see Figure 52 in chap. 17 below). At this level, experience consists in the dialectic between self and others—that is, *reflection* as a signifier function is reflexively connected to *prereflection* as a signified function.

The second step is *phenomenological reduction*, which is a specification of experience in consciousness. At this level, experience displays intentionality in Husserl's sense because it is a consciousness of (signifier) self (signified) as an entailment or reflection. In the plane of prereflection, experience is the consciousness of (signifier) an other (signified) as entailed by the perception of the other.

The third step is *phenomenological interpretation*, which is also known as the hermeneutic step. At this level the analysis turns to the interpretation of consciousness by locating the essential phenomenon in the *preconscious* ground that is the *sign* (signifier/signified) of self in consciousness as part of the plane of reflection. The dialectic relationship in the plane of prereflection is the *unconscious* as the sign (signifier/signified) of the consciousness (signifier) by which an other (signified) is perceived.

Merleau-Ponty's existential method of phenomenology (1962; 1964a, b, c) constitutes a unique semiotic phenomenology when applied to the analysis of conscious experience as manifest in discourse and action (see Figure 53 in chap. 17 below). Expanding on the Saussurean notion of the sign, Merleau-Ponty's phenomenological description of *consciousness* (signifier function) and *experience* (signified function) suggests three levels of inquiry (Lanigan 1972; 1977; 1984).

First, there is the descriptive level of *expression* in which *parole* (speaking), as a signifier, is dialectically related to *langue* (speech act), as signified. The second step is the reductive stage of analysis, wherein *perception* discloses the grounding of *parole* as *parole parlante* (speech speaking) and the reflexive ground of *langue* as *parole parlée* (speech spoken). Third, the interpretive level for *meaning* is the discovery that the lived-body consciousness of the person (*corps propre*) is a sign incarnate in the body-lived (*geste*) experience of *gesture*, also a sign.

Merleau-Ponty concludes that meaning is a synergistic result of the combination of, and relationships among, *signs*. In consequence, a sign per se is meaningless on the same phenomenological ground that a signifier or signified per se is meaningless in the Saussurean sense. The combinatory power of signs in paradigmatic and syntagmatic union is a *radical cogito* for Merleau-Ponty. This *cogito* is a human understanding of the semiotic act; it is the phenomenology of the invisible made visible in the ontology of the *Flesh*.

Chapter Thirteen

Semiotic Phenomenology as a Theory of Human Communication Praxis

A theory of human communication that we practice as an art or science is a philosophy in the classic sense. This philosophy of communication that we apply as communication science is neither novel or new as an idea about discourse and the human condition. For example, Carl Sagan (1978) is among the more recent popular philosophers who remind us that "our learning and our culture would never have developed without speech; our technology and our monuments would never have evolved without hands. In a way, the map of the motor cortex is an accurate portrait of our humanity" (p. 34).

Yet, Plato is the first to see in speech acts (mutatis mutandis, gestures) not just words and skills, but the unique theoretical and practical problem of the *logos* of *logos*. This to say, the problem of theory that is simultaneously and reversibly practice. In a word, this is the problem of *communication*. If we read Plato's dialogue the *Sophist* as communication theorists and practitioners, we find a theoretical account of the discourse praxis that belongs respectively to the statesman, sophist, and philosopher. There is a hierarchy of norms present in these personae ranging from the person whose art applies the science of politics, to the person whose art employs the science of pedagogy, and to the person whose art is the science of right thinking (Lanigan, 1982b; see chap. 17 below). As we read the *Sophist*, we scan the text for signs of logic woven into the conceptual fabric of speech and gesture. We seek in the discussion, as does Socrates, the formula by means of which we can construct an insightful answer to a pervasive question. To put it in human science terms, we seek a means of thematizing the problematic: How does human value become social fact?

DEFINING COMMUNICATION

Such a problematic focuses our expectation for a theory of human communication praxis by anticipating the force of Plato's maxim: "to rob us of discourse would be to rob us of philosophy" (*Sophist*: 260a). Beginning with Plato's maxim and tracing its connection is to contemporary speculations like Sagan's is to display the binary analogue logic in behavior that we call *humane*. The Platonic discovery of the binary analogue logic as the *logos* of *logos* is the foundation for the proposition that defines human communication theory and praxis as a semiotic phenomenology. *Communication is human conscious experience that entails a binary analogue logic.*

$$C_{df}\ \exists \times \supset [(B \cdot A) \rightarrow (E \wedge 0)]$$

Legend:
C_{df} = Definition of Communication (Binary Analogue)
$\exists$ = Necessary and Sufficient Condition (Existential Quantifier)
$\times$ = Relation of Conscious Experience (Hjelmslevian 'Function')
B = First Term Combinatory Functive ("Both" Analogue)
A = Second Term Combinatory Functive ("And" Analogue)
E = Third Term Combinatory Functive ("Either" Digit)
0 = Fourth Term Combinatory Functive ("Or" Digit)
$\cdot$ = Conjunction
$\wedge$ = Disjunction
$\rightarrow$ = Entailment
$\supset$ = Implication

Figure 25. Formalization of the semiotic phenomenology of communication

Communication so defined (see Figure 25) specifies two basic elements of understanding. First, all communication is semiotic by force of being constituted and regulated by systems of signs. All such systems contain formal and structural relationships between *signifiers* (elements of expression) and *signifieds* (elements of perception). These systems are inherently *binary*: the communicative source (terminus a quo) and destination (terminus ad quem) are in fact boundary conditions—the first logically necessary and the second sufficient—for the degrees of normative difference established by relationships in the system—that is, the analogue by degree of one term with another (Lyons 1977, 1:36–37). Second, all communication is a phenomenology of force of being constituted and regulated by conciousness of experience (the signifier) and its entailment as the experience of consciousness (the signified).

THEOREMS OF COMMUNICATION

The uniqueness of the binary analogue logic in behavior grounds both the function and nature of human discursive action as conscious experience. This focus on conscious experience requires a brief discussion of general communication logics (Lanigan 1979b). We are all familiar with the digital logics (either/or choices) in which rectilinear algorithms prescribe choice procedures in a "given" context—that is, data. This is the familiar territory of information theory. Human speech and gesture are a prime exemplar. You either speak or you are silent; you either gesture or remain still. Any choice made provides "information"—that is, a probability for the next useful choice.

By comparison, there are analogue logics (both/and choices) in which recursive algorithms prescribe choice procedures for selecting contexts as "taken"—that is, *capta* (Laing 1967, p. 62). This is the less familiar territory of communication theory. Human speech and gesture are again a prime exemplar. You have both speech and silence when you speak (what is said is concretely contextualized with what is simultaneously not said, but can be said). Also, you have both gesture and its absence (what is done bounds that of which you are capable). Any choice provides a "message"—that is, a defined context of possibility normative for the choice made (see Figure 26 in chap. 14).

We find these two logics, digital and analogue, in the generic systems of machine, animal, and human communication (Eco 1976; Wilden 1980). Human communication, however, characteristically involves both these logics as simultaneous and reversible (a semiology). This one feature of uniqueness is enough to distinguish human behavior from that of machines; but it is not enough to distinguish the human from the animal, because animals do have communication systems that display interacting digital and analogue logics (Sebeok 1977).

If we add the ability to use one logic to code another—for example, coding an analogue logic by a digital logic—we discover the uniqueness of a binary analogue logic. This unique element, which justifies a claim to separate human from animal communication, is the ability to code spatial and temporal placement (or displacement) in one logic by using the second logic to represent placement and displacement, respectively. Spatial and temporal placement and displacement are easily seen in the linguistic element of speech that predicates or ascribes as significative present and past referents or future actions (or gestures that do the same thing in place of speech). Thus, *consciousness* is a referential context that is moved around, fixed, or changed again by mere choice to do so in the coding of the coded system. Yet such consciousness is always bounded by the human agent, the person, who applies the logic of consciousness to consciousness itself thereby creating *experience* (see chap. 8 above).

In short, the concept and practice called "conscious experience" is a normed system of systems, a *logos* of *logos*. Conscious experience combines the binary elements of consciousness and experience, yet distinguishes them as boundary conditions for one another (a phenomenology). Thus, there is a *logic of phenomena* in which we discover the phenomena are themselves a logic. Or if you prefer, there is a discourse (speech) of behavior (gesture) that we understand as consciousness, and a behavior of discourse that we intuit as experience (Lanigan 1979a).

Recall my definition of communication: communication is human conscious experience that entails a binary analogue logic. This definition is itself a construction from four theorems discussed at length in chapter 2, above (Lanigan 1979c).

1. Theorem of intentionality: *Conscious experience is the minimal unit of meaning in communication.*

This theorem derives from Edmund Husserl's (1960) proposition that "subjectivity is intersubjectivity." It is associated with Maurice Merleau-Ponty's (1962) proposition that the *person (corps propre)* is the phenomenon of analysis in conscious experience (Lanigan 1972).

2. Theorem of punctuation: *The reversibility of expression and perception is the minimal system-code for communication.*

This theorem draws from Saussure's (1966) and Barthes' (1968) proposition, based on the language theory of Louis Hjelmslev (1961), that speech entails levels of expression and content (perception) that are individually and jointly the result of sign-production. Eco's (1976) construction of the theory of communicational acts, Jürgen Ruesch's (1972) theory of social communication, and Edmund Leach's (1976) theory of cultural communication on the basis of sign-production further support the theorem (Lanigan 1970; 1979a, b).

3. Theorem of convention: *The transaction is the minimal rule-governed behavior required for communication.*

This theorem expresses the logical elements in discourse discovered by John L. Austin (1962), H.P. Grice (1967), and John R. Searle (1969). The analogue nature of communicative performance provides analytic insights about the constitution of speech communication that are obscured by simply linguistic description (Lanigan 1977).

4. Theorem of Legitimation: *Interpersonal speech competency is the minimal norm in society for communication.*

This theorem formulates a key relationship in which the historical fact/value and individual/mass bifurcations are resolved as a ratio of communicative actions. For Jürgen Habermas (1979b), Karl-Otto Apel (1980), and Hans-Georg Gadamer (1975), the conjunction of hermeneutic and normative actions explains the community achieved by persons in society (Lanigan 1981).

THEORY AND PRAXIS APPLICATION

Theoretical implications and consequent applications as research methods in the study of human communication necessarily rely on a metatheoretical and methodological position (Lanigan 1983a). Yet I shall illustrate the four theorems just presented without regard to metatheory and methodology constraints (see chap. 1 above). I shall exemplify each of the theorems with what I consider to be a study that is theoretically insightful, but geared basically to the newcomer in the area of semiotic phenomenology as an applied research method (see Guba 1981). Suggestions for the direction of communication research will be made.

First, let us examine the "theorem of intentionality" by reference to Ihde's (1977) discussion of Husserl. Husserl's extensive research on the logic of consciousness and tests we might apply for correct judgment are present in Ihde's discussion of the famous Necker cube and other visual objects. By examining the experimental conditions for human perception in an active dialogue with his reader, Ihde demonstrates the observable conditions under which "conscious experience is the minimal unit of meaning in communication." His point is straightforward. In any scientific analysis there is a determinate order of understanding—that is, what we naively assume to be the "real world." This relationship is a normed sequence in which the researcher (a person) engages in certain procedures (acts according to concepts) with a certain subject matter (subjects or objects).

In this sequence of events, there is an isomorphism between (1) the sequence set of (a) researcher, (b) theory/method, and (c) subject/object of analysis (see "Methodology" in Figure 2), and (2) the sequence set of (a) a person's perception, (b) act of conception, and (c) the act of sensation (see "Theory" in Figure 2). As Ihde explains, this "positive" approach is fallacious when experimentally tested. In fact, an examination of a person's logic for constituting phenomena (e.g., visual images) points to just the reverse sequence as between sets 1 and 2. So from a phenomenological point of view, 2-a entails 1-c, 2-b entails 1-b, and 2-c entails 1-a. This is to say, we have an *order of experience* in set 1 (Experiencer/Experiencing/Experienced) and the *order of analysis* in set 2 (Experienced/Experiencing/Experiencer).

The starting point for phenomenological research is a person's perception as the object/subject of analysis, which is a conceptualization used as a theory/method to specify a sensation that is a person's conscious experience—that is, the researcher in situ (Brandt 1970). The consequence by specific reference to the Necker cube is that the cube does not have just two "real" reversible images as precepts, but an infinite number of "real" precepts as possibility—that is, concrete placement or instantiation. The number is directly dependent on the observer's ability to abstract (not generalize!) possibility *from the phenomenon* (to hypothesize), rather than fix probability for change by prior conceptual assumption (to hypostatize).

Eason (1977) illustrates this "theorem of intentionality" in a mass communication context with his analysis of the journalistic problem of reportage in the nonfiction novel. This research approach blends the writing format of the novel with the factual news story to re-create for the reader the contextual message being reported. Due account is taken of the writer's role in the formulation of meaning as the conscious experience through which the reporter lived. A specific study reflecting this methodology is my analysis (see chap. 7 above) of the Attica prison rebellion as reported in Tom Wicker's *A Time to Die* (Lanigan 1983b; see Ablamowicz 1984; Presnell 1983; Sobchack 1984; and Nelson 1986).

Secondly, the "theorem of punctuation" has its best illustration in Spiegelberg's (1975) various essays on methodology that blend an accurate concern for the philosophy of science with the standards of rigorous philosophical analysis. Over the years, his contribution to applied understanding clearly focuses on the theme that "the reversibility of expression and perception is the minimal system-code for communication."

Spiegelberg discusses the methodological issues in the comparison of phenomenology (praxis) to metaphenomenology (theory). He compares this eidetic problematic of the theoretical researcher to the "workshop approach" in which the direction is empirical and pragmatic. In a parallel context, he takes up the field research dimension of the "vicarious experience" of the individual as an interpersonal agent in a social context. Finally, he is a pioneer in explaining phenomenological methods. In his essay, "Existential Uses of Phenomenology" (1975, pp. 54–71), Spiegelberg provides one of the best accounts available of the methodology that is applied in whole or part by phenomenologists. Merleau-Ponty (1962) presents slightly more philosophical account of the procedure covering the three-step method of phenomenological description, phenomenological reduction, and phenomenological interpretation.

Turning to actual communication research, Langellier (1980) and Miller (1980) both explore the reversibility of expression and perception as it occurs within the performance context of the oral interpretation of literature. Miller focuses on the relationships between the performer and text, whereas Langellier's concern is the nature and function of audience. In contrast, Sochat (1978) quantitatively explores the semiotic constraints operating in an instructional setting where interviewing skills are being taught to medical students. A further illustration of the "theorem of punctuation" is the team research project in which student/instructor communication and role-modeling was studied phenomenologically as it occurs in the Southern Illinois University basic interpersonal communication course (Lanigan 1981).

Third, the "theorem of convention" suggests that the transaction is the minimal rule-governed behavior required for communication. One of the most successful illustrations of this theorem is the research methodology developed by William J.J. Gordon (1968). He calls his method "synectics" (a term first suggested by C.S. Peirce), not phenomenology, although even a casual comparison of the synectics method and the descriptive phenomenology of Husserl suggests a direct correlation (see chap. 12 above).

The essential feature of Gordon's method is the use of analogues to compare what is familiar with what is unfamiliar. This is a necessary and critical step in any research procedure faced with an apparently "unsolvable" problem (like the Necker cube). The synectics approach refocuses the problem in terms of the researcher's perception, rather than the conception of the problem. Another main feature of the synectics method is the reliance on group communication in a team format.

Whitsett's (1979) study of Human Sexuality Service division of the Student Health Service at Southern Illinois University exemplifies the "theorem of convention." He used a group communication context to specify phenomenologically how students perceived their conscious experience of sexuality when their conceptions of sexual behavior and norms became dysfunctional within interpersonal settings. Spengler (1975) studied the phenomenon of interpersonal and organizational loneliness using a written survey protocol to gather *capta* from members of a religious order in the Catholic Church. In this study individual respondent's perceptions could be directly compared to the group conception of conscious experience as a member of the religious community.

The "theorem of legitimation" has a focal place in the procedures suggested by Patton (1980; see Anderson 1987) for evaluation research. He explicitly points out that the roots of contemporary qualitative research strategies are in phenomenology and are directly linked to the interpersonal context, especially where interviewing is a primary form of *capta/data* collection (pp. 44–48, 198–200). Patton's detailed review of research methodologies grounds the theme that "interpersonal speech competency is the minimal norm in society for communication." Indeed, his guidelines for writing a research report can be read as an outline of the essential features of a phenomenological description, reduction (analysis), and interpretation that should be part of any such research effort (1980, pp. 340–42; see chap. 10 above).

Although the empirical studies by Whitsett (1979) and Spengler (1975) just discussed apply equally well to the "theorem of legitimation," there are also excellent illustrations of eidetic studies in the work of Peterson, Diekman, and Brooks. Peterson (1980) looks at the normative function of performance as a communication element using the theater as an exemplar. Diekman (1974) explores the process of existential legitimation in the work of Martin Buber, Emmanuel Levinas, and Jacques Lacan. Brooks (1968) examines the original contribution of the philosopher Henry Nelson Wieman to the problematic of "creative interchange." Further examples of appropriate research in this area can be found in Deetz (1981), Cahill (1983), Gomes (1984), and Tsuda (1985).

RESEARCH IMPLICATIONS

I began with the question, "How does human value become social fact?" I suggest that the answer is simply, and thereby profoundly, *communication*. But in an age that obscures both the intension and extension of that term, I propose the definition of semiotic phenomenology, that "communication is human conscious experience that entails a binary analogue logic." Several research implications are apparent in such a thematic position. These implications themselves constitute a set of problematics to be explored.

First, there is the problematic of theory construction. The perspective of semiotic phenomenology asks us to reexamine our heritage in the trivium (see chap. 11). We tend to conceive of logic, rhetoric, and grammar as "conceptions" to be blindly applied to this or that set of *capta/data*. Whether the method of analysis is qualitative or quantitative, the conception still dictates. With the contemporary convergence (in the thematic of *understanding*) of the problems of "text" (in semiology/structuralism) and its "interpretation" (in phenomenology/hermeneutics), we have in the approach of semiotic phenomenology an opportunity to reevaluate the theoretical power of the trivium. It is not once again a digital choice to accept or reject the method of the trivium, but an opportunity to see the analogue power of conjunction. In the communication discipline, we need to study the systemic and systematic connection among logic, rhetoric, and grammar. In applied research this means the science of communication should become the integration of the disciplines of philosophy (logic), communicology (rhetoric), and linguistics (grammar). In short, we should reappraise the trivium in human science terms as a theoretical orientation—that is, as a thematic research praxis.

Second, there is the problematic of human behavior as the *data/capta* we study. Semiotic phenomenology provides a methodology in which the *phenomenon* studied can be handled validly as a perceived object (*datum*) or perceived subject (*captum*) in a modality that is an empirical value (a boundary norm) or an eidetic value (another boundary norm). This is the valence that is the binary analogue whose empirical and eidetic status is combinatory fact. In short, the human sciences do not have to be modeled on the natural sciences. Both a theory and a method for the valid, scientific study of human communication are available in the innovative work of semiotic phenomenology. The research foundation is already in place.

A third problematic, and perhaps the most serious, is the general failure to realize that semiotic phenomenology is a research method with a pedigree that runs as far back as Plato and supports a host of methodological refinements easily rivaling the spectrum of statistical inference models in any good textbook on quantitative methods. There is, in fact, even a school of phenomenology devoted to mathematics (Alperson 1975; Tragesser 1977), so even the procedural ability to formalize *capta/data* is available.

The direct implication for research is the need for adequately trained researchers. Much of the justifiable criticism of semiotics and phenomenology in the U.S.A. stems from research or attempts at research by "one-course wonders" whose entire preparation for phenomenological research is a graduate school lecture course or a self-taught sense of purpose gleaned from a few journal articles or books. In this context also, semiotic phenomenology suffers to a certain extent by being a "research fad." The result is tagging various journal articles as "semiotic" or "phenomenological" or "hermeneutic" in order to gain publication. In most cases, they turn out to be an uninformed use of linguistic theory ("semiotics") or a report on psychological speculation ("phenomenology"). It should not be surprising to learn, then, that in the larger international community of scholars, the leading journals for reporting communication research are *Semiotica* and *Communication* (Paris).

The thematic that emerges from the three aspects of the problematic before us is fairly clear. Just as the discipline of communicology, we need to rethink our uniqueness. We do not need to follow other disciplines, least of all those in the natural sciences. We do need to assert our leadership on the basis of the rather impressive results achieved since the Platonic dialogues and the writing of Aristotle's *Organon*. We need a theory and a method of human science that builds on this history. I think semiotic phenomenology is a good possibility.

Finally, we who use semiotic phenomenology as theoreticians and practitioners need to pool our resources and set some identified standards for the work we do. The first step was taken in a conference at Northwestern University by founding the Society for Phenomenology and the Human Sciences, and adopting *Human Studies* as the society's official research journal. A second step was the founding of the Institute for Human Sciences at Ohio University, with Professor Algis MicKunas as director. The next step will be the applied research we do.

Chapter Fourteen

Semiotic Phenomenology as a Metatheory of Human Communication

Explanations of human communication are by definition projects in metatheory construction. Just as natural languages may be used to describe and explain themselves, the construction rules for communication systems may be used to articulate new paradigms constituting a higher logical type of communication (see Krippendorff 1977).

In this chapter, I want to suggest the way in which certain theory construction rules (exemplar concepts) belonging respectively to *semiology, social systems theory, communication theory*, and *existential phenomenology* can be combined into a *metatheory construction* of communication that is by nature and function *human*. Such a metatheory, I believe, is both a *necessary* and *sufficient* condition for understanding and appreciating the concepts of *signifier* and *signified* as constituents of the concept *sign*. It is the legacy of Saussure that puts these concepts at the center of all communicative behavior that is explained by *communicology*, the process of human expression and perception (Culler 1977; see Hörmann 1971, pp. 109–32).

My analysis will progressively deal with six topics or general hypotheses. First, semiology indicates that the *coding function* in communication relies on the nature of the signifier and the signified. Second, the *nature* of coding (as distinct from its function) is best described by social systems theory. Third, human communication is best accounted for by *communication theory*, not information theory. Fourth, any metatheory of human communication based on the foregoing hypotheses can have only functional (Hjelmslev's sense) models in the social world. Fifth, these two models, which I call the *ecosystem model* and the *phenomenological model*, constitute the *logical universe* of a rigorous *science of communication*. And finally, I state the prolegomena for communication theory and praxis that are human in nature and function.

The usual convention for defining the signifier as a "sound-image" and the signified as a "concept" forgets Saussure's intention that sound-image and concept are precisely the problem to be resolved by the new constructs: "signifier" and "signified" that "have the advantage of indicating the opposition that separates them from each other and from the whole [sign] of which they are parts" (Saussure 1966, p. 67). Together with the *logical theory of coherence*, Saussure further specifies two concomitant principles: (1) the arbitrary nature of the sign, and (2) the linear nature of the signifier. Saussure explains that by "arbitrary" he means the signifier has no *natural* connection with the signified. And he further explains "linear" by noting that the signifier "unfolds solely in time." He further limits the signifier by saying that it "represents a span and the span is measurable in a single dimension; it is a line" (1966, pp. 69–70).

What we have in Saussure's formulations are the often overlooked rules for coding signs as *binary analogues*. Signs do not exist as the behavioristic reductions of sound-image and concept (which in most cases requires an equivocation between "image" and "concept"). Signs do exist as formal boundaries (Wilden 1972, p. 414; Alexander 1972)—that is, logical *forms* that are distinct as class entities (*abstractions, qualities*) and as their combination as a whole (*relations, functions*). In short, Saussure relies on the construction rule that a class cannot contain itself. This condition being the case, signifier and a signified have the status of class identity (they are *reflexive*), the status of a reversible nature (they are *symmetrical*), as either continuity or discontinuity (*rupture*) as boundary conditions of each other, and the status of being *transitive*. These conditions of the signifier and the signified suggest a *synergistic* nature for the sign(s)— namely, that sign-signified relation can be expressed in two functional modalities. First, the relation can be viewed as an open system, where the relationship functions to specify possibilities of signification that are *systemic* and *ontogenic* in nature. Second, a closed system can be expressed, where the relationship is *systematic* and *phylogenetic* in nature. In general, Saussure's discussion of *parole* may be taken as an illustration of the open system, and respectively, his explanation of *langue* may be viewed as the closed system. In both cases the "system" represents a code condition (*langage*) for performance and competence.

The possibilities or boundaries for system performance (and the system infrastructure of "competence") are best articulated with a selected comparison of *communication theory* and *information theory*. In the present context, I will be using *communication theory* to illustrate the open system and *information theory* to exemplify the closed system. The system that is common to both theories is the *entailment* construction rule that communication theory is inclusive of information theory, but not conversely. See Figure 25, in chapter 13, above, for a formalization of this rule.

The logical grounds for this rule are apparent in a brief contrast between the two theories. For simplicity, I conceive of each theory as being a sequential complex of three construction rules: (1) *message*, (2) *context*, and (3) *code*. In the case of information theory (a *digital logic*), which is logically prior to communication theory, message is defined as "sign presence," context is defined as "sign absence," and code is defined as "either sign presence *or* sign absence." The construction rule thereby articulated is that in a closed system *only context of choice* is established. That is, the possibilities of choice are determined, but no one particular choice is specified as appropriate, correct, or the like. The result is the establishment of a system of cultural conventions or *regulative rules* that suggest appropriate choices that are, strictly speaking, arbitrary and linear in Saussure's sense of those terms (Verón 1971).

In short, information theory allows us to account for *langue* as a closed system. That closed system in its general application we normally regard as *culture*. We should note, as Israel points out, that in actual performance human beings do engage in behavior that is explained by such a closed system, although information theory is perfectly suited to the description and prediction of open systems, whether human, animal, or machine signal (signifier/signified *form* is invariant) systems (Israel 1972, p. 145).

Returning now to communication theory (an *analogue logic*), we have a sequential complex that is the opposite of information theory: (1) *code*, (2) *context*, and (3) *message*. In this case, code is "*both* sign presence and sign absence," context is "sign presence," and message is "sign absence." The construction rule generated is that *choice of context* is constituted, thus leaving specific choice to be regulated by social convention. The result is the creation of a system of social conventions or regulative rules that are also arbitrary and linear. At this point, we have a metatheory hypothesis that can explain communicative behavior that is socially variable within culture (*langue*) and culturally variable in society (*parole*), but displays code consistency (*langage*) in either modality.

My explanation so far has considered sign presence and absence as features of both communication theory and information theory. Let me suggest as a postulate that the same analysis can be applied selectively to signifiers and signifieds, thereby generating a theory of logical extension/intension accounting for communication as linguistic connotation/denotation (Alexander 1972) or as nonlinguistic system (Leathers 1976).

It may be helpful at this point to illustrate the information theory/communication theory connection in a diagram indicating the arbitrary, linear sense in which communicative competence allows for communica-

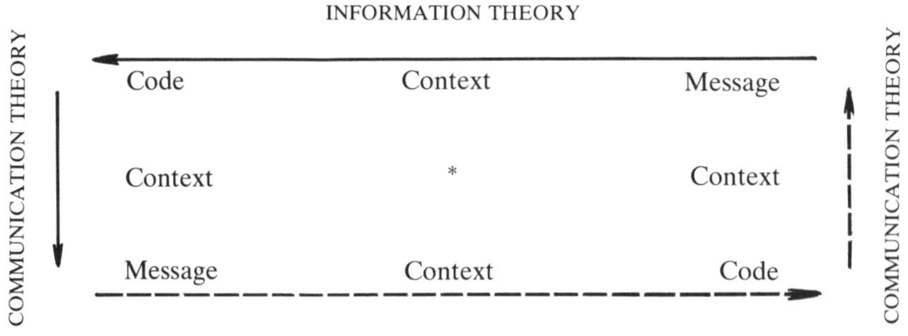

Fig. 26 Communication praxis

Note: 1. Communication Theory = Synchronic [consciousness] and Polychronic [behavior].
2. Information Theory = Diachronic [consciousness] and Monochronic [behavior].
3. Legend: * = Synchrony [person's conscious behavior] which is either Egocentric or Sociocentric.
-- = *Gemeinschaft/Gesellschaft* Function.
—= *Lebenswelt/Weltanschauung* Function.

tive performance as a metatheory phenomenon (cf. Habermas 1970a, b). In Figure 26 the [*] indicates the locus of a person's conscious behavior, which in a cultural, performance sense will be either *egocentric* or *sociocentric*, or, if you will, the consistency of "context" located in a person or in a group is the movement from code to message to code ad infinitum as it occurs in human interaction. In linguistic terms, we may think of *langage* as the cultural connection between persons (*Lebenswelt*) and their cultures as institutions (*Weltanschauung*). I have illustrated this process with a solid line [————] in Figure 26. In other words, a cultural system of messages exists when a person is born into the culture. Those messages contextualize individual performance (*parole*), and the repetition of performance contextualizes new messages appropriate to the system.

In more technical terms, information theory represents the *Weltanschauung* as a closed system that is *diachronic* (cultural consciousness; e.g., myth) and *monochronic* (cultural behavior; e.g., social convention). Yet the existence of the person as a cultural agent allows the generation of communication theory from the information theory base. Thus, communication theory represents the *Lebenswelt* as an open system that is *synchronic* (personal consciousness; e.g., my lived reality) and *polychronic* (personal behavior; e.g., my intentional acts). Thus, we move to an explanation of the ways in which cultures determine the *context of* choice for persons who always make choices *in context* (Fisher, Glover, & Ellis 1977).

The other connection that needs explanation is the social mediation between culture and person, and vice versa. This process is illustrated in Figure 26 by the broken line [------]. In this case the relationship is between a person as a member of a society (*Gesellschaft*), whose conscious behavior is a functional norm, and as a member of a community (*Gemeinschaft*), whose conscious behavior is a natural norm. Again, in a technical sense, information theory represents the *Gesellschaft* as a closed system that is diachronic (social consciousness; e.g., Western values) and monochronic (social behavior; e.g., American norms). In turn, communication theory represents the *Gemeinschaft* that is synchronic (group consciousness; e.g., family attitudes) and polychronic (group behavior; e.g., classroom activities).

It does not take much analysis to see that the relationships I have described are functions in time, but the relationships per se cannot be compared as to their essential nature. Hence as I previously suggested, the nature is achronic (indeterminate), and the function is determined by chronological condition. It is this fact that allows a system to alternate its *function* between a state of "openness" and "closedness" (Blackwell 1976).

I am now in a position to suggest my third point, that human communication is best accounted for by communication theory as I have defined it. Four key relationships are involved with this hypothesis. First, *metaphor* and *morphogenesis* must be viewed as a condition of *discontinuity* for the signifier, and the relationship of *metonymy* and *homeorhesis* as a condition of *continuity* for the signified. In turn, the continuity of the signifier is explained by the *analogue/homeogenesis* relationship, and the discontinuity of the signified is illustrated by the *digit/homeostatis* condition. These basic relationships are diagramed in Figure 27.

In this diagram, I combined concepts based on their logical nature and their system function. The first combination is metaphor and morphogenesis. Metaphor is a relational process of one-for-one substitution of attributes and is usually, but not exclusively, an analogue based on a difference of degree. Morphogenesis is a process of constant change resulting from a sensitivity to *noise* and is consequently a condition of ultrastability. A working paradigm of morphogenesis is *society*—that is, a collection of sociocentric nature and function, or what Hall (1976, p. 91) calls a "high context"society.

The second combination is metonymy and homeorhesis. Metonymy is a relational process of the substitution of an attribute for a substance, usually (but not exclusively) a digit based on difference of kind. Homeorhesis is a process of selection and combination within the given norms of a system; it is a form of morphostasis. In brief, *morphostasis* is a process of massive redundancy that reduces noise to insignificance and prevents change. It is a condition of instability in a system, and a working

SIGNIFIER	
DISCONTINUITY	CONTINUITY
METAPHOR MORPHOGENESIS	ANALOG[ICAL] HOMEOGENESIS
METONYMY HOMEORHESIS	DIGIT[AL] HOMEOSTASIS
CONTINUITY	DISCONTINUITY
SIGNIFIED	

Fig. 27. Communication theory

Note: Communication Theory Entails Information Theory.

paradigm is a *person*—that is, an egocentric nature/function, or Hall's (1976) "low context" society.

The third grouping is the analogue and homeogenesis. An analogue is a relational process that suggests *both* the static condition of elements *and* their reversible combination; it is a choice of context. Homeogenesis is a homologous process that is also homeomorphous—that is, homeogenesis is a form of morphostasis.

The fourth combination is the digital and homeostasis. A digit is a relational process that suggests *either* the static condition of elements *or* their reversible substitution; it is the context (known choices) for a choice. Homeostasis is a steady-state process in which a system and its environment are in balance, but in a condition of change. It is also a form of morphostasis.

The schema articulated in Figure 27 suggests the communication theory rules by which a person communicates as a member of a society. In Figure 27 the movement from signifier discontinuity to signified continuity is the movement from *parole* to *langue*. In a linguistic sense, this means having many words (e.g., words in several languages) for the same referent. The parallel movement from signifier continuity to signified discontinuity (again *parole* to *langue*) suggests, in my example, that one word can have many referents. The same illustration holds true if we shift the perspective to the signified and move through continuity or discontinuity to the signifier.

Such movement is precisely why Saussure insists that the signifier and signified are *forms* in a system. Such a process reversal as I just described is not possible if the relationships are defined as sound-image and concept within *one* natural language. It is in this context that information theory is found wanting, for this theory presumes one finite system in which there is only one form for all functions—that is, a rule of disjunction for elements (sound-image cannot be a concept, etc.). An interesting illustration of this point is the American diplomatic response in World War II with the Japanese word *mokusatsu* (Alexander 1972, pp. 11–12).

My fourth basic point in this chapter is that, given the preceding analysis, there are only two functional models permitted by the theory that can operate in a *social world* of persons. Both *models* represent a metatheory of human communication, for they prescribe both the nature and function of the system as *direction*: either "open" or "closed." These directions are, respectively, the *rectilinear* and the *curvilinear*. In detailing them it may be helpful to examine Figure 28, which is a progressive elaboration of Figures 26 and 27.

		SIGNIFIER					
OPEN SYSTEM [SYSTEMIC]		DISCONTINUITY		CONTINUITY			CLOSED SYSTEM [SYSTEMATIC]
	ONTOGENESIS	Multifinality CURVILINEAR Morphostasis	METAPHOR MORPHOGENESIS	ANALOG[ICAL] HOMEOGENESIS	Equifinality [RECTI]LINEAR Morphogenesis	PHYLOGENESIS	
		Equifinality [RECTI]-LINEAR Morphogenesis	METONYMY HOMEORHESIS	DIGIT[AL] HOMEOSTASIS	Multifinality CURVILINEAR Morphostasis		
		CONTINUITY		DISCONTINUITY			
		SIGNIFIED					

Fig. 28. Communication metatheory

Note: 1. Phenomenological Model = All Oppositions are Reversible and have a Dialectic Function.
2. Ecosystem Model = All Oppositions are Vectors and have an Analytic Function.
3. Oppositions = Vertical or Horizontal Movements of Relation [Form] in the Schemata.

The rectilinear direction in a system is characterized by *equifinality* and morphogenesis. In this sense rectilinear refers to a directional motion in time and space (*consciousness* and *behavior*), is a *linear process* (closed system) or a *multilinear process* (open system) [see Figure 3]. We can conceive of this structure as functionally *arithmetic*, where its nature is an equivalence between system output and antecedent input. The foundation for the rectilinear construction rules is information theory. Thus, equifinality is a final state that may be reached from different initial states or by different paths. Put another way, choosing a context of choice counts as a choice—a point proven by its contradiction—namely, that not choosing is a choice function by nature. Recall that morphogenesis is a condition of ultrastability exemplified above as *society* or a sociocentric system condition.

On the other hand, the curvilinear direction is a cycle motion in time and space that is a *helical process* (open system) [see Figure 5] or *circular process* (closed system) [see Figure 4]. We can think of this structure as functionally *geometric*, where its nature is a condition of output that is greater than its antecedent input. The base for the curvilinear direction and construction rules is communication theory. Therefore, the curvilinear process is characterized by multifinality and morphostasis. *Multifinality* is a process state by which similar initial conditions, or routing by different paths, may lead to dissimilar end states. For example, the same choice in one context will be unlike the same choice in another context—a point also proven by its contradiction—that is, the same choice cannot be repeated in the same context, for each unique choice alters the context. Most paradoxes depend on forgetting this principle. Also recall that morphostasis is a condition of instability illustrated previously by the concept of *person* or an egocentric condition.

At this point I should like to move to my fifth topic. To be specific, I want to characterize the model with rectilinear direction as the ecosystem model. In turn, I describe the curvilinear direction as the phenomenological model. It is not possible, given the confines of this chapter, to proceed through a detailed proof for my construction of these models. So I must limit myself to an outline description of the key elements in each model, which will then allow me the privilege of making some assertions about future theory construction as it pertains to human communication. I also should note that Merleau-Ponty makes a similar argument; see chapter 4, above.

First, let me suggest that I am using the concept of *ecosystem* in the way Wilden develops it (1972, p. 39 and passim). With this understanding, I want to contend that the rectilinear direction has four rather exclusive functions in human communication. First, it can describe the *digital* nature of *intrapersonal communication*. Such communication can be illustrated by a person's own perception of distinct expressions, such as the difference between "my" *writing* and "my" *speaking*. Secondly, the model can describe digital *interpersonal communication*. Here a good illustration is the distinction between the perceived interaction that is "speech," such as a conversation, and the interaction that is "language," such as one encounters in a newspaper item. Thirdly, the model can explain *analogical* intrapersonal communication—for example, the difference between *writing* and *speech*. Contrast, as an illustration, how my personal letter-writing presumes a context much like that in which my speech occurs. Indeed, how often do we receive letters devoid of context? Yet it rarely happens in a face-to-face conversation. Fourthly, the model can describe analogical interpersonal communication. In this case we have the example difference between *speaking* and *language*. This category is illustrated by situations in which your language is corrected by others when you are speaking, or you do not have the words that will make your speaking express your actual meaning, and so forth.

In this sketch I have taken some care to make the parts of speech correspond with system functions—that is, nouns suggesting a static condition with rectilinear direction, present participles as action conditions that are nominal in a curvilinear sense, and so on. In addition, I have mixed semiotic forms, writing versus speaking, and I haved mixed code-systems, language versus speaking. All this is to suggest the metatheory conditions that presume theory conditions. Thus, the main point of the ecosystem model is its utilization of an information theory approach, where a natural language is the governing paradigm for theory construction.

The phenomenological model, by comparison, is grounded in communication theory that displays the curvilinear direction in systems. In this particular discussion I am using "phenomenological" in its philosophic sense (Lanigan 1977). In similar fashion, with the ecosystem model I want to characterize four basic functions for human communication. In what follows, the basic point of the phenomenology model is the use of a communication theory approach where conscious behavior is the governing paradigm.

1. The phenomenology model can describe digital intrapersonal communication. Such communication is exemplified by a person's tendency to be "conscious of behavior," where the norms of society (sociocentric) are compared to those of nature/history (egocentric), or the tendency to behave "consciously," where historical norms are compared to cultural preferences.

2. The model can describe digital interpersonal communication. This type of communication illustrates self-conscious behavior (what is existential to the organism) as compared with the consciousness of an other's behavior (what is empirical and mechanical—often as display *technique* for behaving).

3. The model explains analogical intrapersonal communication, where "being conscious of behavior" (norms in society/nature) becomes an existential function of the organism (e.g., ego and alter-ego, or self-concept and body-image, etc.).

4. The model describes analogical interpersonal communication. Here the use of historical/cultural norms to "behave consciously" allow for technique as intention to become "real" (empirical/mechanical). For example, the psychiatric technique of *free association* allows a person to behave consciously, yet utter basic feelings, attitudes, and so forth, that are repressed (see chap. 5 above). A linguistic example would be some-

thing like a performative utterance, such as saying "I do" in a marriage ceremony. The utterance is the historical norm made empirical by intention to do so.

By way of connecting the ecosystem model and the phenomenology model with the initial analysis in this chapter, let me point out that in Figure 28 the operation of the models would have the following characteristics. First, all oppositions in the diagram are conceived in the phenomenological model as being reversible. Hence, communication is *dialectical* in a logical sense. Second, the ecosystem model conceives of all oppositions as *analytical* and not reversible. Communication is *rhetorical* in this context (see Lanigan 1974, 1984; Eco 1976).

My last point in this chapter is the general prolegomena for human communication theory and praxis. Given the metatheory conditions I have outlined (see Figure 28), I believe theory construction must take account of *semiology*, which as a discipline focuses on the nature of digital codes functioning in an analogical context. The primary benefit in this orientation is the ability to describe interpersonal conditions that define the person in an empirical sense. By contrast, the discipline of phenomenology focuses on the analogue nature of codes used in digital contexts. The gain here is the ability to describe personal conditions of existence that define interpersonal situations that are likewise empirical.

In specific terms of *communication praxis*, the phenomenology model provides us with a *methodology* of (1) *description*, (2) *reduction* (i.e., definition of description), and (3) *interpretation* (i.e., reduction of definition) (Lanigan 1977, pp. 84ff.). The ecosystem model, on the other hand, provides us with a *technology* consisting of (1) *information* (i.e., *data* generation as cognition), (2) *communication* (i.e., *capta* generation as affection), and (3) *legitimation* (i.e., *acta* generation as conation) (Lanigan 1972; cf. Rosenthal 1977; Toulmin 1977; & Culler 1976, pp. 103ff.). Both models presume a semiotic base in which (1) description and information are *code* conditions (*langage*), (2) reduction and communication are *context* conditions (*langue*), and (3) interpretation and legitimation are *message* conditions (*parole*) (Lanigan 1978). It is in the framework of these prolegomena that I contend that human communication is by definition a project in metatheory construction.

[Section Two: EMPIRICAL RESEARCH]

Chapter Fifteen

The Semiotic Phenomenology of Speech and Linguistic Discontinuity

Many of the presuppositions that one encounters in the philosophic literature on the phenomenology of human communication suggest a useful parallel to the linguistic concept of discontinuity. The structuralist view of language, in which discontinuity occurs either as a paradigmatic or syntagmatic function of sentence use, bears a close theoretical resemblance to the phenomenological thesis that an "intentional object" in speech displays a separation and reversibility of language as (1) the act of speaking, and (2) the act of speech perception—for example, Merleau-Ponty's (1968) use of *écart* and *chiasme*. In this chapter, I should like to explore in a brief way exactly how the linguistic concept of *discontinuity* or *rupture* compares with the phenomenological concepts of *separation* and *reversibility* in speaking.

CONTRAST AND FREE VARIATION

As Lyons (1969, p. 73) suggests, every linguistic unit has a potentiality of occurrence in a certain context wherein two types of structural relationships are possible. First, any language unit that can occur in the same context as another given unit enters into a paradigmatic relationship. For the linguist it is not critical whether the relationship of units is by "contrast" or whether they are in "free variation." This is a rather important point inasmuch as the phenomenologist is concerned only with units in free variation, or what is historically called "imaginative free variation."

Secondly, a linguistic unit occurs on the same level with other units and these other units constitute its context, thereby amounting to a syntagmatic relationship. The similar idea in phenomenological philosophy is the synergistic relationship of expression and perception in speaking, which is present as an intentional object—that is, an object of consciousness in which linguistic performance and competence are coincident. In this connection, linguistic competence refers to a person's tacit understanding of the rule system of the language that person speaks, whereas linguistic performance relates to the essentially social use to which the rule system is applied. As B. Bernstein (1971, p. 229) elaborates, "competence refers to man abstracted from contextual constraints. Performance refers to man in the grip of the contextual constraints which determine his speech acts."

Given a basic understanding of paradigmatic and syntagmatic relations in the context of the present discussion, it is appropriate to examine *discontinuity*, which is fundamentally a rearrangement of the relationship between linguistic units. Such a rearrangement comes to constitute a new set of paradigmatic and syntagmatic relations. For the linguist, the new set of relationships either exhibit a contrast with the original relationship or are a product of the free variation of comparable units (Lyons 1969, p. 223).

Thus in linguistics, discontinuity offers a tool for determining the structural possibilities of language unit occurrence within specified contexts. The procedure is essentially negative in that it provides an internal criterion of unit nonoccurrence, derived from natural languages and their statistical features of unit occurrence, for application to any respective natural language. In other words, a given language is taken as a set of relationships that determine how sentence generation is possible. Where the linguistic unit generation does not occur as an expected probability within the limits of possibility, discontinuity can be readily identified as the violation of linguistic potentiality.

The point to be made about the linguistic use of the discontinuity concept is that speaking or language use is delimited by a negative process of definition. Discontinuities are used for the determination of the limits of possible usage. It is this view that allows for the functionally equal acceptance of contrast and free variation as modalities for determining paradigmatic and syntagmatic relationships. Contrast is accepted as a criterion of discontinuity because it is a direct indicator of probable potential in speech acts. There is an observable difference of unit kind indicative in the relationship of units per se. The phenomenologist views "contrast" in this context as basically a negative criterion, because the semantic value of the relationship is determined by analytically constituting a difference, and utilizes the functionally positive concept of separation (*écart*). What is meant by separation is that the intentional object is a synergistic relationship of related (similar or dissimilar) units of speech.

Equally acceptable to the linguist as a methodological criterion is the restriction on language use implied by the concept of free variation. Given the structural characteristics of speech, only certain variations will be within the limits of the potentiality of use in a natural language. Violations of potentiality simply do not count as speech acts for the linguist. This is to argue that the linguistic view of "free" variation exists as free only in the negative sense that violations of rule relationship are not to be counted as an acceptable description of how language is constituted. "Free variation," then, is a rather restricted linguistic concept that is best understood only as "variation by rule" or "variation that is use-specific." It is precisely this limiting conception that the phenomenologist tries to avoid by not utilizing a concept comparable to "contrast" and by qualifying the use of "variation" as "free and imaginative" in a positive sense.

The problem that emerges from using a negative definition of discontinuity is that linguistic analysis must restrict its theoretical investigation to descriptions of actual utterances of speech, whether initially as research paradigms or as pragmatic proof examples within theoretical constructs. From a linguist's point of view this restriction may be quite acceptable in describing language. But from a philosopher's point of view, it is a limitation that obscures the criteria by which speech possibility, over and above speech potentiality, can be specified in such a way as to constitute conditions in which the activity of speaking and listening (linguistic perception) are coincident phenomena—that is, the linguistic synergism that is the speech act (Gardiner 1951).

SEPARATION AND REVERSIBILITY

Perhaps some of the ambiguities raised in the analysis thus far can be clarified by a closer examination of the phenomenological view of speech with respect to the functions of *separation* and *reversibility* (imaginative free variation) in the determination of *intentional objects* in speech. Recall that these relationships parallel the linguistic view that *contrast* and *free variation* account for structural *relations* that are paradigmatic and syntagmatic.

Within the context of speech or language use, the phenomenological idea of separation (*écart*) suggests in a conditional sense that the occurrence of any linguistic unit marks itself as distinct from the context in which it occurs, not as a division of units but as their juxtaposition. The resulting distinction is meaningful only when it is understood that the individual linguistic unit and the context mutually and dialectically derive their meaning from one another. The relationship indicating this meaning is not a product of contrast or comparison. Rather, the relationship is a synergism in which the joint occurrence of the context and the linguistic unit provide a meaning greater than the sum of the meaning contained individually by the unit or by its context.

The linguistic concept of a *paradigmatic relationship* would appear to amount to the same assumption made by the phenomenologist. However, this is not the case. The phenomenologist views the synergism of a linguistic unit and its context literally as a *gestalt*. To change the linguistic unit with another unit that is functionally equivalent is to destroy the particular synergism and create a new one. In this situation, the linguistic concept of contrast is a procedure that automatically and by definition destroys the paradigmatic (in the phenomenological sense of gestalt) relationship of the unit and its context. Because of this result, the phenomenologist does not accept the idea of contrast as an acceptable methodology for determining paradigmatic relationships in speech.

The phenomenological view of contrast as a methodology for determining *syntagmatic relations* in language use is much the same as what was just said about paradigmatic relations. For the linguist, the syntagmatic relation occurs when a linguistic unit appears on the same level with other units that constitute a context for the original unit. In other words, the linguistic unit or those units making up its context are always in a state of contrast, for their very definition as units is by mutual, collateral descriptive difference. This view of the syntagmatic relationship is generally unacceptable to the phenomenologist, because any given language unit in speech is taken to be its own meaning regardless of context. This is to suggest that a linguistic unit (whether morpheme, phrase, sentence, or other systemic unit) is its own signification. Put another way, one might say that a syntagm represents a gestalt and to separate a unit from its context (in the linguistic sense) is to arbitrarily make an analytic division of the syntagmatic relation. Obviously, such an analytic division creates contrast *per force*. This division destroys the phenomenological meaning present in the linguistic unit. It destroys the gestalt in the sense that the separation creates other phenomena whose significance is unique. This is to say, the mere addition of unit phenomena to context phenomena (or vice versa) does not account for the original gestalt, but rather suggests a newly constituted phenomenon.

Reversibility is the phenomenologist's term for "imaginative free variation," which superficially sounds like the linguistic idea of "free variation." But it is only a peripheral resemblance of nomenclature. As briefly mentioned before, the phenomenologist is most actively interested in the use of reversibility to determine the possibilities of what (rather than potentialities of how) speech acts are. Reversibility refers to the conscious possibility of manipulating the linguistic units within a given phenomenon of speech to determine which are the necessary and sufficient elements that will constitute the communicative phenomena per se. This is to say that the phenomenologist arranges the linguistic units into varying syntagmatic and paradigmatic relations regardless of their acceptability as potential relationships in terms of the natural language matrix in which they first occur. In this phenomenological sense the variation is truly "free" where, by contrast, the linguistic meaning of "free" implies movement only within the permissible cultural limits of the specified natural languages(s).

Also, a word needs to be said about the phenomenological implications of the term "imaginative" with respect to the discussion of variation. Imaginative variation is the movement in a dialectical sense, not only of the language units constituting a speech phenomenon, but a movement of the *perspective* of the use of language, as Plato first noticed (see chap. 17, below). For example, the phenomenologist would be concerned to specify the possibilities of variation from the perspective of a speaker expressing speech and a listener perceiving speech, of these expression/perception processes when the language units are also in variation, and so on throughout the range of interacting possibilities. Thus, any one perspective might be occurring as an actuality, whereas the dialectical perspectives connected to it are imaginative possibilities. These imaginative possibilities may well constitute the actuality of a given speech phenomenon when the perspective shifts. In linguistic terms, imaginative free variation would constitute the active comparison and contrast of competence and perfomance on an intrapersonal, interpersonal, and public level to determine the necessary and sufficient conditions for the potential of syntagmatic and paradigmatic relationships as dependent variables of one another.

PRESENCE AND ABSENCE

The combined implication of the phenomenological concepts of *separation* and *reversibility* is what has been referred to previously as the *intentional object* or that of which one is conscious as the synergism coincident in speech expression and perception. With regard to the linguistic idea of discontinuity, the concept of an intentional object requires a brief discussion of the "presence" and "absence" of phenomena.

When a person is conscious of an object (such as a linguistic unit), it is because that object is present within a phenomenal situation (the act of speaking). Such a situation not only presents the object as *there*, but also suggests what objects are not there—that is, objects that *can be there*. In terms of a linguistic illustration, the existence of a syntagmatic relationship between linguistic units has meaning precisely because a paradigmatic relation is also possible. In a similar way, the occurrence of a paradigmatic relation is possible because of the presence of a syntagmatic relation. In either of these cases, the presence of one type of relationship precludes the simultaneous presence of another unit of the same type, but that such other units are possible is implicitly given also (an "absence"). In short, the intentional object is composed of both a presence and an absence, but it is more than an item and its context. The coincidence of a presence and an absence has a synergistic meaning—namely, the limits of possibility as distinguished from the limits of potentiality (which are strictly determined by the presence of a linguistic unit only).

Discontinuity from a phenomenological point of view, therefore, represents an intentional object that is a possible way of speaking (exactly the function of *tone* in C. S. Peirce's system of type, token, and tone; see chap. 12). Unlike the linguist's view of discontinuity, there is no implication of a structural deviation from the acceptable potential of a natural language. Discontinuity in this context could be conceived only in analytic terms where the reversibility of presence and absence (of linguistic units) is arbitrarily separated into presence versus absence, thereby eliminating the very significance of the relationship. This arbitrary step is precisely what the phenomenologist attempts to avoid.

In a tacit sense, the phenomenologist is primarily concerned with utilizing the existent relationships in speech to ascertain the significance of the speech act viewed as the interplay of human expression and perception. This is to suggest rather directly that the phenomenologist is concerned with the place of speech in the definitive process of human being and becoming, and not conversely. The linguist, on the other hand, is concerned with the semantic implications associated with the linguistic relationships themselves. For the linguist it is important to be able to separate language units within a relationship, for this analytic division becomes the basis of description within a given natural language. In other words, linguists are concerned to discover *how* humankind uses language to symbolize its behavior, whereas phenomenologists direct their inquiry toward discovering *what* part of the human being is, indeed, phenomenally present in speaking.

Thus, discontinuity represents a feature of language usage that helps the linguist determine how language functions and, within natural limits, can function. Discontinuity or *rupture* for the phenomenological philosopher represents a phenomena of speech that helps determine what the human act of speaking is per se. The linguistic tools of contrast and free variation within paradigmatic and syntagmatic relations between linguistic units suggest how language conceptually operates, whereas the phenomenological concepts of separation and reversibility suggest how a human being experiences speech as an intentional object in a world with other persons.

Chapter Sixteen

A Treasure House of Preconstituted Types

Alfred Schutz on Communicology

On June 6, 1922, Edmund Husserl began his London lectures entitled "Phenomenological Method and Phenomenological Philosophy." The opening lines of his first lecture announce his thesis—namely, to explicate "a transcendental sociological phenomenology having reference to a manifest multiplicity of conscious subjects communicating with one another" (1970c, p. 18). Ten years later, in 1932, Alfred Schutz concludes his major work *The Phenomenology of the Social World* with the same thesis: "The primary task of this science is to describe the process of meaning-establishment and meaning-interpretation as these are carried out by individuals living in the social world" (1967, p. 248). The book presents a discussion of "interpretive sociology" that is, of course, a human science application of Husserl's (1931; 1970a) phenomenology to various issues concerning communication and exchange (catallactics; see Schutz 1967, p. 245) thematized in the writings of Max Weber.

What is generally overlooked in this classic Schutz text is the explicit semiotic stance it takes in two important philosophical senses: (1) the transcendental element of Husserl's semiology is set aside, and (2) the reinterpretation of Husserl's semiology in terms of the human science of communicology (as opposed to transcendental philosophy) theoretically grounds much of the innovation usually associated with and reserved to the much later work of Louis Hjelmslev (1961) and Schutz's New School colleague, Roman Jakobson (Holenstein 1974).

Both Husserl and Schutz anticipated what is today the new human science of Communicology. With its historical roots in the classical Greek texts of Plato and Aristotle on the social function of rhetoric and the logical form of semiotic, the discipline of communicology finds its contemporary human science grounding in the theory and methods of phenomenology. This phenomenology of human communication is an eidetic science in Husserl, yet it becomes an empirical science in Schutz (Wagner 1983, pp. 43–44). I propose to explicate this eidetic-to-empirical development of phenomenology that Schutz offers us in his consideration of the ground and application of the human sciences. It is, without exaggeration, a major contribution to the ongoing refinement of Human Communication Theory.

The main thesis of my analysis is the unique *semiotic phenomenology* that Schutz specifies as a *communicology* within the problematic of the "meaning-context of communication" (1967, pp. 129, 216). My thematic analysis divides into two parts. There is a discussion, first as a problematic, of the general process of human *communication*. This discussion comes mainly from Schutz's essays, (1) "Language, Language Disturbances, and the Texture of Consciousness," (2) "Symbol, Reality, and Society," (3) "The Well-Informed Citizen: An Essay on the Social Distribution of Knowledge" (Schutz, 1973, I & II), and (4) partially from *The Phenomenology of the Social World* (1967). The second section of my analysis concerns the Schutzian thematic of *meaning-context*. It is expressed basically in the "Postulate of Meaning-Adequacy," a specific entailment of the "Postulate of the Coherence of Experience," both of which are discussed in *The Phenomenology of the Social World*.

COMMUNICATION: THE PROBLEMATIC OF A MEANING-CONTEXT

The original contribution that Schutz makes to the history of communicology as a science is his specification of *time* as an essence of human communication (cf. Hall 1959). This is an eidetic element of description. Yet the eidetic core locates its empirical horizon as the essence called *speech*. Schutz gives us an explicit definition of speech communication as the conscious experience—that is, "time-process"—of language:

> Here we simply want to indicate that it is of the essence of language that normally any linguistic communication involves a time process; a speech built up by sentences, a sentence by the step-by-step articulation of successive elements (polythetically, as Husserl calls it), whereas the meaning of the sentence or the speech can be projected by the speaker and grasped by the listener in a single ray (monothetically). The stream of articulating cogitations of the speaker is thus simultaneous with the outer event of producing the sounds of speech, and the perceiving of the latter simulta-

> neously with the comprehending cogitations of the listener. Speech is, therefore, one of the intersubjective time-processes—others are making music together, dancing together, making love together—by which the two fluxes of inner time, that of the speaker and that of the listener, become synchronous one with the other and both with an event in outer time. The reading of a written communication establishes in the same sense a quasisimultaneity between the events within the inner time of the writer and that of the reader [1973, 1:324].

Although it is commonplace these days to dismiss the description of communication as common knowledge, I quote Schutz at length to sharpen our awareness of the key elements of human communication that are quickly and easily overlooked by the naiveté of the natural attitude. It is, indeed, our task as phenomenologists to invoke the *epoché*, most especially were the typification of the taken-for-granted conscious experience of spoken language is at issue (Wagner 1983, pp. 224–25).

Schutz grounds his definition with *four principles* that constitute "communication proper" (1973, 1:321–23). These principles serve as a way of focusing on Schutz's semiotic description (see Figure 29) of the *patterns of consciousness* in "appresentational situations" and subsequent *world typologies*—that is, the "world within my reach and its dimensions, marks, and indications" with "myself as a center" (1:306, 319).

Recall that *appresentation* is a technical term in Husserl's vocabulary; it means the *pairing* or *coupling* of phenomena in consciousness. It is neither the usual notion of analogical inference nor that of induction, but rather an eidetic and empirical form of confirmation. It is what Peirce calls *abduction*: "we experience intuitively something as indicating or depicting significantly something else" (Schutz 1973, 1:296; see chap. 12). With "appresentational relations" as the theoretical or *structural typology* of communication, Schutz presents what I shall refer to as the *Law of Typicality* with its four "postulates" as the methodological criteria for eidetic and empirical research on the world typologies experienced in human communication.

I should note here that these postulates are the theory construction keystone of two leading graduate textbooks in the discipline of communicology. First, B. Aubrey Fisher in his *Perspectives on Human Communication* (1978, p. 22) cites the Schutzian postulates of relevance, adequacy, consistency, and compatibility as the methodological foundation for social science research. Second, Anderson (1987) makes Schutz in particular and phenomenology in general the focus of his discussion of "qualitative research" (pp. 237–244) in his *Communication Research: Issues and Methods*. Polkinghorne's (1983) *Methodology for the Human Sciences: Systems of Inquiry* echoes Fisher's and Anderson's position by also affirming the Schutzian view of the human sciences as an account of

PATTERNS OF CONSCIOUSNESS	WORLD TYPOLOGY	STRUCTURAL TYPOLOGY	PRECONSTITUTED TYPIFICATIONS	LAW OF TYPICALITY
APPRESENTATIONAL SITUATION	SELF AS CENTER {Semeion}	APPRESENTATIONAL RELATIONS	TROPIC LOGIC [ABDUCTIONS]	POSTULATES
[1] APPERCEPTUAL SCHEME	MY REACH {Sign}	PRINCIPLE OF VARIABILITY	[METONYMY]	RELEVANCE
[2] APPRESENTATIONAL SCHEME	ACTUAL REACH {Icon}	PRINCIPLE OF RELATIVE IRRELEVANCE	[METAPHOR] [SIMILE]	ADEQUACY
[3] REFERENTIAL SCHEME	POTENTIAL REACH {Symbol}	PRINCIPLE OF FIGURATIVE TRANSFERENCE	[IRONY] [SYNECDOCHE]	CONSISTENCY
[4] CONTEXTUAL-INTERPRETATIVE SCHEME	RESTORABLE REACH {Index}	PRINCIPLES OF RELATIVE IRRELEVANCE & FIGURATIVE TRANSFERENCE	[OTHER TROPES]	COMPATIBILITY

Figure 29. The Phenomenological Structure of Schutz's communicology.

[Bracketed Numbers] in all Figures indicate appropriate relations among all Figures.
[Brackets indicate my interpolations]

research procedure. Nor should we forget that Kelly (1981) opens his theory book *A Philosophy of Communication* with a chapter devoted to Schutz and the place of communication in the everyday life-world.

In this context, Schutz suggests the phenomenological problematic for the human science of communicology: "We may interpret the prescientific human language as a treasure house of preconstituted types and characteristics, each of them carrying along an open horizon of unexplored typical contents" (1973, 1:285). These *preconstituted typifications* are the *semeion* (sign-act) of human communication, which we designate in contemporary theory as a "tropic logic" (White 1978; Foss, Foss, & Trapp 1985) and our method of using them is *abduction*, to borrow the appropriate term from the American existential phenomenologist, Charles S. Pierce (Anderson 1986).

Principle 1: "The sign used in communication is always a sign addressed to an individual or anonymous interpreter" (Schutz, 1973, 1:321). It is important to note Schutz's extraordinary scholarship with regard to the concept of the *sign* in human communication. He cites the opening passage of Aristotle's *De interpretatione* (16a4ff.), which, of course, introduces the *Rhetoric* and *Poetics*, to specify that spoken and written words are respectively primary and secondary "symbols" (*symbola*), but that the spoken symbols are the *sign* (*semeion*) of consciousness (1973, 1:291). This first principle of communication, thus, incorporates the first order of *semiotic phenomenology* whose characteristics are schematized in Figure 29, row 1.

Conscious experience emerges as an *apperceptual scheme*. This scheme situates an object of consciousness "experienced as a self" without any appresentational reference. From a communicative point of view, it is our "personal biographical situation" that becomes the motive for discovering the uniqueness or atypicality of a phenomenon in the typical world of everyday society (1973, 1:299, 327). The world typology begins as the *here*, as the embodied world horizon of embodied *reach*. Such a communicative context is governed semiotically by "the principle of variability of the appresentational meaning" (1973, 1:304). This is a context in which an appresented object X (or, to use contemporary terminology, a *Signified* = Sd) paired with an appresenting object A (a *Signifier* = Sr) enters into a new pairing with an object B (another Sr). The object A is dropped. In short, several signifiers (like A and B) may have different signifieds (the meaning of A and B), but signify the same object (like X).

We must be cautious here to remember that in symbolic communication (which is all human communication!) we are *not* dealing with a simple Saussurian "sign" composed of a signifier and a signified. Rather, we have a Hjelmslevian sign whose *signifier* represents a signifier/signified and whose *signified* represents a signifier/signified (Eco 1976; 1979). From the perspective of a *tropic logic* (White 1973; 1978), this principle exemplifies the discursive relationship of *metonymy*: one attribute (a Sr/Sd) substitutes for another (a Sr/Sd) in the representation (either a Sr or a Sd) of a substance (sign). Schutz gives this example: "The Commander in Chief of the Allied Armies on D Day 1944, the author of the book *Crusade in Europe*, the thirty-fourth President of the United States, are all proper names denoting Dwight D. Eisenhower, but each appresentational reference is a different one." To generalize this point as a methodological procedure, principle 1 incorporates what Schutz calls the *Postulate of Relevance*: "The formation of ideal types must comply with the principle of relevance, which means that the problem once chosen by the social scientist creates a scheme of reference and constitutes the limits of the scope within which relevant ideal types might be formed" (1973, 2:18).

Principle 2: "The sign used in communication is always preinterpreted by the communicator in terms of its expected interpretation by the addressee" (1973, 1:322). This second principle of communication, thus, incorporates the second order of semiotic phenomenology whose characteristics are schematized in Figure 29, row 2. Conscious experience emerges as an *appresentational scheme*. This scheme locates an object of consciousness that refers to something other than itself, because it is a member of an appresentational pair and is not experienced as a self. These objects are not apprehended in themselves, but rather "call forth" or "evoke" a reference (1973, 1:299, 327). The scheme is the embodied world of my *actual reach* that is outside the self and is the "manipulatory sphere" of the self.

Here the communicative context is governed semiotically by "the principle of the relative irrelevance of the vehicle" (1973, 1:303). In this case, an appresented object X (Sd) originally paired with appresenting object A (Sr) has a new pairing with object B (Sr). Schutz considers two options as an information theoretic/digital logic: (1) *Either* object A and B continue and function as "synonyms" in all senses (not just linguistic); (2) *Or* the object X is detached from object A and X is forgotten as an original reference. Ritual communication is an illustration (Lévy-Bruhl 1985).

There are many other semiotic possibilities that Schutz does not consider, but I shall not detail them here for they do not bear directly on his thesis (see Eco 1976; Lanigan 1986). From a tropic logic point of view, the "synonym" function of (1), above, is the condition of *metaphor* as an abduction that uses preconstituted typifications. But the (2) function, above, is a case of *simile* tropically defined. That is, an object X (Sd) becomes attached to any expression (any Sr) that occurs in the presence of object X. It is in this sense that ritual works (the Sr evokes an Sd) or fails (the Sr does not "waken" the appresented object, as Schutz would say).

As a methodological procedure, principle 2 uses what Schutz calls the *Postulate of Adequacy*—that is, "each term used in a scientific system referring to human action must be so constructed that a human act performed within the life-world by an individual actor in the way indicated by the typical construction would be reasonable and understandable for the actor himself as well as for his fellow-man" (1973, 2:19).

At this point, we should note one of those fascinating historical coincidences of parallel thinking. Reacting to Max Weber just as Schutz does, the French philosopher (and anthropologist, sociologist) Lucien Lévy-Bruhl (1985) published in 1910 his classic work *Les fonctions mentales dans les sociétés inférieures* in which he explicates the *Law of Participation*. This law is now appreciated as the sine qua non of field research, especially that which involves the description of culture and communication together with their symbolic presentation. The law is identical to Schutz's own "postulate of adequacy" in human science research.

In the present context, I also want to mention the extraordinary empirical phenomenological research on narrative communication as conducted by Tom McFeat and reported in his *Small-Group Cultures* (1974). In Schutzian fashion, McFeat's research focuses on the temporal nature and function of the human group as a *communication medium*! To my mind, McFeat's model of social communication and related work deserve to be better known: his work is an empirical prototype of what excellent qualitative research in the phenomenological tradition can be.

Principle 3: "Successful communication is possible only between persons, social groups, nations, etc., who share a substantially similar system of relevances" (Schutz, 1973, 1:323). This third principle of communication illustrates the third order of semiotic phenomenology whose characteristics are schematized in Figure 29, row 3. Conscious experience emerges as a *referential scheme*. This scheme locates an object of consciousness that refers to a paired object by analogy, whether in the "reality of everyday life" or in such other "subuniverses" as science, art, religion, politics, fantasms, or dreams (1973, 1:299, 328–29). The scheme is the *potential reach* of my embodiment and "constitutes the zone of my potential manipulations or, as we prefer to call it, of my potential working acts" (1973, 1:307). Hall's (1959) empirical research on cultural communication is the best illustration, especially his "high-low context" model of cultural meaning (1979, pp. 88–89).

In Schutz's perspective, the communicative context of reference is regulated by "the principle of figurative transference." As the opposite of the principle of relative irrelevance, figurative transference occurs where an appresenting object A (Sr) paired with an appresented object X (Sd) entails another object Y (Sd), and another Z (Sd), and so on. Schutz again argues that other information theoretic/digital possibilities exist: (1) *Either* an original appresentational reference (A-X) continues to coexist with a new coupling (A-Y) or more (A-X, Y, Z, . . .); (2) *Or*, "the original appresentational reference (A-X) is obfuscated or entirely forgotten, and merely the new one (A-Y) preserved" (1973, 1:305).

Given the context of a tropic logic, (1), above, functions as a theoretical definition of *irony* and accounts for the change of valence that often occurs with the situational use of words in everyday discourse. Indeed, Schutz calls attention to this communicative fact as the ground for "any form of tropes in the broadest, not merely linguistic, sense." Again, it is important to note that Schutz in his 1955 essay "Symbol, Reality, and Society" offers a more sophisticated version of the tropic logic than does Kenneth Burke (1969) who sketched his idea of "master tropes" as an appendix in his 1945 volume *A Grammar of Motives*. By comparison, (2), above, illustrates the tropic function of *synecdoche* in which a part-whole relationship functions to accommodate the contextual "shift of meaning" that occurs in everyday discourse. For example, the English term "xerography" (whole = process), which is formally a word in the United Nations International Scientific Vocabulary, has become merely "xerox" (part = product) in everyday discourse because of the new meaning attachment to Xerox Corporation. Once again, there are many other semiotic possibilities with the Principle of Figurative Transference that Schutz does not consider. They have been discussed elsewhere (see Lanigan 1986; Eco 1976).

Principle 3 as a methodological procedure expresses the *postulate of logical consistency*. As Schutz remarks, "the system of ideal types must remain in full compatibility with the principles of formal logic" (1973, 2:19). Recall that Schutz is careful to remind us that Aristotle grounds his logic in the linguistic practice of semiotic and rhetoric. This is to say, the call for consistency is an argument for discovering and appreciating the "treasure house" of prescientific human language. Schutz does not substitute logical validity for material confirmation.

Principle 4: "To be successful, any communication process must, therefore, involve a set of common abstractions or standardizations" (1973, 1:323). Speech becomes the empirical, experiential manifestation of language as an eidetic essence of consciousness. The conscious experience of human discourse, in Schutz's view, becomes the paradigm and prototype of the communication process. "Typification is indeed that form of abstraction which leads to the more or less standardized, yet more or less vague, conceptualization of common-sense thinking and to the necessary ambiguity of the terms of the ordinary vernacular" (1973, 1:323). Typification is the communication theoretic/analogue logic of differentiation by combination. Only human discourse articulates the combination of consciousness and experience while differentiating them. Typification is *both* the authentic existential discourse of the person *and* the sedimented conventional discourse of society. Typification is, in fact, the process of meaning-adequacy that grounds the coherence of experience, and conversely.

Thus, the fourth principle of communication illustrates the fourth order of semiotic phenomenology whose characteristics are schematized in Figure 29, row 4. Conscious experience emerges as a *contextual or interpretational scheme*. The scheme situates the object of consciousness as a reflexive condition of appresentational reference. That is, we experience the relationship that per se connects the appresentational and referential schemes together—that is, *typology as typification*. As both Schutz and Husserl explain, the appresentational relationship is our system of reference as lived. A person may take any relationship as the ground or context of interpretation in communication such that "the Other (as communicator or addressee) will apply the same appresentational scheme to the appresentational references involved in the communication as I will" (1973, 1:328).

Of course, the best example is "the medium of the vernacular of ordinary language." Communicating persons in this context live in a world within *restorable reach*. As Schutz (1973, 1:308) emphasizes, this world is a general idealization of embodiment, the idealization Husserl names in the revelatory phrase: "I can do it again." From the perspective of a tropic logic, any trope in the classic sense of a "figure of speech" can be utilized as the ground of a preconstituted typification in the human sciences (Ijsseling 1976; Valesio 1980; Deely 1986; Eco 1979). Again, the extensive cross-cultural research by Hall (1959) illustrates the phenomenological range of empirical communication possibilities that Schutz labels the "world of restorable reach." Indeed, Hall's opening chapter in *The Silent Language* (1959), entitled "The Voices of Time," might well have been written by Schutz!

From the procedural perspective, principle 4 illustrates the *Postulate of Compatibility*. As Schutz defines it, "The system of ideal types must contain only scientifically verifiable assumptions, which have to be fully compatible with the whole of our scientific knowledge" (1973, 2:19). This statement is absolutely clear in the specification of phenomenological procedures as grounded in the theory of human science. It is this fact that leads Fisher (1978, p. 23) to comment: "The term *social science* does not exclude humanistic studies, phenomenological techniques, or 'the literary tradition'. . . . It does exclude unsystematic inquiry that leads to no generalizable results or explanations that can never be applied to reality."

Throughout his *Collected Papers* (1973), Schutz offers many varied examples of the typification process and product. As a relevant illustration of two generalizable typologies (Figure 30), I want to turn to Schutz's examples of (1) the *Arts* generally and *Music* in particular within the *preknowledge typology*, and (2), *Human Communication* in general, along with my interpolation of the *Speech Communiation* discipline in particular, in the *knowledge typology*. For the sake of comparison, I divide the typologies into "socially derived" and "socially approved" categories. As Schutz argues, the communication process of typification can be *offered in communication* (socially derived) or *accepted in communication* (socially approved) by a "communicator" and an "addressee." This focus and terminology, of course, suggest a compatibility with the model of communication made famous by his colleague at The New School for Social Research, Roman Jakobson (Rutkoff & Scott 1986; Holenstein 1976).

In the example of *music*, Schutz (1973, 2:133, 168) makes the existential elements of—conation, affection, cognition—and their social institution counterparts—aesthetics, morality, politics—come together in a coalescence of intersubjectivity. Communication is both a personal and social act with epistemological and axiological consequences. This is why Schutz's terminology of *creator* and *beholder* is especially indicative of the human discourse that occurs in the respective "appresentational situations" (compare Figure 29, rows 1–4 and Figure 30, rows 1–4). In short, the *writer* and *reader* (Figure 30) illustrate the "apperceptual scheme" with its respective typologies and typicality (Figure 29). In turn, the *composer* and the *player* connect with the "appresentational scheme," the *performer* and the *listener* exemplify the "referential scheme," and the *executant* and the *nonexecutant* represent the "contextual-interpretive scheme."

The example of *human communication* where, following Husserl subjectivity is intersubjectivity, Schutz (1973, 2:132–33) describes the process from the *perspective of the beholder*. Hence, the appresentation situations are respectively described from the point of view of the *analyst*, the *eyewitness*, the *insider*, and the *commentator* as an Other who beholds the communicative situation as offered, or, as a Self whose very beholding is accepting. In my view, incidentally, Schutz has anticipated and described here the "constative-performative" speech act distinction in the "linguistic phenomenology" of the "communicational situation" later made famous by Austin (1962).

As a way of extending Schutz's example and also illustrating the comparative *perspective of the creator* in the human communication process, I offer the interpolation of *Speech* (act of speaking) in Figure 30. The comparison of socially derived and approved appresentational situations allows the following formulations: (1) *speakers* and *listeners* constitute the "apperceptual scheme" with all its characteristics (see Figure 29, row 1); (2) *audience* and *auditor* utilize the "appresentational scheme"; (3) *moderator* or *actor* and *orator* or *critic*, respectively, use the "referential scheme"; and (4) *teacher* or *director* and *student* or *producer* represent the "contextual-interpretive scheme." Other examples are possible, but I

PRE-KNOWLEDGE TYPOLOGY		KNOWLEDGE TYPOLOGY	
The General Example of the ARTS; The Specific Example of MUSIC		The General Example of HUMAN COMMUNICATION; [The Specific Example of SPEECH; an interpolation]	
SOCIALLY DERIVED	SOCIALLY APPROVED	SOCIALLY DERIVED	SOCIALLY APPROVED
CREATOR	BEHOLDER	OFFERED in Communication	ACCEPTED in Communication
[1] WRITER	READER	Other as ANALYST [SPEAKER]	Self as ANALYST [LISTENER]
[2] COMPOSER	PLAYER	Other as EYEWITNESS [AUDIENCE]	Self as EYEWITNESS [AUDITOR]
[3] PERFORMER	LISTENER	Other as INSIDER [MODERATOR; ACTOR]	Self as INSIDER [ORATOR; CRITIC]
[4] EXECUTANT	NON-EXECUTANT {e.g., Conductor}	Other as COMMENTATOR [TEACHER; DIRECTOR]	Self as COMMENTATOR [STUDENT; PRODUCER]

Figure 30. Examples of Schutz's communicological typifications.
[Brackets indicate my interpolations]

have cited the historically familiar ones for the speech communication discipline.

Given the specification of human communication as the problematic of Schutz's notion of meaning-context, we can now turn to a specific analysis and discussion of meaning-context as thematic. This is to say, the conditions (which I call the "Law of Typicality") for a human science of communicology can be explored. The postulates of relevance, adequacy, consistency, and compatibility (a phenomenological description) are integrated by Schutz (a phenomenological reduction) into the two postulates of "Meaning-Adequacy" and the "Coherence of Experience." Last, these two postulates are discovered (a phenomenological interpretation) to be identical as reflexive (Schutz 1967, pp. 82, 231–32, 234). Put more pointedly, Figures 29 through 32 can be overlayed showing that rows 1–4 in all figures are the same combinatory illustration of a hermeneutic of hermeneutic—that is, *existential representation* as the eidetic and empirical essence of communication as human (a *Logos* of *Logos*; see chap. 17 below).

MEANING-CONTEXT: THE THEMATIC OF COMMUNICATION

Meaning-context and communication are mutual entailments in the phenomenology of lived-experience according to Schutz. In this section of my analysis, what I first propose is an examination of the notion of *meaning-context* as Schutz thematically characterizes it in his *Postulate of Meaning-Adequacy* (Figure 31). Second, I look at the specific entailment of *communication* by this postulate. The entailment, thus, comes to be the important thematic dimension of the meaning-context—namely, the *Postulate of the Coherence of Experience* (Figure 32).

The postulate of meaning-adequacy, according to Schutz (1967, p. 206), "states that, given a social relationship between contemporaries, the personal ideal types of partners and their typical conscious experiences must be congruent with one another and compatible with the ideal-typical relationship itself." The postulate relies on a view of temporality that is *existential* rather than transcendental, thereby anticipating the later development of embodiment as temporality by Merleau-Ponty (1981).

As illustrated in Figure 31, Schutz suggests the status of conscious experience as that which is *present* (note the temporal-spatial ambiguity in English!). There is a positive ambiguity in the use of the word "Now" to mark the temporality of existence, because "now" contains simultaneously the meaning-context of the "present" as a boundary place on the diachronic scale of history. The present is the boundary between past and future; it is the "historicality" (to use Foucault's [1972] term) *from which*

TEMPORALITY	PERSONS	INTERSUBJECTIVITY	LIVED WORLD	SPATIALITY
THEN {Past; Absent}	[1] PREDECESSORS [Langage]	WE-RELATIONSHIP	VORWELT [Historicality]	BECAUSE-MOTIVE {Pluperfect = 'had been'} {Terminus a quo}
NOW {Present; Presentation}	[2] CONSOCIATES {ASSOCIATES} [Parole]	CONCRETE WE-RELATION	UMWELT {Directly Experienced Social Reality}	HERE [Synchronic; Static]
		PURE WE-RELATION		
	[3] CONTEMPORARIES [Langue]	THOU-ORIENTATION	MITWELT {Mediated Social Reality}	THERE [Diachronic; Dynamic]
		THEY-ORIENTATION {Reciprocal}		
THEN {Future; Absent}	[4] SUCCESSORS [Langage]	THEY-ORIENTATION {One Sided}	FOLGEWELT [Historicity]	IN-ORDER-TO-MOTIVE {Future Perfect = 'shall have been'} {Terminus ad quem}

Figure 31. Alfred Schutz's postulate of meaning-adequacy (as described in The Phenomenology of the Social World). [Brackets indicate my interpolations]

the person exists—in Cicero's rhetoric it is speech as the terminus a quo (Schutz 1973, 2:11). On the synchronic scale of personal existence, "presentation" is the boundary place between conditions of temporal absence such as birth and death. Presentation is the *now* of "historicity" (Foucault's term) *toward which* the person is existing—again, in Cicero's rhetoric it is speech as the terminus ad quem (Schutz 1973, 2:11). Hence, the binary concepts *now/then* are fixed by Schutz within an analogue logic in such a way that *now* is a floating boundary condition on the infinite scale of *then*. In this sense, conscious experience is an existential condition of the person that stands as the ideal-typical relationship itself. "Activity is an experience which is constituted in the phases in the transition from one Now to the next" (Schutz 1967, p. 56). Unlike positive science and unlike Husserl's eidetic model, time for Schutz is not the measure of space. Rather, as we shall come to understand, temporality is the condition of spatiality.

Recall now another condition for the postulate of meaning-adequacy—namely, that the personal ideal types of partners and their typical conscious experiences must be congruent with one another. Schutz specifies this condition for *persons* in his famous division of temporal human relationships. First, there is the life-world of *predecessors* (Figure 31, row 1). They are persons with whom I share no experience of time or location, although I live in the shadow of their discourse—I share their symbolic universe (Merleau-Ponty's [1962] *langage*). They have lived and died prior to my living. The absence of their conscious experience is a testimony to the presence of my own conscious experience. I can be an analyst (see Figure 30). Secondly, there are *consociates*—or *associates* as Schutz occasionally calls them—who are persons with whom I share both time and location. We share the conscious experience of interpersonal communication in the face-to-face situation of shared activity (Figure 31, row 2). Our mutual sense of Now constitutes an intersubjective present. I can be a witness (see Figure 30). It is a discursive present that constitutes experience as lived—in Merleau-Ponty's phrase, it is speech speaking (*parole parlante*) as a refinement of Saussure's *parole*.

A third type of person is the *contemporary* (Figure 31, row 3). This person shares time by living when I do, but is displaced from me. At best, our discourse is merely symbolic and sedimented, *speech spoken* (*parole parlée*), as Merleau-Ponty describes it in contradistinction to Saussure's *langue*. Locality is not shared; we have never met or shared our experiences. We are merely ideal types of partners and our consciousness displays a typicality. I can be the insider (see Figure 30). *Successors* are the fourth category of persons (Figure 31, row 4). Successors, like predecessors, are persons with whom I do not share time and space. Yet they are uniquely marked by the fact that I could share time and location with them. I can be the commentator (see Figure 30). The ideality of our relationship has the potential to become actual as "power" in the same way that I share the discourse of predecessors as "desire" (Foucault's [1972] *langage*).

What is truly unique in the lived-taxonomy (Foucault's *genealogy*; Jakobson's *paradigmatic axis*) of persons that Schutz creates is the fact that he offers the first modern notion of "qualitative data," or if I may use the historically correct qualitative term, *capta*—namely, that which is taken (as opposed to given) in discovery (Foucault's *archaeology*; Jakobson's *syntagmatic axis*). Only now are the human sciences becoming aware of the fact that the pejorative rhetoric of the positive sciences hides the *person* as the real and ideal "unit" of analysis and synthesis. The person as *captum* offers an unlimited source of research that is quite apart from the equally restrictive view of the pure arts and humanities. Schutz's modest four-part action-classification of persons is the beginning, and there are signs of significant work in this context, especially in the discipline of communicology. I have already mentioned the innovative work by McFeat (1974), which specifies the *human group* as the cultural medium of communication, hence another type of *capta* to be used. And there is my own empirical application of *eidetic practice* as *capta* to discourse and rhetoric (Lanigan 1984; see chap. 8 above).

Building on the classification of persons, Schutz constructs a model of *intersubjectivity* in which the "we-relation" derives from my knowledge that I have of predecessors. Thus, my experience of consociates first emerges as I notice that the other person and I have differences in our conscious experiences. As Schutz (1967, p. 168) explains the "concrete we-relation," the "partner, for instance, may be experienced with different degrees of immediacy, different degrees of intensity, or different degrees of intimacy." Natanson (1965) provides an excellent discussion of the communicative consequence that consociates make in the "claim to immediacy."

But just as temporal absence suggests presence, differences in conscious experience are balanced by similarities in the "pure we-relation": "The face-to-face relationship in which the partners are aware of each other and sympathetically participate in each other's lives for however short a time" (Schutz, 1967, p. 164). In the world of contemporaries, I first discover the "thou-orientation" and with it the problem of the other. I am confronted with other persons who are not in face-to-face contact with me, but could be. I have the expectation of encounter. I sense the ideal typicality in which the other person removed in space can come to share my location, can enter into the we-relationship. The full range of communicative elements that contextualize the Schutzian we-relationship are discussed in Von Eckartsberg's classic article, "Encounter as the Basic Unit of Social Interaction" (1965).

Where the occasion of encounter remains impossible, we discover the realm of the "they-orientation," which is either reciprocal or one-sided. When it is reciprocal, the other person and I are aware of one another. But when the orientation is one-sided, I alone am aware of the other. At this juncture, I am entering the world of successors: they are that class of distant others whom I can come to know, but do not know in the Here and Now.

The *lived-world* and the construction of human spatiality—that is, the existential element of conscious experience, can now be summarized. First, the world of predecessors (*Vorwelt*) is our usual conception of historicality, of those persons who came before us, yet with whom we have only a discursive relationship. The influence of the world of predecessors functions in the meaning-context as the "because-motive". Schutz suggests that we can discursively understand this motivation by looking at the pluperfect tense in language (*langage*). Language records the existential condition of predecessors, of their speech activity, which *had been* and which we share as an ideal typicality of language and action because we can speak and act as they did! The *because-motive* directly grounds our spatial sense of here. It is now, here that we share in consciousness our mutually experienced social reality (*Umwelt*). As consociates living in the midst of we-relations, we live the subjectivity of intersubjectivity in Husserl's sense.

By contrast, our spatial sense of *there* grounds the world of contemporaries (*Mitwelt*). Our sense of the other is located. And we begin to derive from it a sense of the future that is absent from us, but *shall have been*. Thus, Schutz records the world of successors (*Folgewelt*) with the use of the future perfect tense in language. The *in-order-to motive* is for Schutz the activity that is grounded in the spatial consciousness of *there*. What we have, then, in the postulate of meaning-adequacy, is a philosophical conception of human activity as a source of both eidetic and empirical research derived from contexts of *meaning* as a "sign-system" (see Figure 32). In other words, Schutz gives us the criteria by which to judge context—conscious experience in the social world. We have a measure of adequacy for human reality. What remains, therefore, is the problematic of meaning per se in "sign-vehicles."

Before undertaking a specific discussion of the postulate of the coherence of experience, it is helpful to review both the formal and material definitions that Schutz gives for the philosophical idea of *coherence*. In more precise philosophical thinking, we have the necessary and sufficient conditions for a coherence theory of truth—that is, the criteria by which to judge the modalities of meaning in conscious experience as human activity. Contexts of meaning in the semiotic form of schemes of experience are formally defined "by identifying the mode of their constitution as a synthesis of a higher stage out of polythetic Acts of once-lived-through experience" (1967, p. 82).

This formal definition entails the function of the *sign-vehicle* as a necessary condition for meaning. By comparison, the sufficient condition for meaning—its material definition—entails the *sign-system*. Schemes or *patterns of experience* acquire a material definition "by referring to the total object which comes into view when such syntheses are viewed monothetically" (Schutz, 1967, p. 82). In short, the semiotic phenomenology consists of sign-vehicles in sign-systems that constitute a coherence of experience. "By this we mean (a) their mutual conditioning of one another, (b) their synthetic construction into higher-level patterns, and finally (c) the meaning-configuration of these patterns themselves, namely, the 'total configuration of our experience in the actual Here and Now'" (p. 82; see chap. 8 above).

In order to avoid confusion at this point, note that I am equating the notion of sign-vehicle(s) with the Husserl/Schutz notion of *polythetic acts*, whereas the idea of a sign-system is treated as a *monothetic act*. This reading is consistent with the entailment suggested by Schutz whereby "metaschemes" and sign-systems are reversible temporalities.

We also need to be cautious, again, in the case of human communication to recall that we are not just in a monothetic action where a one-level hermeneutic operates—that is, "the appresenting and appresented members of the pair and the interpreter pertain to the same level of reality, namely, the paramount reality of everyday life." Rather, we are in a polythetic action that requires us to "redefine the symbolic relationship as an appresentational relationship between entities belonging to at least two finite provinces of meaning so that the appresenting symbol is an element of the paramount reality of everyday life" (1973, 1:343). Now, we can turn directly to the postulate of the coherence of experience (Figure 32).

The eidetic nature and function of the "sign-vehicle" as both a *coordinating scheme* and a *metascheme* is indicated by Schutz's definition of a semiotic scheme: "A scheme of our experience is a meaning-context which is a configuration of our past experiences embracing conceptually the experiential objects to be found in the latter but not the process by which they were constituted" (1967, p. 82). The process of constitution is, of course, the sign-system. The sign-vehicle as a coordinating scheme involves the combination of the "sign" per se (*actio*; *Handeln*; action) as an enactment (*Akt*) leading to a *signatum* (*actum*; *Handlung*; act/project). We can express this *static* process (terminus a quo) simply by saying that *activity* is an *acting* that results in an *action*, but "action" in this usage is not a dynamic process (terminus ad quem) in communication. When we consider the sign-vehicle as a metascheme, a meaning-endowing act (*Sinngebung*; see chap. 4 above) combines with the "sign-act" or object-act (appresenting) with an "artifact" (appresented). That is, the sign-act as the universe of discourse always combines with its own

SEMIOLOGY	PATTERN OF EXPERIENCE	COMMUNICATION	MEANING
SIGN-VEHICLE	[1] COORDINATING SCHEME	AKT {Enactment}	SIGN {Actio; Handeln}
			SIGNATUM {Actum; Handlung}
	[2] METASCHEME	SINNGEBUNG {Sense-endowing -Act-character}	SIGN-ACT {Universe of Discourse}
			ARTIFACT {Symbol}
SIGN-SYSTEM	[3] INTERPRETIVE SCHEME	SIGNIFICATIVE FUNCTION	SINN {Meaning Establishment}
			BEDEUTUNGEN {Objective Meaning}
	[4] EXPRESSIVE SCHEME	EXPRESSIVE FUNCTION	BEDEUTEN {Subjective Meaning}
			BEZEICHNUNG {Meaning Interpretation}

Figure 32. Alfred Schutz's postulate of the coherence of experience (as described in The Phenomenology of the Social World).

artifact—a symbol (= sign-system). As Schutz (1967, p. 120) comments, "the boundary between the two is absolutely fluid."

This distinction between sign-act and artifact is a combinatory differentiation in which the interpretation (typology) of signs and significations is a product of previous interpretations (typifications). Hence, the distinction is a metascheme of which the obvious example is *discourse* in its combinatory modality as a *dynamic*, fluid boundary (terminus ad quem) between phonology and orthography in the act of articulation—a thesis suggested, but not proved, by Husserl in Investigation III of the *Logical Investigations* (1970a; see chap. 8 above). Indeed, on this point, Schutz has unwittingly characterized the ground of the long debate on discourse as between, first, the phenomenologists and structuralists, and now, as between the hermeneuticists and poststructuralists (see chap. 11 above).

Turning to the empirical nature and function of the "sign-system," Schutz distinguishes *interpretive schemes* and *expressive schemes* (Figure 32). The interpretive scheme is the social worldview. It is the receptive world of the *beholder* (Figure 30) where "socially approved" communication occurs for readers, listeners, and so on. As a receptive activity, the interpretive scheme accounts for the *significative function* in communication situations. The interpreting addressee as beholder contends with activity as a process of sense-making (*Sinn-*) where the intent of the communicator as *creator* is to establish meaning in the character of the act (*-gebung*) by contrasting that act with its context—that is, with *Objective Meaning* (*Bedeutung*)— with "that which is meant"—namely, a discursive function of expression. Reversing the situation of activity—that is, focusing on the creator (see Figure 30) —we have the expressive scheme in the sign-system. Here the *expressive function* operates to specify the *subjective meaning* (*Bedeuten*) used by writers, composer, speakers, and so on, and the occasional reference of *meaning interpretation* (*Bezeichnung*) that the act constitutes as a function of perceptual expression for the performer, executant, actor, teacher, and so on.

Last, we should recall that sign-vehicles always occur in sign-systems so that the analytic scheme represented by Figure 32 should itself be considered a *scheme* in Schutz's sense. This realization then permits our understanding that Figure 31 and Figure 32 are, respectively, eidetic and empirical schemes (polythetic) of a unitary (monothetic) human activity. Conscious experience becomes coterminus with social reality; communication guarantees subjectivity as intersubjectivity. Expressed in terms of the Schutzian postulates, meaning-adequacy becomes the coherence of experience, yet experience constructs a coherence of consciousness as meaningful (1967, pp. 233–34).

Schutz gives his own summary in his characterization of the discipline and methodology of interpretive sociology, which we can read as a generalization about all the disciplines of the Human Sciences and which I have read as a specification of the discipline of Communicology:

> the primary task of this science is to describe the process of meaning-establishment and meaning-interpretation as they are carried out by individuals living in the social world. This description can be empirical or eidetic; it can take as its subject matter the individual or the typical; it can be performed in concrete situations of everyday life or with a high degree of generality. But, over and above this, interpretive sociology approaches such cultural objects and seeks to understand their meaning by applying them to the interpretive scheme thus obtained [1967, p. 248].

The Law of Typicality with its postulates of *relevance*, *adequacy*, *consistency*, and *compatibility* are a phenomenological description of the human sciences. The phenomenological reduction that Schutz conducts on this description yields the two postulates of *meaning-adequacy* and the *coherence of experience* that make sciences human, the reality of everyday living. The phenomenological interpretation of this reduction specifies *communication* as the science of meaning for persons whose very act of living is the reflexivity of consciousness and experience—that is, *time*. From the treasure house of preconstituted types, Alfred Schutz has taken the coin of human exchange, of human speech. That coin is the person in the lived-world of communication whose symbol is time.

Chapter Seventeen

Semiotic Phenomenology in Plato's Sophist

The dialogue *Sophist* is often regarded as the most difficult of Plato's writings. In part, it is ambiguous in taking up the problem of the Being of Not-Being. Also, it attempts an explanation of the One and the Many that is an enduring philosophical and empirical paradox. Last, the dialogue is an oral illustration of Platonic method (maieutic) as purported in the Seventh Letter. The presence of these varying threads in the one dialogue suggests a major shift from the conversational tone of inquiry present in the early dialogues to the argumentative mode of analysis in Plato's later thinking. The chief result is the creation of an object of consciousness within interpersonal experience that is open to analytic justification as an empirical experience.

My argument in this chapter attempts to explicate the main features of the Platonic thesis in order to establish that the *model* of *discourse analysis* is semiotic in nature and phenomenological in function. I am using the term *model* in its technical theory construction sense as an "exemplar" (combined "paradigm" and "prototype") in a theory.[8] Thus in a Heideggerian (1972, p. 51) view, "What a model as such is and how

8. Heidegger (1972, p. 51): 'A thinking which thinks in models must not immediately be characterized as technological thinking, because the word "model" is not to be understood in the technological sense as the repetition or project of something in smaller proportions. Rather, a model is that from which thinking must necessarily take off in such a way that that from which it takes off is what gives it impetus. The necessity for thinking to use thinking is related to language. The language of thinking can only start from common speech. And speech is fundamentally historico-metaphysical. An interpretation is already built into it. Viewed from this perspective, thinking has only the possibility of searching for models in order to dispense with them eventually, thus making the transition to the speculative.'

its function for thinking is to be understood can only be thought from an essential interpretation of language." The dialogue *Sophist* relies on a binary code that is cast within a rhetorical situation grounded in an analogue logic. The binary coding is made clear with the illustrative use of a modified version of the Barthes model of discourse. That model is grounded in Hjelmslev's (1961; 1970a, b; Garvin 1954) theory in which he describes the structure of language and similar systems with the following theorems:

> (1) A language consists of a content and an expression. (2) A language consists of a succession, or a text, and a system. (3) Content and expression are bound up with each other through commutation. (4) There are certain definite relations within the succession and within the system. (5) There is not a one-to-one correspondence between content and expression, but the signs are decomposable in minor components. Such sign components are, e.g., the so-called phonemes, which I should prefer to call taxemes of expression, and which in themselves have no content, but which can build up units provided with a content, e.g., words [1970b, p. 35].

Barthes's model of Hjelmslevian theory allows a direct comparison between the stages of Platonic method and Barthes's concepts of connotation, denotation, and reality as set in a signifier or rhetoric system and signified or ideology system (Lyons 1963). The analogue logic is equally applicable in the respective correlation to Merleau-Ponty's (1962) phenomenological model of description, reduction, and interpretation. In short, the logic for a *semiotic phenomenology* is provided in the dialogue *Sophist* and it points the way for viewing the speaking subject as an agent provocateur in the sociocultural context where empirical reference must give way to the production of analytic signification. As Heidegger (1972, p. 51) specifies: "Speaking about ontic models presupposes that language in principle has an ontic character, so that thinking finds itself in the situation of having to use ontic models for what it wishes to say ontologically, since it can only make something evident through words."

My analysis does not represent an effort to claim that Plato is either a semiologist or a phenomenologist. Rather, I argue that the dialogue *Sophist* offers a long-neglected textual model of binary analogue thinking that is foundational to many of the issues current in the discipline of communicology, especially in the study of the philosophy of communication where semiology and phenomenology intersect as the problematic of analysis. Indeed, many of the basic elements in the Platonic investigation are being unnecessarily reinvented by contemporary theorists. By addressing the fundamental problem of the being of not-being, Plato provides a semiotic phenomenology of discourse in which he demonstrates the acceptability of analytic proofs as the concrete analysis of empirical communication acts. Thus, the dialogue *Sophist* represents a critical, but often ignored, theoretical foundation for an empirical examination of the sign relationship between the ontology of the speaking subject and the epistemology of the discourse system.

As a dialectic examination, my analysis has four steps. First, I review the exemplar of maieutic that Plato provides in Letter VII. Then I indicate the parallel between the Platonic model and the one that Barthes (1968) offers. The point of this comparison is to demonstrate that Barthes adopts a view of "rhetoric" and "ideology" (and the subsequent view of "text") that is dysfunctional if we concede the force of Plato's analysis. Third, I examine the Platonic model as it is applied in substance to the productive art of discourse in the dialogue *Sophist*. Last, I suggest the way in which Merleau-Ponty's (1962) existential phenomenology offers a praxis model of philosophic discourse that meets the Platonic standard for theory construction and grounds *rhetoric* in a dialectic logic consistent with modern Hjelmslevian (1961) notions in communication theory. That is, I am concerned to argue that Plato gives us a coherent logic of discourse as a grounding that we readily perceive as information theory.

Barthes utilizes this theory and is trapped by its structure—namely, that context always provides for choice, but concrete choice is systematically ambiguous. By comparison, Plato helps us discover that the inclusion of the human agent in the use of information theory sets the criteria for communication theory, in which a person makes a choice that systemically constitutes a context. But in specifying the problem in order to locate the solution, Plato stops short of disclosing the condition for choice in context. For such an illustration of completed theory, I turn to Merleau-Ponty's (1962) philosophy of communication and my own extensions of his basic model (Lanigan 1970; 1972; 1979a, b).

One other feature of these various comparisons needs to be mentioned before proceeding. In Plato, Barthes, and Merleau-Ponty the basic philosophic pair of concepts at issue is "rhetoric" and "ideology." In this regard, it is important to recognize the signification that attaches to these concepts as they are used in dialectic analysis. In brief, *ideology* should be viewed as a condition of discourse that constitutes the *context of choice*—namely, "information." By comparison, *rhetoric* is the practice of discourse that constitutes a *choice of context*—namely, "communication." Indeed, it is the very irony of the dialogue *Sophist* that in seeking out the axiological characteristics of sophistry, we apparently locate the philosopher's condition and thereby discover the logic of human discourse with its full ontological import (Kerferd 1954; 1981).

THE SEVENTH LETTER

Plato addresses his letter to the companions and friends of Dion. The letter is occasioned by Plato's attempt to maintain his neutrality in the struggle for power at Syracuse between the exiled Dion and the ruling Dionysius I. We need not encumber ourselves with the history of Syracuse, but it is of consequence to recall that in the dialogue *Sophist* the discussion begins epistemologically with the problem of distinguishing among the sophist, the statesman, and the philosopher. Plato's intellectual problem in the dialogue has its vivid practical illustration in Letter VII, which recalls the threat to his personal existence during the boat trips between the Greek mainland and Sicily. To be sure, the existential flavor of Plato's thinking is all too clear in the repeated mention of his recurrent, urgent need to get a boat out of town!

With less facetiousness, I also need to recall that Socrates pursued the question "What is knowledge?" in the dialogue *Theaetetus*, which ends with a promise to complete the discussion the following day (Klein 1977). But the next day Socrates is arrested and brought to trial. The consequence is that the discussion of knowledge resumes while Socrates is in prison awaiting execution (cf. chap. 7). The resumed dialogue is the *Sophist* (Sallis 1975, p. 457).

In the key passage of Letter VII, Plato announces the exemplar that informs the Socratic method of maieutic:[9]

> For everything that exists there are three classes of objects through which knowledge about it must come; the knowledge itself is a fourth, and we must put as a fifth entity the actual object of knowledge which is the true reality. We have then, first, a name, second, a description, third an image, and fourth, a knowledge of the object [342b–343c].

Later he adds:

> Furthermore these four [names, descriptions, bodily forms, concepts] do as much to illustrate the particular quality of any object as they do to illustrate its essential reality because of the inadequacy of language. Hence no intelligent man will ever be so bold as to put into language those things which his reason has contemplated, especially not into a form that is unalterable—which must be the case with what is expressed in written symbols.

9. While I follow the standard codex practice of using Stephanus numbers for textual citation, the edition of translations I am using is Hamilton and Cairns (Plato 1961). It should be further noted that I am using Letter VII for convenience of explication; I realize that the authenticity of authorship for this letter is in dispute. It simply offers a concise statement of issues with which to begin my analysis of the dialogue *Sophist*, which is the text of concern.

The fact that this model is communicated in a written letter points to a momentary paradox. Yet, we recall that in the *Sophist* the contemplated model is in fact articulated according to Plato's criteria for production (Isenberg 1951).

Plato offers us an illustration to demonstrate the model's utility. The example is the concept "circle." First, the articulate use of "circle" is a word that names. Second, we use nouns and verbal expression to describe the circle and thereby suggest its *logos*: "The thing that has everywhere equal distances between its extremities and its center." Third, we discover a class of objects—for example, the graphic object that we can draw and erase or the wooden object we can turn on a lathe and then destroy. Fourth, we come upon another thing that is not found in sounds or in the shape of bodies, but in the mind. This concept has a degree ranging from knowledge to understanding to current opinion, each displaying a "particular quality." Fifth, there is the real circle, what Plato in his idealism calls the "essential reality."

We immediately perceive that the clear, but epigrammatic, presentation of the exemplar in Letter VII is an assertion in want of proof. The desired demonstration of the model occurs in the *Sophist*, where Plato addresses the question of knowledge and its method—that is, the *logos* of *logos* (Sallis 1975, p. 456; Kerferd 1954). But before examining this detailed argument, I should like to compare the Platonic model to that of Barthes (1968).

THE BARTHES MODEL OF DISCOURSE

The Barthes (1968) model consists in a developmental approach to the question of knowledge that is in spirit like the Platonic quest. In particular, both Plato and Barthes are concerned to formulate a method for discovering and utilizing knowledge that is produced and comes to us in the form of discourse. Also, both theorists provide for a modification in their method when discourse proves to be an inadequate guide. This modification is, of course, the use of myth. As I subsequently suggest, it is the Barthes (1972) model for myth analysis that points to a serious defect in the structuralist theory of *rhetoric* in general and of *text* in particular. It is a defect that is exposed initially by using the Platonic model for epistemology (see chap. 5 above).

In chapter 4 of Barthes's *Elements of Semiology* (1968) we have the now classic presentation of the semiotic model of discourse. The model is constructed to account for the production of signification. By comparison, Eco (1976, pp. 54–56, 268–69) presents a less flawed process model of the Hjelmslevian theory and subsequent diagrammatic presentation. Following Hjelmslev, Barthes calls the first element in the system the *plane of expression*. The second element is the *plane of content* and the connection between the two planes is simply the *relation*. He proceeds to argue that the expression/relation/content or ERC condition exists on the two levels of "connotation" and "denotation," this latter being a metalanguage function. Barthes offers two illustrative expressions of this model: one is a symbolic calculus and the other is a pictorial diagram. Finally, there is a third diagrammatic illustration of the model that shows the combined models of connotation and denotation as based in the Real System. It will be useful to compare the symbolic and diagrammatic versions (mutatis mutandis, existential graphs) of the models to indicate the logical limitations built into Barthes's approach.

The symbolic version of the model in a propositional calculus is quite simple and straightforward (Figure 33). The first system (noted in "1" in Figure 33) ERC becomes the plane of expression of the second system (noted as "2" in Figure 33), so the formulation now reads *(ERC)RC*. In this case we have the connotation, because the place of expression in the first system (ERC) becomes the signifier (Sr) of the second system—that is, *(ERC)* substitutes for E in the second *ERC*. This structure is reversed in the case of denotation, thereby becoming a metalinguistic function. Here (Figure 34) we have the plane of expression in the first system by commutation for the plane of content in the second system. That is, the formulation reads *ER(ERC)*, in which the signified *(ERC)* replaces the C in the first system of ERC. Both connotation as a signifier and denotation as a signified are apparent in the existential graphs (Figures 35 and 36).

At this point a problematic issue arises. If we take Barthes's (1968) symbolic presentation of connotation *(ERC)RC* and denotation *ER (ERC)* as combinatory, it should be possible to express the formulation as *(ERC)R(ERC)*. Why is this formulation not presented by Barthes? If we graphically present the combinatory formula (Figure 37), it becomes quite apparent. Barthes gives us only one commutation set (Figure 37), although there is at least one other necessary set (Figure 38), and multiple sufficient sets (Figures 39 and 40). In fact, Barthes suggests the possibility of an answer when he distinguishes "rhetoric" (Figure 37) from "ideology" (Figure 38). Yet there is no discussion of the production of ideology; it is simply asserted.

The best explanation for the use of the linear ratio *(ERC)RC:ER-(ERC)* (see Figure 41) rather than my entailment model *(ERC)R(ERC)* (or more elegantly $[ERC]^2$) is that such an entailment (see Figure 42) discloses that discourse is dialectic (ontologically reversible) and should be grounded in a theory of the speaking subject (Kristeva 1975, p. 5; Merleau-Ponty 1962, p. 174; Eco 1976; Hikins 1977). In contrast, Barthes solves the problem of the ontological status of discourse by making *language (langue)* the ground for Being. For Plato, language is the ground

2 E R C

1 ERC

Figure 33. Barthes's 'connotation' expressed in his propositional calculus

Figure 34. Barthes's 'denotation/metalanguage' expressed in his propositional calculus

Sr		Sd
Sr	Sd	

Figure 35. Barthes's 'connotation' graphically produced

Sr	Sd	
	Sr	Sd

Figure 36. Barthes's 'denotation/metalanguage' graphically produced

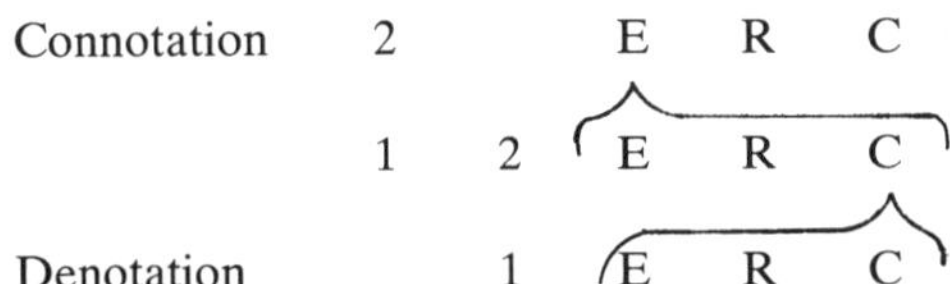

Figure 37. Combinatory overlay of Barthes's propositional calculus for 'connotation' and 'denotation' where the metalanguage function is produced: Rhetoric

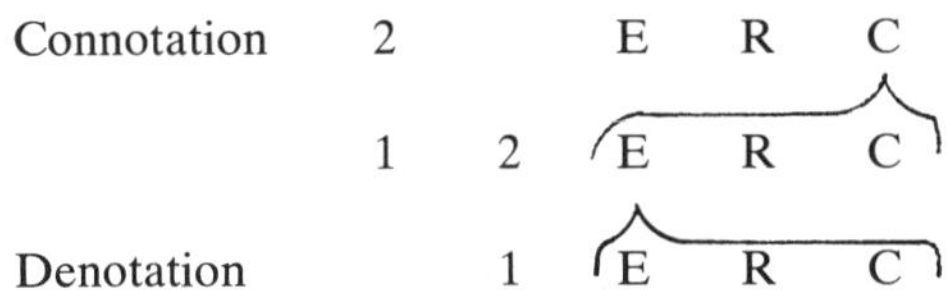

Figure 38. Combinatory overlay of Barthes's propositional calculus for 'connotation' and 'denotation' where the metalanguage function is produced: Ideology

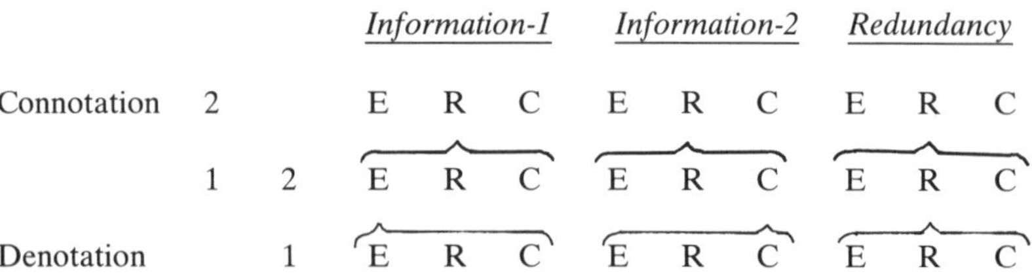

Figure 39. *Examples of combinatory sufficient condition sets that can be demonstrated in communication theory*

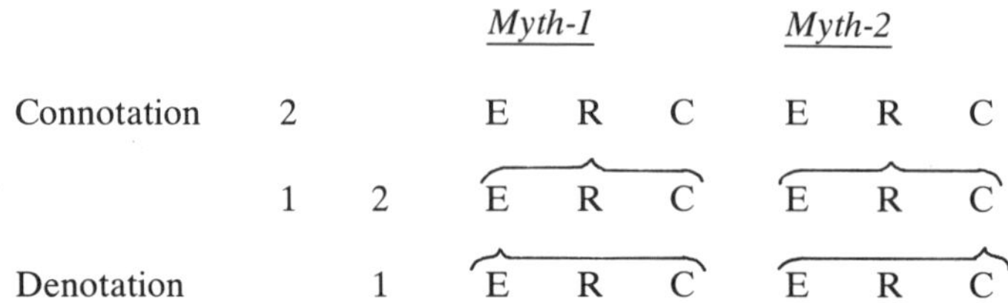

Figure 40. *Examples of combinatory sufficient condition sets that can be interpolated in communication theory*

for Not-Being. As one might guess, Barthes's view is that of the classical sophist, to whom Plato points his many objections.

As a limited demonstration of my argument, I suggest a comparison between Barthes's (1972, p. 115; 1982) use of his model for myth analysis (Figure 43) and one of the sufficient variations of my entailment model (see Figure 40: Myth-1), which reveals an identity of formulation. I am confident about the accuracy of my interpretation: Barthes (1972, p. 109) specifically argues that "myth is a type of speech," to which he adds the operational definition: "Innumerable other meanings of the word 'myth' can be cited against this. But I have tried to define things, not words." If we follow Barthes's intent in providing this definition of "myth" and "speech" as deriving from a "thing," we instead should expect the formulation presented in Figure 40, Myth-2, which indicates such content signification. The fact that Myth-2 is asserted—that is, "to define things, not words," when Myth-1 is used (Figures 41 and 43), merely confirms the error by omission found in the original model in the *Elements of Semiology* (see the "ideology" system in Figure 42). However, for immediate purposes of comparison with Plato's analysis, I use the complete model (Figure 41) that Barthes presents in the *Elements of Semiology* (1968). I think the Platonic argument is clearest if simply formulated according to Barthes's construction principles, for the comparison thus illustrates the concrete differences involved between the two theorists.

For Plato, the "plane of expression" consists of what I shall call the *verbal form* (Sr) in relation to what Plato calls the object or *bodily form*

3 Connotation	Sr: rhetoric		Sd: ideology
2 Denotation: Metalanguage	Sr	Sd	
1 Real System		Sr Sd	

Figure 41. Barthes's complete model in Elements of Semiology *(1968: 93)*

3 Connotation	Sr: Rhetoric		Sd: Ideology	
2 Denotation: Metalanguage	Sr	Sd	Sr	Sd
1 Real System		Sr Sd	Sr Sd	

Figure 42. Lanigan extrapolation of Barthes's model

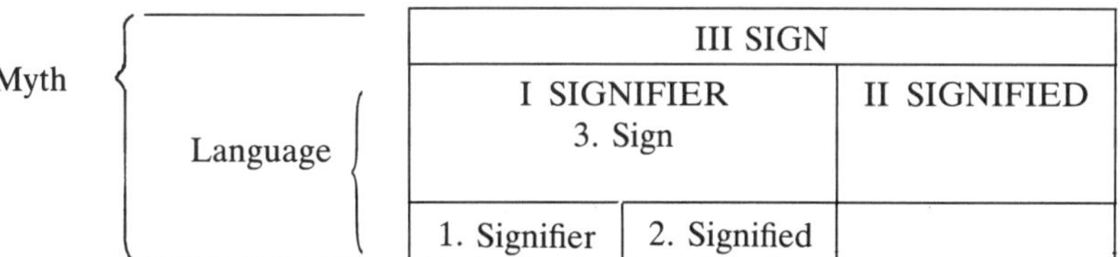

Figure 43. Barthes's interpolation model in Mythologies *(1972: 115; graph inverted)*

(Sd). We have now the simple ERC formulation. For Platonic connotation, the *name* stands in relation to *description*, and this pair becomes the signifier in place of the "verbal form" (Figure 44; cf. Figures 35 and 33) or *(ERC)RC*. For denotation and the metalanguage function we have the signifier/signified relationship of "name" and "description" where "description" is produced by the relationship of *knowledge* and *essential reality* (Figure 45; cf. Figures 36 and 34) of the formulation *ER(ERC)*. At this point, we can compare the two possible sets represented by the formula *(ERC)R(ERC)* or $(ERC)^2$. The commutation set hypostatized by Barthes (1968) as "rhetoric" is apparent in Figure 46. The key factor to be recognized, as Plato argues, is the signifier function, the *verbal form* that is always a characteristic (Figure 47), that is, a "particular quality."

Before proceeding, it is helpful to look at my construction of the set that Barthes (1968) suggests is "ideology" (Figure 48). Or, it may be useful to visualize the arrangement of sets as specified by my formula $(ERC)^2$ in Figures 42 and 49. I believe that it is apparent that the diacritical sign production process of this formulation is consistent with

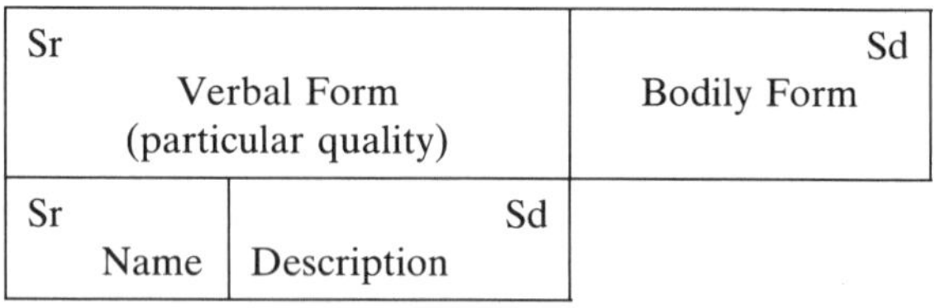

<table>
<tr><td colspan="2">Sr
Verbal Form
(particular quality)</td><td>Sd
Bodily Form</td></tr>
<tr><td>Sr
Name</td><td>Sd
Description</td><td></td></tr>
</table>

Figure 44. *Platonic categories formulated according to. Barthes's model of connotation*

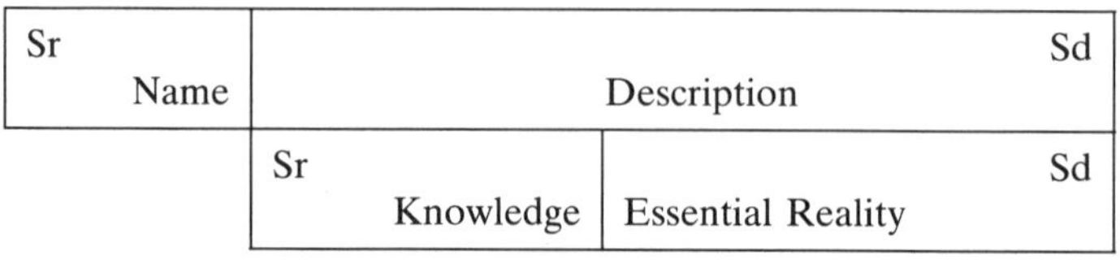

<table>
<tr><td>Sr
Name</td><td colspan="2">Sd
Description</td></tr>
<tr><td></td><td>Sr
Knowledge</td><td>Sd
Essential Reality</td></tr>
</table>

Figure 45. *Platonic categories formulated according to Barthes's model of denotation*

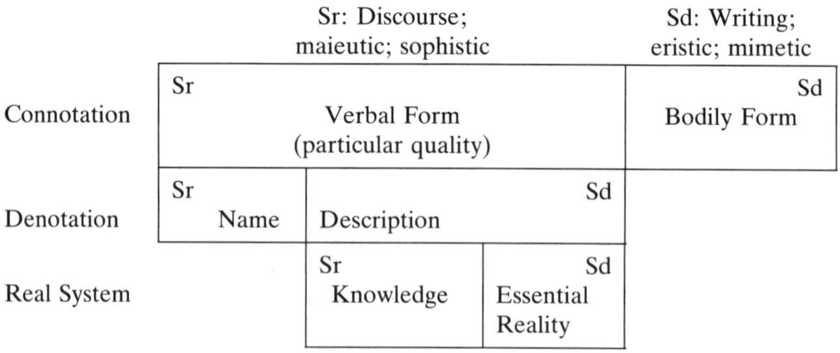

<table>
<tr><td></td><td colspan="3">Sr: Discourse;
maieutic; sophistic</td><td>Sd: Writing;
eristic; mimetic</td></tr>
<tr><td>Connotation</td><td colspan="3">Sr
Verbal Form
(particular quality)</td><td>Sd
Bodily Form</td></tr>
<tr><td>Denotation</td><td>Sr
Name</td><td colspan="2">Sd
Description</td><td></td></tr>
<tr><td>Real System</td><td></td><td>Sr
Knowledge</td><td>Sd
Essential Reality</td><td></td></tr>
</table>

Figure 46. *Platonic categories formulated according to Barthes's model*

the logical and phenomenological principles of paradigmatic/synchronic and syntagmatic/diachronic production established by Saussure and elaborated by Jakobson in the context of communication theory (Lanigan 1979b; Holenstein 1976; Alperson 1975).

Plato's model for knowledge, used as a test of Barthes's model, therefore, allows us to recognize with Plato that an ambiguity exists when dealing with words, actions, or thoughts. This is the Platonic problem of distinguishing sophists, statesmen, and philosophers. Or more to the point, we have the problematic ambiguity of speaking, writing, and thinking as the labor of sign production (Eco 1976). Here is the philo-

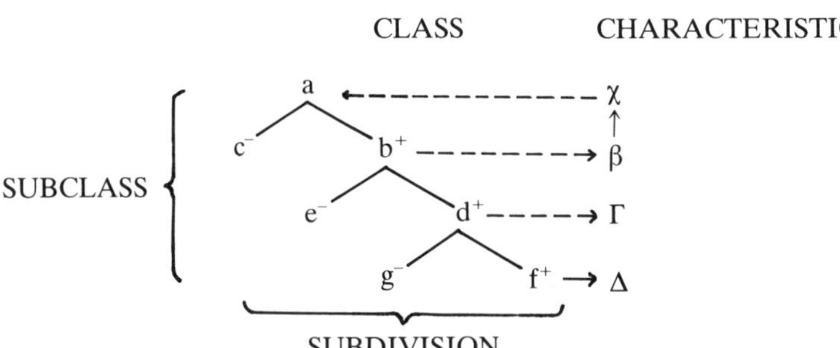

Figure 47. Plato's method of definition by genus (CLASS) *and differentia (CHARACTERISTIC)*

Sd: Writing (Text)

<table>
<tr><td>Sr
Verbal Form</td><td colspan="3">Sd
Bodily Form</td></tr>
<tr><td></td><td colspan="2">Sr
Name</td><td>Sd
Description</td></tr>
<tr><td></td><td>Sr
Knowledge</td><td>Sd
Essential Reality</td><td></td></tr>
</table>

Figure 48. Lanigan extrapolation of Barthes's model applied to the Platonic categories

<table>
<tr><td colspan="3">Sr: Discourse
(consciousness)</td><td colspan="3">Sd: Writing
(experience)</td></tr>
<tr><td colspan="3">Sr
Verbal Form
(particular quality)</td><td colspan="3">Sd
Bodily Form</td></tr>
<tr><td>Sr
Name</td><td colspan="2">Sd
Description</td><td colspan="2">Sr
Name</td><td>Sd
Description</td></tr>
<tr><td></td><td>Sr
Know-
ledge</td><td>Sd
Essential
Reality</td><td>Sr
Know-
ledge</td><td>Sd
Essential
Reality</td><td></td></tr>
</table>

Figure 49. Lanigan model for Platonic categories: Discourse and writing

sophic issue. Barthes (1968) resolves the ambiguity by choosing *writing* as a *context* that punctuates both speaking and writing as choice procedures (Lemert 1979). Plato, on the other hand, suggests, as a communication theorist might, that we probably should choose thinking to contextualize speaking and writing (the philosopher's method of maieutic). Or perhaps a second Platonic choice would be to select speaking as a context for writing and thinking (the sophist's method in rhetoric).

Let me digress slightly to indicate that in the *Sophist* Plato suggests that speaking can produce many differential qualities, so that just as we might perceive that the speech of philosophers is like the speech of the gods (which for Plato is a correct assessment), we may mistake the pedagogical speech of sophists for those speakers (ideologues) who engage in eristic. As distinguished from philosophers and sophists, Plato has no label to mark the eristic practitioners (see Figure 48), who are mere bodily forms for whom there is no verbal form—that is, they have no *name*, because the description of their acts is not produced by any knowledge of essential reality. These "ideologues," as I call them, are embodiments of eristic. They are speakers (particular quality) who are marked by their skill at deception (a denial of essential reality). Yet philosophers, sophists, and statesmen (Kerferd 1981) are speakers (essential reality) who are to a degree skilled at knowing (particular quality). Barthes's notion of "myth" seems to be an exemplar of Plato's notion of eristic where "III SIGN" (Figure 43) is identical to "bodily form" (Figure 48). In the present context, however, to make the extension that the concept of "text" becomes the "verbal form" attached to the "bodily form" is an error (Figure 49). It is to confuse the very production of ideology with rhetoric (Sallis 1975, pp. 110–17).

We might speculate that we now also have an explanation for why Barthes's (1967) "writing degree zero" or "third meaning" is so difficult to detect as an explicit object of production (an "essential reality"); or why Lévi-Strauss avoids contemporary social analysis (Charbonnier 1969; Lévi-Strauss 1967, p. 49).

With this comparison between Barthes and Plato and with my assertion that Plato's dialectic should be the received logical interpretation, I now turn to the argument that Plato offers for the justification of maieutic.

THE *SOPHIST*

The *Sophist* stands as a ready illustration of Burnyeat's (1979, p. 56) comment that "Plato's dialogues are a miraculous blend of philosophical imagination and logic." On the one hand, the *Sophist* entices us to contemplate how we know things by looking to our experience with those persons who articulately profess imagination—that is, the sophist, statesman, and philosopher. There is a hint of argument by degree in this approach whereby Plato uses the personae of the dialogue to display a scale (of distinctions) of knowable experience. The dialogue opens with Theodorus, a mathematician, introducing the Eleatic Stranger (a philosopher who knows the sophistic method) to Socrates, who spontaneously mistakes the Stranger for a god in playful recognition of the demeanor that a philosopher should have.

Art in its fundamental sense is the practice of knowledge that begins with the gods and has its first reflection in number, the art of mathematics. So philosophers, who are like gods in the practice of knowing, must be skilled in the *logos* of *logos*—that is, the understanding of *collection* and *division*. Hence from the perspective of the dialogue personae, we know that the analysis of knowledge (Figure 47) will proceed by the philosopher's ability (the art of distinction) to combine and divide the characteristics of the sophist (representing the acquisitive arts) from those of the statesman (representing the productive arts). In short, the personae represent an analogue logic of degree in which the choice of the philosopher prescribes a context belonging differentially to the sophist or the statesman. This binary analogue model of choice/context construction is, strictly speaking, our contemporary understanding of communication theory (Runciman 1973, pp. 200–201; Lanigan 1979b; Marcus 1974).

On the other hand, the *Sophist* shows a concern with logic as separate from philosophical imagination. In Plato's phrase, there is "the art of discerning or discriminating" (226c). It is clear that Plato assigns the *art of controversy* to the sophist (232b) and the *art of imitation* to the philosopher (235b). The logical approach indicates one kind of knowledge that can be distinguished from another, so the kind of dialectic used by the sophist can be contrasted with that used by the philosopher. Within the context of dialectic possibilities (Sallis, 1975, p. 478), speakers make choices in discourse that display "controversy" (that which is over against, in opposition to, *logos*) or "imitation" (that which is identical). As opposed to "controversy," which is digital (Prior 1979), "imitation" is binary by degree in either "likeness" (235d) or "semblance" (236b).

In contemporary terminology, Plato is asserting the conditions required by information theory, in which digital choices ascribe a context of choice. That is, the formulation reads: *either x or y* is true *in context z*. One makes a particular choice in a preestablished context; a context of choice predicates a choice in context (Lanigan 1979b). Thus, Plato's notion of "controversial" choice is parallel to the technical concept of information "bit," whereas the idea of "imitation" is akin to "redundancy" (see Figure 39).

Plato undertakes to explore the differences between Being and Not-Being, philosopher and sophist, by exploring the binary oppositions that are discovered in the image (bodily form) that the sophist projects through *discourse* (see Figure 46). Plato's goal is to demonstrate that the *Being* (bodily form) of the sophist can be discovered in his discourse (verbal form), which is produced by the "name" and "description" that can be the "knowledge" we have of the "essential reality" in question. This procedure (Hunt 1921) is the famous academic method (derived from Plato's use of Socratic maieutic in the Academy) of definition by genus and difference (Figure 47). Taylor provides a concise summary of the method:

> In principle the procedure is this. If we wish to define a species x, we begin by taking some wider and familiar class a of which x is clearly one subdivision. We then devise a division of the whole class a into two mutually exclusive sub-classes b and c, distinguished by the fact that b possesses, while c lacks, some characteristic β which we know to be found in x. We call b the right-hand, c the left-hand, division of a. We now leave the left-hand division c out of consideration, and proceed to subdivide the right-hand division b on the same principle as before, and this process is repeated until we come to a right-hand "division" which we see on inspection to coincide with x. If we now assign the original wider class a and enumerate in order the successive characters by which each of the successive right-hand divisions has been marked off, we have a complete characterization of x; x has been defined [1956, p. 377].

Plato begins his maieutic analysis by saying of the sophist, "He is clearly a man of art" (219a). The investigation is rather long and involved, and I shall not trace it out, because Sallis (1975) provides an excellent schematic illustration (Figure 50), and because this analysis by division is abandoned as merely a discovery of *logos* instead of the sought definition of knowledge—that is, a *logos* of *logos*. But it is important to list the defining characteristics of the sophist that Plato discovers. First, the sophist uses flattery. Second, he is a merchant of knowledge regarding virtue. Third, he uses the knowledge of others as a merchant. Fourth, he makes use of one's own knowledge of virtue. Fifth, the sophist makes money by teaching argumentation. And sixth, the sophist is skilled in the educational practice of cross-questioning.

Unfortunately, as I indicated, this analysis proves inadequate. It is apparent that Plato, in the person of the Eleatic Stranger who conducts us through this long division, is thinking as an information theorist. His digital choices of names and descriptions turn out to be only a *context of choice*, rather than choice per se. Thus it is painfully obvious to Plato that the six characteristics belong to the philosopher as well as to the sophist. There is no difference in contextual kind between the philosopher and the sophist. As Plato argues, there is only a difference of degree—for instance, let us take the fifth characteristic whereby the sophist makes money by argumentation and the philosopher is seen to lose money in the same way!

Plato's judgment is that the analysis has gone astray because it started with the division of characteristics from the perspective of "controversy"—that is, a digital division. Instead, we should start again with the perspective of "imitation" as the basis for a new series of divisions that in fact are "collections." In short, Plato shifts the dialectic into a binary analogue form of combinatory logic in which a *choice of context* is made—that is, the communication theory perspective: *both x and y* are true *of context z*. This is to say, a choice of context gives context in choice (Lanigan 1979b). Thus, certain pairs of defining characteristics will be *both* present (a collection) *and* separate from each other (a division). For example, Plato suggests the typical dilemma of the information theorist: things must be said to be *either* hot *or* cold. This is not a paradox for the communication theorist, who realizes that the Being of things can possess *both* hot *and* cold in any given situation, that is, differentiation by combination (243b).

It is clear to Plato that one should not mistake a difference of kind for a distinction by degree. This is to say, a collection is a difference by contiguity (a distinction and combination) that entails a difference by division (a distinction by disjunction and separation), because the reverse implication disallows a process presence—that is, a separation cannot lead to a concrete combination. Foucault writes:

> In this sense, the diagnosis does not establish the fact of our identity by the play of distinctions. It establishes that we are difference, that our reason is the difference of discourses, our history the difference of times, ourselves the difference of masks. That difference, far from being the forgotten and recovered origin, is this disperson that we are and make [1972, p. 131; see 1977, pp. 35–36].

The same point is made by Peirce (Savan 1976, p. 16) who says, "a sign is something by knowing which we know something more."[10]

Plato confirms the basis for his new choice of division grounded in collection by taking up the problem of distinguishing among *Being*, *One*, and *Whole* (244d). He discovers that the collection "Being-One-Whole" is found in the division of both "Being-Whole" and "One," where the collection "Being-Whole" is a division of both "Being" and "Whole." Plato is quite explicit (253–58) in suggesting that the binary analogue logic of communication theory is the dialectic discourse that identifies both the sophist and the philosopher as opposed to those who practice eristic—

10. I am indebted to Professor Luis Perez, University of Saskatchewan, for bringing this point to my attention.

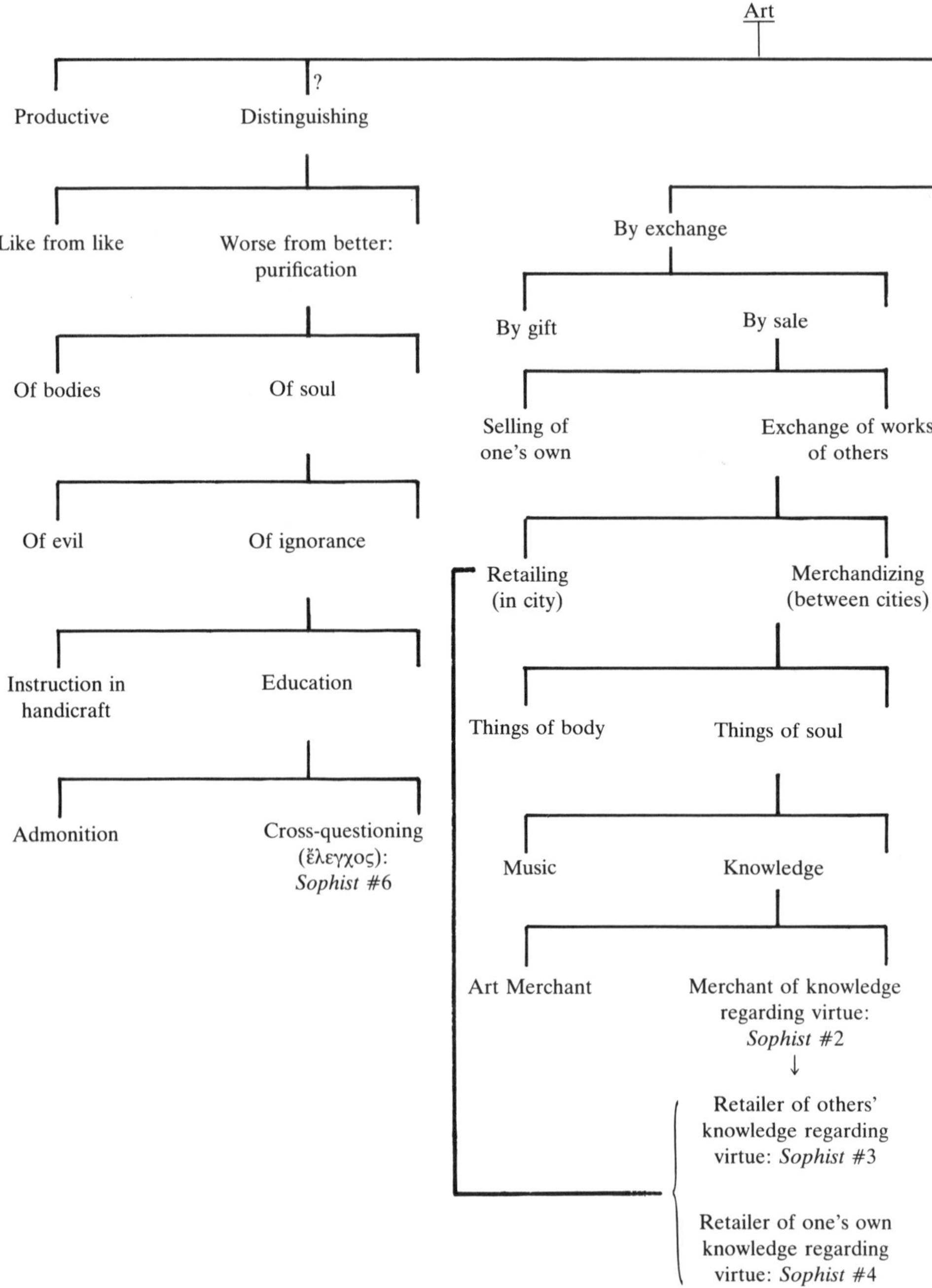

Figure 50. The preliminary divisions from Sallis (1975: 470–471)

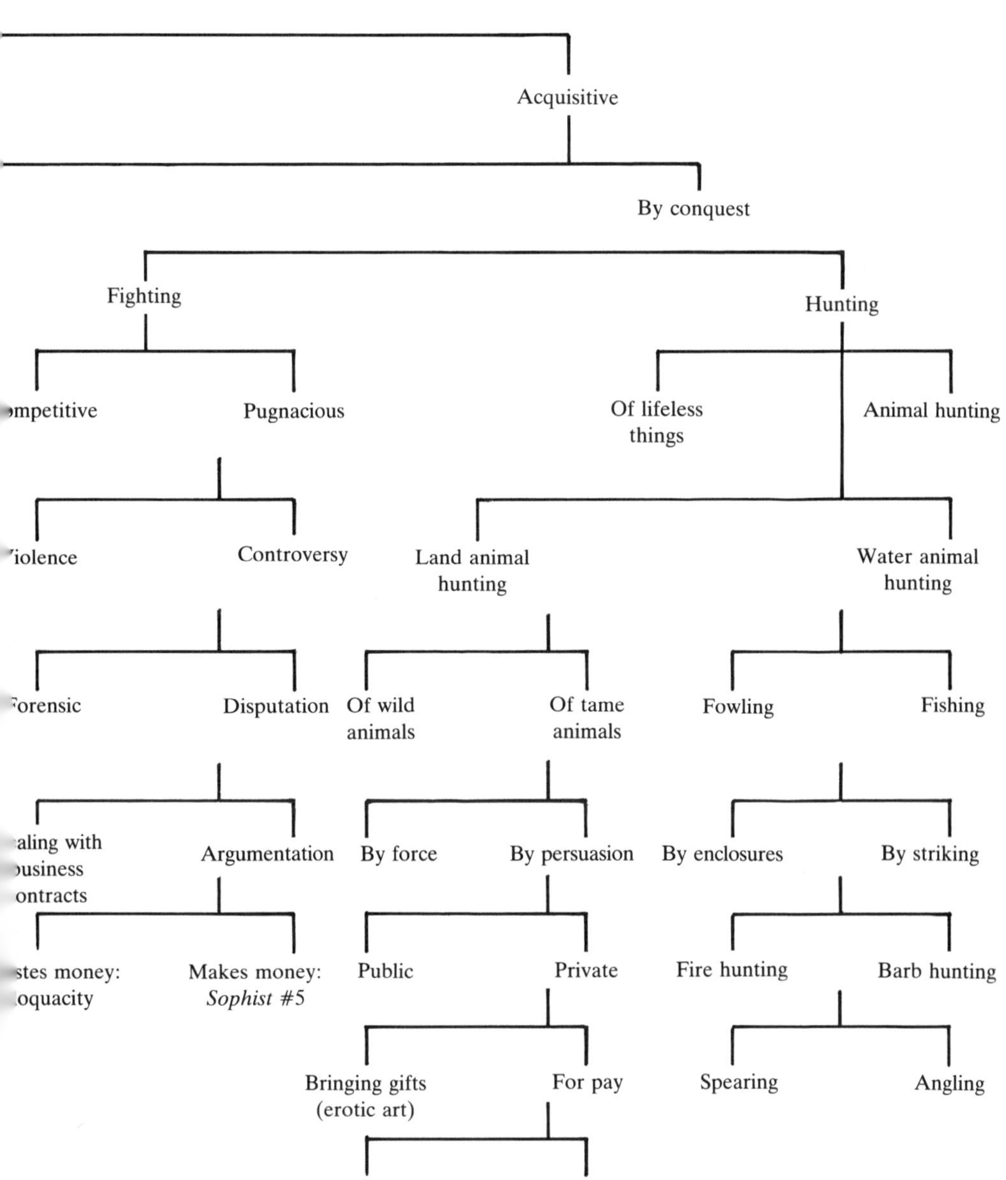
Acquisitive
By conquest
Fighting
Hunting
ɒmpetitive
Pugnacious
Of lifeless things
Animal hunting
'iolence
Controversy
Land animal hunting
Water animal hunting
'orensic
Disputation
Of wild animals
Of tame animals
Fowling
Fishing
ːaling with ɔusiness ontracts
Argumentation
By force
By persuasion
By enclosures
By striking
stes money: ɔquacity
Makes money: Sophist #5
Public
Private
Fire hunting
Barb hunting
Bringing gifts (erotic art)
For pay
Spearing
Angling
Flattery
Sophist #1

that is, "ideologues" who rely on the use of information theory to invent their knowledge (Kerferd 1981, pp. 59ff.).

Plato proceeds to an elaborate proof of his thinking by showing how the conditions of *Being*, *Movement*, *Rest*, *Same*, and *Other* combine and divide. In brief, he argues that being and not-being become mutual proofs of each other by their status as binary boundaries that punctuate knowledge (Figure 51). The proof recognizes two oppositional pairs: *Movement* and *Rest*; and *Same* and *Other*. Either one or the other in each pair is recognized as the Being against which the Not-Being is contrasted when one member of the pair is initially selected as a defining characteristic. For example, in the pair Movement/Rest we could select Movement as characteristic of Being. In turn, Rest is thereby equally characteristic of Not-Being (i.e., not being in motion). Thus, we discover that the Being and Not-Being of Movement is the *Same*, and that the Being and Not-Being of Rest is *Other* than Movement (Sallis, 1975, pp. 514ff.).

Plato's basic illustration for his argument is *language*, where he reviews many of these logical features in terms of language at both the phonological and syntactical levels. And he offers a review of language in terms of paradigmatic and syntagmatic shifts—that is, the analogue function of the *One* and the *Many* (253d–e). It is plain that the competence of the philosopher matches the performance of the sophist (253b). The speaking subject is the source of Being (263a–e). As proof, Plato offers a comparison between the following sentences:

(1) "Theaetetus sits."

(2) "Theaetetus, whom I am talking to at this moment, flies."

Plato tells us that several judgments are possible. First, as Theaetetus remarks about both utterances: "They are about me and belong to me." Hence, (1) is true and (2) is false. And we know that the second utterance is one of the shortest that conforms to the definition of a sentence. The first contains both *name* and *description* in Being, whereas the second prescribes Being in the *person* of Theaetetus ("whom I am talking to at this moment"), not-being in his *name*, "Theaetetus," which is true, and Not-Being in his *description* ("flies"), which is false.

It may be helpful to review this example with the aid of Figure 49. The first sentence *divides* discourse (Sr: verbal form) and the person of Theaetetus (Sd: bodily form); Not-Being (Sr) is combined with Being (Sd). By contrast, the second sentence *combines* discourse and the person (Sr: verbal form and bodily form); Being (Sr) is distinguished from Not-Being (Sd: "flies"). The word "flies" becomes the bodily form of Not-Being. Recall Barthes's comment about myth as things that are speech! Thus, Plato establishes the dialectic of collection and division as conditions of Being and Not-Being that are mediated by the *speaking*

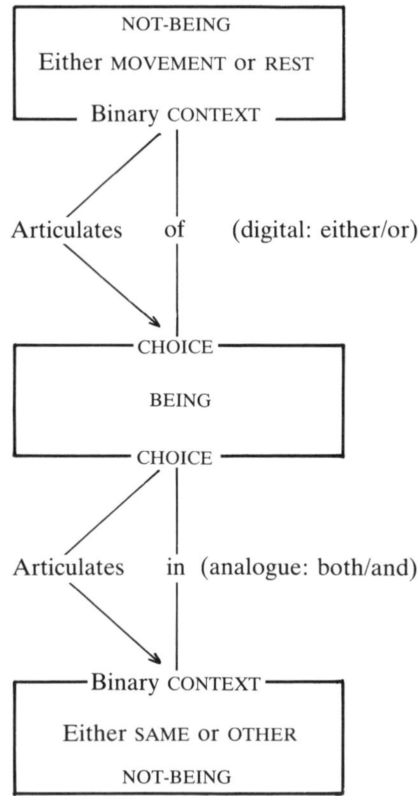

Figure 51. Plato's entailment of communication theory and information theory in the categories of Being/Not-Being, Movement/Rest, and Same/Other

subject, not by language. Mediation by language is myth. As Taylor remarks:

> The satisfaction of these conditions depends on our native acumen and our acquaintance with the subject-matter, and no rules can be given for it, precisely as no rules can be given for the discovery of a promising explanatory hypothesis. The method, like all scientific methods, will not work *in vacuo* [1956, p. 377].

Thus does Plato remark that "to rob us of discourse would be to rob us of philosophy" (260a).

There is more to note here. We have an illustration of how the philosopher and the sophist use thinking to produce discourse. The reverse, using discourse for thinking, is eristic—that is, bad philosophy and bad sophistry. Indeed, eristic is the crime for which Socrates stands falsely condemned. The *Sophist* explains the philosopher's method and hence the innocence of Socrates. In accord with the quest for a *logos* of *logos*, the explanation comes through the last-minute speaking of a sophistic philosopher, the Eleatic Stranger!

Thus far in this chapter, I compared Plato's model of discourse analysis to that of Barthes (1968). Second, I indicated certain errors in structuralist thinking in Barthes's analysis by reexamining the detailed argument that Plato gives in the *Sophist* with respect to the method of discursive analysis. I should now like briefly to suggest the way in which Merleau-Ponty (1962) builds on the Platonic argument by utilizing the speaking subject as the source of sign production to combine the methods of semiology and phenomenology.

MERLEAU-PONTY AND SEMIOTIC PHENOMENOLOGY

Discourse, according to Barthes (1968), exists on the levels of connotation, denotation (metalanguage), and the real system. The object of his structural analysis is *language (langue)* or its artifacts: *text* and *myth*. By comparison, Merleau-Ponty's (1962) phenomenological analysis takes the consciousness of the person as the object of analysis (see chap. 7 above). The result is the development of a model of analysis consisting of (1) description, (2) reduction, and (3) interpretation (Lanigan 1972; see chap. 1 above).

Utilizing this method, I now want to construct a model of discourse that is a semiotic phenomenology. By describing the key features that Plato offers to us and reducing them to essential characteristics in the comparison between Barthes and Plato, I generate a hermeneutic of discourse for the speaking subject. In this model (Figure 52), there are two reversible commutation systems: (1) the *reflective system* of the signifier (Sr) and (2) the *prereflective system* of the signified (Sd). Each system has three levels (boundaries): the punctuation of *expression* (comparable to Barthes's "connotation"), the punctuation of *perception* (comparable to "denotation"), and the punctuation of *meaning* (comparable to "real system"). These three paradigmatic levels exist in both the Sr and Sd systems.

The signifier system of *reflection* illustrates the phenomenological perspective that discourse is a production of the *speaking* subject. In this system, *expression* is the *self-experience* that is constituted by *consciousness of self* or, in Platonic terms, expression is the "particular quality" of verbal form that is *named* in the *description* of self (see Figures 49 and 52). Thus, expression is constituted by perception. In turn, *perception* derives from a *meaning* infrastructure that is the *preconscious*. Again in

	Sr: Reflection		Sd: Prereflection	
Expression	Sr Self Experience		Sd Experience of Other	
Perception	Sr Consciousness (of)	Sd Self	Sr Consciousness (of)	Sd Other
Meaning		Sr Sd Preconscious	Sr Sd Unconscious	

Figure 52. Semiotic phenomenology of human communication. Vertical relationships display communication theory: analogue choice, binary coding, metaphor, symbol, and paradigmatic/synchronic condition. Horizontal relationships display information theory: digital choice, binary coding, metonymy, sign, and syntagmatic/diachronic condition

Platonic terms, the preconscious is equivalent to the knowledge I have of an essential reality. We can see that the phenomenological method of Merleau-Ponty (1962) has the same logical structure as the Platonic dialectic. That is, the methodological *description* of self-experience is *reduced* to consciousness of self, which allows the *interpretation* of what has meaning in the preconscious. Recall Plato's method of analysis for oral sentences (1) and (2) above.

Where Plato and Merleau-Ponty differ is the ontological status of the *maieutic*. For Merleau-Ponty (1962) discourse is a proof of the person, the speaking subject, as the incarnation of consciousness. For Plato the analysis shows that the person is an image [bodily form] of an ideal form ("essential reality") that is true.[11] For Plato this image can be known through discourse that is oral (knowledge)—that is, an oral report of what was said (understanding), or written (opinion). But writing converts the "essential reality" into a "particular quality"—that is, writing as an instrument replaces the "person as instrument" just as mimicry of another uses the voice as an instrument to replace my discourse (266d–267e). Opinion is mistaken for knowledge in writing.

Eco (1976, p. 171) illustrates the semantic sense in which propositional meaning requires a *perceptum* from the communicative point of view of an addressee, which is precisely the point of Plato's view that writing

11. Edmund Husserl's phenomenology, with its emphasis on the transcendental Ego, would be compatible with the Platonic ontology in a way that Merleau-Ponty's existential phenomenology clearly is not. It is also important to recall that the Greeks did not have our ontological tendency to separate signifiers and signifieds: 'Even a non-human object can, in the archaic period, take on a life of its own—as when an inscription on a pot reads "I greet you"' (Havelock 1978, p. 99).

requires (erroneously) the reader to invent, rather than discover, a *perceptum*. Sebeok and Rosenthal (1981) ingeniously point to this same principle (historically found in magic acts of the theater) as the "clever Hans" fallacy in scientific research procedures. Thus although Plato and Merleau-Ponty differ on the ontological status of persons and discourse, they are agreed that discourse, not language, is a dialectic knowledge of the person.

The signified system of *prereflection* illustrates the phenomenological view that subjectivity in discourse must be viewed as intersubjectivity. That is, in the Sr system, expression comes from the *speaking* subject (experience of self), which entails that expression in the Sd system is the speaking *subject* (experience of other). For Plato this is simply another way of suggesting that Being is founded in Not-Being. Or from the linguistic point of view, it is Saussure's distinction between *parole* (*speaking* subject) and *langue* (speaking *subject*). The Sd system of *prereflection* is thereby the experience of the *other*, which is constituted by the *consciousness* I have of the *other*. Or in Platonic terms (Figure 49), experience of an other (bodily form) is *named* by my conscious *description* of the other. Expression of the other is constituted by my perception. In turn, consciousness derives from the grounding of the *unconscious*. In Platonic terms (265b–266d) the unconscious is equivalent to the knowledge we have of an object's absence in essential reality. Or more precisely, we have the Not-Being of Being as Same or Other (Figure 51). In a phenomenological perspective the unconscious is the Not-Being of my consciousness or Being. In turn, this knowledge of my being at the meaning level of the Sd system allows me to constitute the perception level in which my consciousness (Being) constitutes the other (Not-Being [of me]).

Foucault provides a concrete illustration of the present analysis in his discussion of the therapeutic force of imitation in "theatrical representations":

> The fulfillment of delirium's non-being in being is able to suppress it as non-being itself; and this by the pure mechanism of its internal contradiction—a mechanism that is both a play on words and a play of illusion, games of language and of the image; the delirium, in effect, is suppressed as non-being since it becomes perceived as a form of being; but since the being of delirium is entirely in its non-being, it is suppressed as delirium. And its confirmation in theatrical fantasy restores it to a truth which, by holding it captive in reality, derives it out of reality itself, and makes it disappear in the non-delirious discourse of reason [1965, p. 191].

Foucault's analysis, interestingly enough, draws on a previous exploration (see chap. 5 above) by Merleau-Ponty (1962, pp. 291, 334) of the place of the rationality of the speaking subject in the problematic of hallucination and delirium (Levin 1979; Lanigan 1979c).

I trust that it is apparent at this point that Merleau-Ponty adopts Saussure's concept of, and Jakobson's elaboration of (Holenstein 1976), paradigmatic/synchronic and syntagmatic/diachronic shifts to illustrate the reversibility of analysis that occurs at each level of the system. That is, expression, perception, and meaning in the Sr or Sd system are paradigmatic/synchronic shifts, and there is a simultaneous syntagmatic/diachronic shift between Sr and Sd expression, Sr and Sd perception, and Sr and Sd meaning. I illustrate this process in Figure 53 by citing

<table>
<tr><td></td><td colspan="2">Sr: Consciousness</td><td colspan="2">Sd: Experience</td></tr>
<tr><td>DESCRIPTION
[Expression]</td><td colspan="2">Sr
Parole
(speaking)</td><td colspan="2">Sd
Langue
(social language)</td></tr>
<tr><td>REDUCTION
[Perception]</td><td>Sr
Parole
(speech)</td><td>Sd
Parlante
(speaking)</td><td>Sn
Parole
(speech)</td><td>Sd
Parlée
(spoken)</td></tr>
<tr><td>INTERPRETATION
[Meaning]</td><td></td><td>Sr Sd
Corps Propre
(person: lived-body)</td><td>Sr Sd
Geste
(gesture: body-lived)</td><td></td></tr>
</table>

Figure 53. Merleau-Ponty's model of human discourse. All relationships are combinatory; this is critical to recall with reference to 'parole parlante' and 'parole parlée'.

Merleau-Ponty's categories as they constitute a semiotic phenomenology of discourse—that is, a *communicology*. I have detailed Merleau-Ponty's philosophy of communication in chapter 3, above. It informs the content of the schematic in Figure 53 (Lanigan 1970; 1972; 1977; 1979).

In brief summary, let me say that the *Sophist* provides a *maieutic* analysis of philosophical imagination that in large part we methodologically recognize as the contemporary school of *existential phenomenology*. At the same time, however, the dialogue also gives us a discussion of the logic in human conscious experience that we may readily call the human science of *semiology*. Indeed, the very argument that I am making for the existence of a *semiotic phenomenology of discourse in the speaking subject* (*corps propre*) comes from the mouth of the Eleatic Stranger, who tells us: "Knowledge is also surely one, but each part of it that commands a certain field is marked off and given a special name proper to itself. Hence language [discourse] recognizes many arts and forms of knowledge" (257d).

Chapter Eighteen

The Convention of "Conventions"

A Phenomenological Reflection on the Ideological Practice of Discourse in Professional Mass Communication

Human communication, both as a concept and as practiced, is arbitrary and conventional. Communication is *arbitrary* at the personal and social level because the currently used concepts and behavior displays could be different. Although concept and behavior are not individually determined, they do arise through some personal choice process. Concept and behavior are *conventional* because they are commonly understood and preserved in society with sufficient uniformity to be available to the next generation as theory and praxis (McFeat 1974). This uniformity is precisely what Znaniecki (1969, p. 137) calls the "humanistic coefficient."

Exactly because of this arbitrary and conventional nature, communication both as a concept and behavior is inherently ideological. Both the idea and action develop at a particular point in time, in a particular culture, and within particular theories, and are retained to the exclusion of potential competing concepts and behaviors, as discussed in chapter 6, above. Both the concept and behavior interconnect with beliefs and values that make up our particular social milieu. The particular ideological commitments implied in our everyday action and interaction are usually taken for granted as the standard background practices from which we constitute our engagements with other persons (Bourdieu 1977).

To follow Karl Mannheim, the term "ideology" is the most appropriate for describing this constituted communication background (Brown 1978, p. 16). As he indicates: "There is implicit in the word 'ideology' the insight that in certain situations the collective unconscious of certain groups obscures the real conditions of the society both to itself and to others and thereby stabilizes it." (See chaps. 9 and 16).

Speech communication conference/conventions, though being special contexts for mass communication, are like everyday interaction in their conventionality and implied ideological commitments. This conventionality, like that of everyday life, assures a reasonable amount of unreflected orderly discourse, but systematically distorts experience in favor of certain kinds of ideas and activities over others (Johnson et al. 1982).

In this chapter I wish to characterize this type of discourse as the convention (discourse; practice) that takes place at a convention (meeting)—a phenomenological description. In other words, my analysis seeks to display the conventionality of convention discourse. In so doing, I critically deconstruct the ideological commitments of speech communication conventions (meetings) and look at the particular type of experiences these commitments self-select for the participants—a phenomenological reduction. Last, I discuss a more appropriate ideological basis for professional meetings as a critical form for mass communication—a phenomenological interpretation (i.e., the "mass" critically considered as the "communicative community" that it is [Apel 1981]). In order to explicate my thesis, I begin with a discussion of ideology, conventionality, and conventions.

IDEOLOGY AND CONVENTIONALITY

In a general sense, *ideology* is a systematic body of concepts arising within culture, which describe or explain culture or, more particularly, human life. In the particular sense in which I am interested, ideology is a set of behavioral practices reflexively used to describe or explain themselves (O'Sullivan et al. 1983, p. 107; see Ritter 1979). As Habermas (1979) explains, "In filling out the double structure of speech, participants in dialogue communicate on two levels simultaneously. They combine communication of a content with communication about a role in which the communicated content is used" (p. 42).

Note that Habermas is not describing the relationship between a metalanguage and an object-language (Lyons 1977). Rather his concern is for the creative or productive element in communication that is *performance* (Merleau-Ponty 1962, p. 383; see Nelson 1986). When a person communicates with another person, there is a performance such that the act of saying something both says something and produces the context (audience, situation) in which it can be said.

The double structure of action and conception is based on, but conceals, ideological commitments. Ideology represents the unexplicated normative behavior of individuals whose communication is constituting their society as a culture (see chap. 6 above). Or, to be particular to my immediate concerns, a person who reads a paper at a professional meeting helps to constitute a select society whose values include being learned. For the professoriat, a less anxiety-provoking example is the rhetoric of town meetings (Potter 1957).

In an unsophisticated sense, *convention* is thought of as a rule of conduct. As a historical criterion, in the study of convention, a distinction is made between conduct that is (1) constituted and/or (2) regulated by rules (Lanigan 1977). But in understanding conventions, this constitutive/regulative distinction falls victim to the same type of analysis that Habermas warns against in the object-language/metalanguage distinction. More accurately, personal behavior becomes a social performance (by constitutive rules) that is simultaneously controlled by cultural expectations (in regulative rules). Thus, the focal concern is once again the double structure of communication. I shall use the term *conventionality* to refer to an *adherence* to rules of conduct by participants.

Conventionality displays a double structure inasmuch as any communication that occurs simultaneously confirms its legitimate value by comparison to past behaviors of a similar nature and function (Verón 1971). Hence, a precedent is confirmed. "Indeed, precedent is merely the source of one important kind of salience: conspicuous uniqueness of an equilibrium because we reached it last time" (Lewis 1969, p. 36). To put it more simply, a state of conventionality occurs where and when a regularity in performances is manifest. Such a regularity is the creative or productive process that links the individual act (constitutive rules) to the social—that is, intersubjective—conception (regulative rules).

Having laid out the grounds for understanding ideology and conventionality, I can now turn to conventional ideologies. This is to say, I can expose the salient features of the annual professional conference commonly known as the *convention*. To a certain extent, my goal is to demythologize the communicative behaviors that are produced and consumed as the process of creating meaning between communicology professionals in such ecosystems as the annual (or better yet, the international fifth-year) meeting of the International Communication Association, or similar "professional" and "academic" associations.

Inasmuch as convention (meeting) forms are generally assumed rather than made explicit, it should be useful to spend a moment comparing some alternative ecosystems (Wilden 1980), principally to be found in the history of European practice. Alternative models are important because they display ideological conventionality that offers some context for looking at convention forms by negative definition (Foucault 1972). That is, we may find out what we do and why, by looking at what could be done (but is *not*—Foucault's concept of *exclusion*) and the reasons for it. To be specific, let us compare professional gatherings that are variously called a *symposium*, a *conference*, and a *congress* (see Figure 54).

In developing a sense of ideological conventionality, I begin with the symposium and culminate with the congress for reasons that will become apparent. Because I am dealing with an ideological conventionality, I am in the peculiar position of attempting to describe what we do by doing it, a sort of performing performance (Peterson 1980). However, for the conceptually oriented in our ecosystem, I refer you to the O.E.D. for documentation of the relevant terms.

A *symposium* is a specially called meeting for the purpose of discussing a common subject. In particular, it is a meeting, organized around a special topic, which attempts to locate some common ground among diverse participants. In short, the symposium is a problem-centered gathering, rather than the product of a special interest group as typically found *within* a discipline. If you like, a symposium is usually an attempt to get conflicting interests resolved for the common good.

As a frequent practice, the symposium is as much a social as professional event, often facilitated by the abundant drinking of special beverages—if you remember your Platonic dialogues. In the typical convention, drinks tend to signal the switch from problem— to social-centered talk. The conventional success model follows the practice of the "business cocktail" where making contacts for some future discussion is facilitated by the drink rather than an enhancement of the present experience.[12]

A *conference* is a more formal version of the symposium. It is still a problem-centered meeting, but one cast within the limits of a given discipline. The basic idea of a conference is consultation and discussion by persons who have a special interest in formulating the boundaries of a particular problematic. Once the problem has been stated, work on a solution can begin.

One possible approach to the conference is a dialectic one. In this model the attempt is to put aside the particular characteristics of the participants in an effort to reach a common understanding. Thus, the problem can be stated in such a manner that a solution can be found or at least criteria for a solution can be stated. The hope is that a group can reason through reality to reach some certainty as to which solution is correct.

12. An interesting illustration is the dilemma of the City Council in Carbondale, Illinois that voted to change the name of its proposed "convention center" to "conference center" since the facility was *not* intended for large, national groups who would require extensive hotel, drinking, and eating accommodations. However, the "conference center" was duly re-renamed the "convention center" when it was discovered that federal tax legislation does not permit the public funding of anything except a "convention center" (Tax Rule, 1984).

INSTITUTION	PERSPECTIVE	DEGREE	RESEARCH REPORTING [1 to 9 hierarchy; A to B causality]					
			A. WRITING FORMS			B. SPEAKING FORMS		
			Topics	Issues	Relationships	Topics	Issues	Relationships
Scholar	Personal	B.A. B.S.	Abstract 1–A	Précis 4–A	Prospectus 7–A	Recitation 1–B	Course 4–B	Symposium 7–B
Profession	Communal	M.A. M.S.	Research Report 2–A	Thesis 5–A	Dissertation 8–A	Tutorial 2–B	Seminar 5–B	Conference 8–B
Discipline	Social	Ph.D. D.Sc.	Article 3–A	Monograph 6–A	Book 9–A	Lecture 3–B	Proseminar 6–B	Congress 9–B

Figure 54. The Structure of research reporting. The structure is followed closely by European scholars, largely because of the paradigmatic organization of the University of Paris in the 13th Century and its German successors in the 14th and 15th Centuries. The structure is relatively unknown to American (USA) scholars and is seldom followed with any understanding of its intent as a communication channel. (See Overfield 1984 and Ferruolo 1985)

In the convention (as opposed to the symposium or conference) discussion is primarily rhetorical, rather than dialectical (Rosenfield et al. 1976, pp. 234–38). At conventions, solution upon solution is offered for an ill-stated and often obscured or forgotten problem. The speaker's presence, academic credentials, past research, and research design are marshaled together to make a case for the acceptance of one of the solutions. Both the content and process differ in (1) a dialectic process aimed at understanding (in symposia and conferences) or (2) in a rhetorical process aimed at agreement (in conventions). Ideology is clear in this differentiation (Habermas 1984).

Finally, a *congress* is a formal assembly of specialists to settle some outstanding question. Congresses are not annual affairs, they are frequently held in four-year cycles—like the World Congress of Philosophy—so that breakthroughs in special disciplines can be announced. The main purpose of the congress is to detail the manner in which the specific solution can be applied to concrete, secondary problems. Europeans who attend congresses expect to come away with new technical information that will enable them to finally resolve practical problems.

The popular press occasionally prints findings reported at the last "convention," but they are rarely conclusions or breakthroughs. Usually it has to do with an isolated study using a method or making an unusual statement about an old subject that the reporter found interesting or at least thought the reader or listening audience would. Rather than blame the reporter, it would appear that the reporter is true to conventionality behavior.

To sum up, the models of the symposium, the conference, and the congress differ from the convention in that the participants in these first three types of meetings are interested in producing concrete experience, whereas convention-goers are interested in consuming it. A convention is an *association*, a meeting place of persons rather than ideas, and it is the interaction of persons, not ideas, that stands out as interesting. The association is with "famous" persons with the hope that there is magic in knowing them by name, rather than an encounter with great ideas where we first remember what was said, and then who said it (see chap. 17, above).

All this is not to suggest that every professional association should have a "congress." I only wish to make clearer what a convention is by contrasting it with other forms of professional meetings. We choose to have conventions for practical-social-cultural-historical reasons. Those who attended the first (and as yet only) ICA World Congress on Communication Science in Berlin might recall reporters waiting outside for a session to end. At the conclusion, they would ask a panelist what had been concluded. When the American panelist answered that there had been papers on this topic and that topic, neither the panelist nor the reporter had any idea of what to say next. What I am arguing is that the choice of a meeting format is an ideological one (see Figure 38). Now let me turn to the nature of these ideological commitments.

By negative dialectic, the conventional ideology of the American convention (meeting) is precisely convention defined as an ideology. What is the "convention" as an ideology? By a fortunate turn of thinking, the answer is provided in the very context of performing performance—that is, in this case the researching of research:

> Beyond its social and ritualistic functions, the annual convention is important both to the organization which sponsors it and to the members who attend. Ideally, the annual convention provides a rhetorical situation in which the needs of individual members and the needs of the organization meet on common ground. For an organization, the convention offers a mechanism for conducting its business, an opportunity for increasing its membership, and an index of its vitality and strength. For individual members, the convention affords a chance to present their views, enhance their professional expertise, and maintain friendships with colleagues of similar interests [Larson and Hensley 1978, p. 206].

Thus, Larson and Hensley characterize systematically the values present in their study of the Central State Speech Association held in Detroit in April 1977. The convention as a communication event suggests the typicality of conventionality. That is, we find adherence to rules of conduct: "Ideally, the annual convention provides a rhetorical situation in which the needs of individual members and the needs of the organization meet on comon ground." In turn, the typicality of ideology is displayed: "For an organization the convention offers a mechanism for conducting its business" "For individual members the convention affords a chance to present their views."

At this point, the relationship among communication, ideology, and conventionality is fairly explicit as it occurs in the annual convention. In this relationship, we have a coherent picture of *mass communication* as the individual and organizational actions that become the manifest conceptions in such a professional gathering. My concern now is to explore the extension of ideology and conventionality beyond the convention event to the discipline of communicology itself. Although, it might appear at least epigrammatic to speak of this extension as the "spread of conventional wisdom," I shall reserve the term *conventionalism* for this mass communication function, Apel's (1981) *Verständigung*.

CONVENTIONALISM AS IDEOLOGY AND CONVENTIONALITY

The use of the term *conventionalism* is as historically problematic as it is practical to my present explication. The concept is historically "reserved for an attitude to the methodology of natural science" (Kolakowski 1968, p. 158). Nonetheless, the same attitude makes its appearance in the *human sciences* as well. And it is this human science view that interests me. In particular, I am concerned with the method by which ideology and conventionality at a professional convention form the communication values in the discipline generally as an "interpretive community" (*Kommunikationsgemeinschaft*). As might be anticipated, one major reason for this line of analysis is the circular and cumulative nature of professional behavior that leads back to the annual convention.

Our discussion of conventionalism is easier if we examine the standard view in the physical sciences and then translate it into the human science view. In this transformation please recall that I am discussing the *attitude* (ideology) contained in *methodology* (conventionality):

> The fundamental idea of conventionalism may be stated as follows: certain scientific propositions, erroneously taken for descriptions of the world based on the recording and generalization of experiments, are in fact artificial creations, and we regard them as true not because we are compelled to do so for empirical reasons, but because they are convenient, useful, or even because they have aesthetic appeal. Conventionalists agree with empiricism on the origin of knowledge but reject empiricism as a norm that allows us to justify all accepted judgments by appealing to experience, conceived of as a sufficient criterion of their truth. Or, to put the same point somewhat more accurately, the data of experience always leave scope for more than one explanatory hypothesis, and which one is to be chosen cannot be determined by experience. Rival hypotheses accounting for a given aggregate of facts may be equally sound from a logical point of view, and hence our actual choices are accounted for by eidetic (non-empirical) considerations [Kolakowski 1968, pp. 158–59; see J. Berhstein 1978].

The most efficient way to translate this physical science attitude and method into the communicological view of ideology and conventionality as a human science is to briefly cite the theory construction work by Lewis (1969). He offers the following definition (of what I am calling conventionalism), which he confirms analytically using a standard propositional calculus:

> A regularity *R* in the behavior of members of a population *P* when they are the agents in a recurrent situation *S* is a *convention* if and only if it is true

that, and it is common knowledge in *P* that, in almost any instance of *S* among members of *P*,

(1) almost everyone conforms to *R*;
(2) almost everyone expects almost everyone else to conform to *R*;
(3) almost everyone has approximately the same preferences regarding all possible combinations of actions;
(4) almost everyone prefers that any one more conform to *R*, on condition that almost everyone conform to *R*;
(5) almost everyone would prefer that any one more conform to *R′*, on condition that almost everyone conform to *R′*, where *R′* is some possible regularity in the behavior of members of *P* in *S*, such that almost no one in almost any instance of *S* among members of *P* could conform both to *R′* and to *R* [p. 78].

This rather formal explanation of conventionalism should become clear as we look at the five conditions enumerated in the definition. In particular, we can take these conditions and exemplify them in a progressive movement from the phenomenological description of conventionalism as (1) a social form, (2) to the phenomenological reduction of that disciplinary description, and (3) the phenomenological interpretation of the annual convention meeting as a fundamental structure of discourse (see Figure 2).

Conventionalism as a Social Form

I have already discussed the cultural differences between models of the symposium, conference, and congress as opposed to the convention. In all cases, however, there is a common element and that is for Lewis "a regularity *R* in the behavior of members of a population *P* when they are agents in a recurrent situation *S*." The *necessary and sufficient conditions* that constitute the professional meetings under their various methods of problem-stating or -solving is that "(1) almost everyone conforms to *R*" and that "(2) almost everyone expects almost everyone else to conform to *R*."

I can illustrate these two conditions of conventionalism as a *phenomenological description* by recalling that attendance at an American convention is preeminently a social and ritualistic activity.[13] Attendance calls for a certain style of behavior. Styles are considered here as "idioms of knowledge and communication. They suffice for communication in so far

13. A good humorous illustration is the comment in Ian Hay, *Paid with Thanks* (1925, pp. 66–67): "But first let us be clear as to what a convention is. In England the conventions are unwritten rules and regulations which you defy or conform to according to your sense of humor. But a convention in America is a concrete, living, palpitating fact. In England we should call it a conference, or a Beanfest, or a blend of both. . . ." I am indebted to John D. Peters, Stanford University, for this reference.

and for so long as they are understood by convention (*samketa*); elsewhere or at another time, they must be learnt before the art can be deciphered" (Coomarasway 1956, p. 85). Compare, for example, the dress, hotel selection, and climate of Speech Communication Association conventions as compared with those of the International Communication Association (or any two disciplinary associations you care to choose). Compare the technical specialists in the discipline whose styles of professionalism are radically different (e.g., the rhetorical critic and behavioral scientist), yet are at least social equals in one *discipline*. In *symposium form*, the annual convention creates a common ground for communication and other social behavior. The specialists are of the same social form; they conform and expect conformity.

In *conference form*, the annual convention is a rhetorical situation giving the specialist circle a common ground. You must be a technical specialist in this group in order to *confer*. You must have a specific style of adhering to the subject matter and the persons who discuss it. At the annual convention the boundaries of style are present as the various divisions of the professional association. Of course, each division has several programs that take the style to the level of the *congressional form*. Specialists attack a very specific problem, often so that they can become even more methodologically specialized at attacking the problem, rather than solving it in a concrete, applied manner. If we can use the social systems metaphor, the annual convention represents a method of creating meaning in organisms that are themselves constituted by cells (programs), organs (divisions), and systems (regional and national professional associations).

Conventionalism as Disciplinary

The annual convention also establishes and maintains a certain control over participants and subject matter. That is the nature and function of a discipline. As a *phenomenological reduction* in terms of the Lewis model, the third and fourth necessary and sufficient conditions are met. That is, "(3) almost everyone has approximately the same preferences regarding all possible combinations of actions" and "(4) almost everyone prefers that any one more conform to *R*, on condition that almost everyone conform to *R*." Or as we previously noted in the Larson and Hensley (1978) version: "For an organization, the convention offers a mechanism for conducting its business, an opportunity for increasing its membership, and an index of its vitality and strength" (p. 206). A quick mental review of the membership categories in our professional associations, the procedures for holding administrative positions in the association, and the history of the connection between these and annual conventions, gives you a clearer picture of disciplinary conventionality.

What is often less clear is the ideological commitment to consumerism (Lanigan 1981; see chap. 6 above). You begin by purchasing your membership, and frequently that is done as a prerequisite for getting into the annual convention. And then there is good value for money spent by attending the convention. As Larson and Hensley naively suggest in their study, attendance is not random, but is representative of those "persons whose professional interests and/or financial resources warranted their attendance at Detroit. Thus, while the convention-goers may not have been a random sample representative of *all* CSSA members, it is likely that they *did* represent a sample of the most professional, interested, and active persons in the organization." Of course this includes those seeking employment or different employment, recruitment of graduate students, status reports of departments and persons, and the selling of T-shirts and textbooks.

How different this is from a scholarly society whose membership is by invitation or nomination on the basis of research accomplishment and whose conferences are not conventions arranged on the fraternal model of the "Elks," the "Lions," or the "Rotary Club" in American society.

Conventionalism as Recurrent Structure

There is in the annual convention an opportunity to grow and change. The convention is an open system. Yet, it is a system with very specific change conditions that are nicely stated in Lewis's fifth condition for conventionalism as a *phenomenological interpretation*. That is, "(5) almost everyone would prefer that any one more conform to R', on condition that almost everyone conform to R', where R' is some possible regularity in the behavior of members of P in S, such that almost no one in almost any instance of S among members of P could conform both to R' and to R." In more familiar language, Lewis explains formally that if one person is going to do something unexpected, it is permissible if we would all prefer that change to our usual practice. This is the ideology of the buzz word and the "latest" research fad in the "mainstream."

The best illustration of conventionalism as a recurrent structure is the process of making presentations at conventions. Let us suppose you are responsible for chairing a program panel. Such a program is R'; it is a new situation that must have all the structural features of R (the usual program) to be acceptable to the membership (P) at the annual convention (S). Typically there is no problem in mounting such a program, because the new subject matter is plugged into the old structure. The R to R' shift represents more consumption of a familiar product. We experience the same old format with the same old faces. We come to hear Person X "do his thing" again and we judge this year's performance. The competitive selection process, even more clearly than that of the "old boys' club," assures that the free marketplace of ideas will be filled with "new improved" varieties of name brand products. This type of conventionalism enforces a kind of procedural sublimation where having done something in the right way is seen as an adequate substitute for having done something right.

By way of summarizing conventionalism as ideology and conventionality, three distinct empirical relationships emerge under *phenomenological analysis*. These relationships prescribe the ideological constituents of conventionalism as an ideology of mass communication. First, there must be regularity in behavior. Convention participants do the same thing in the same way. Those who do not are devalued by banishment to the nondivisional program. Second, there must be a recurrent population. Those who do not attend regularly are rarely elected to office or appear on a panel. Third, there must be a recurrent situation. Basically this situation is the annual gathering but, more specifically, it is the traditional assignment of three panels to this division, and four to that one, and so on. If you cannot find a division you like, you must look for another association to join. Given these ideological conditions, How do we go about legitimizing our continued involvement in conventionalism? After all, there is a presumption that our activities can be personally and professionally justified.

REFLECTED AND UNREFLECTED IDEOLOGIES

Whether or not we can justify an ideological claim is the precise nature of the contemporary idea of *legitimation*. That is, conventionality leads to the establishment of an ideology, and conversely. In either case, the conjunction of an action and a conception are united as a normative condition or value. The manner in which the union occurs is its justification. As a usual practice, it is possible to distinguish justifications as either reflected or unreflected. Recall that I cited this difference in the very beginning of the paper with Habermas's comment that communication contains the *double structure* of combining content and function in one action. Yet such a communication act may be reflective in that I am aware of the manner in which I am joining content to function. Or the act remains unreflected if it is merely functional or substantive because I am unaware of the method of my manner. Or to put the issue in Hjelmslevian (1961) terms, the communicative action is reflective if it is a *function*, whereas it is unreflective if it is a *functive*.

In their dicussion of "special audiences," Perelman and Olbrechts-Tyteca (1971) point out that the unreflected conventionality and its ideological consequences exist because "there are agreements that are peculiar to the members of a particular discipline, whether it be of scientific or technical, juridical or theological nature. Such agreements constitute the body of a science or technique. They may be the result of certain conventions of adherence to certain texts, and they characterize certain audiences" (p. 99). In particular, such audiences use a technical language that displays "an aggregate of acquired knowledge, rules, and conventions."

The only point at which participation in the discipline is a reflective process is when a person initially joins the profession. One must literally learn by reflection how to profess the discipline. Perelman & Olbrechts-Tyteca provide an excellent illustration:

> Entry into a specialized group requires initiation. While a speaker must normally adapt himself to his audience, this is not true of a teacher responsible for teaching students what is accepted by the particular group they wish to join. In this case, persuasion is preliminary to initiation. It must secure submission to the requirements of the specialized group, for which the teacher is the spokesman. Initiation into a given discipline consists of communicating its rules, techniques, specific ideas, and presuppositions, as well as method of criticizing its results in terms of the disciplines own requirements [1971, pp. 99–100].

Hence the annual convention becomes a testing ground for candidates wishing initiation into the discipline (see chap. 9). Even at the convention stage, we can distinguish the reflective and unreflective legitimation process at work. Those graduate students still caught up in the reflective process are the tag-on co-authors of papers bearing the names of high-profile conventionalists. The so-called successful initiates, those who are part of the standard unreflective process, are present to delivery their solo papers on special "debut" programs.

In the process I am describing there is a *legitimation crisis*. A symbolic relationship is created whereby *criticism* is transformed into *commentary*, and explicit values offer not justification but neutrality (Foucault 1972). As Perelman & Olbrechts-Tyteca (1971, p. 335) suggest, "speech acts on what it states." Commentary is the unreflective process of *testing* the *regulation* of members of a population when they are agents in a recurrent situation (the Lewis model). Here *commentary* is the ureflected process of evaluation—literally to fix or determine the value of the speech communication within the boundaries of the technical language and action of the discipline. By comparison, *criticism* is the reflective process of *analyzing* the *constitution* of behavior of the members of a population when they are agents in a recurrent situation (see Grossberg 1978).

In the normal course of events at an annual convention, we witness critique turn into commentary as the initiate turns professional. And we see criticism subverted into commentary as conventionalism ensures that only accepted methods will be used to explore new subject matters; indeed, speech acts on what it states. Normal science in Kuhn's sense reigns supreme, or at least governs such an ideology as dominant.

What is apparent in the dialectic between commentary and criticism is the value neutrality of conventionalism. There is an absence of any system of justification inherent in the subject matter of the discipline. Hence, justification is abstracted from the behavior of the members of the discipline. The resulting legitimation process is a crisis state because the annual convention legitimizes the professional, not the profession. The scholar as famous name is valued rather than the discourse of creative research (Merleau-Ponty 1962, p. 362). The growing use of so-called blind reviewers in the selection and publication of research products is at the very least a recognition, if not a confirmation (because it is just "so-called"), of this legitimation crisis. Nor do we need to explore the ironic fact that the reviewer must be blind in order to see in an ideologically correct way. Because of this situation, some professional journals have recognized the *academic* and *scholarly* importance of *signed* reviews.

RECONSTRUCTIVE LEGITIMATION

Habermas (1979, p. 204) suggests a theoretical solution to a legitimation crisis like the one we are concerned with in conventionalism. He argues for a program of "reconstructive legitimations." "The reconstruction of given legitimations can consist, first, in discovering the justificatory system, *S*, that allows for evaluating the given legitimations as valid or invalid is *S*." In other words, we need to discover in a systematic way exactly *why* we, as a profession, have an annual convention (see Beale 1978). I have examined the many personal reasons that offered justification for participation in the discipline, but there is no system of values that points to the inherent existence of a discipline. Given this situation, a "justificatory system" should be created.

There are at least signs that this is happening: the creation of workshops, "masters' sessions," and seminars preceding conventions, doctoral honors seminars in isolation from conventions, and special conferences that are problem-specific (Bitzer and Black 1971; Miller and Simons 1974). The "bottom line" is that *professional associations* must adopt the "justificatory system" that is typical of *learned societies*. The legitimation of the discipline should develop from the profession in the professional, not from the personalities at the party convention.

The need for an effort at reconstructive legitimation is familiar and obvious when set in the concrete world of convention-goers and -doers. In the "publish or perish" atmosphere of institutionalized, corporate academia, the annual convention should be a recognized and positively valued mark of professional contribution. It should provide valuable critique for research, rather than the present tendency to offer commentary by lack of mention in this year's convention directory. The annual convention should be a practical context for judging a scholar's readiness to be promoted and not a "market" for advertising the latest "products" of the scholar. The annual convention should consistently address itself to the concrete social responsibility the discipline has to itself and to the general public. The convention should motivate public praise and criticism rather than foster private cynicism. In this context, the convention should be a testing ground to expose the rampant ideological neutrality that sustains the failure of social commitment and lack of political involvement.

The fantasies of the ivory tower to the contrary, our discipline of communicology is in the middle of the contemporary social and political arena of discourse and we must take responsibility for it. It will no longer do to make research claims and simultaneously deny responsibility for their social importance. As a discipline functioning within the institution of education, we are part of the reflective process. We cannot pretend to unreflected neutrality by hiding our objective world in a technical language (Perelman & Olbrechts-Tyteca, p. 212). "In constrasting the natural and the human sciences, or quantitative with qualitative knowledge, we construct a classification of kinds of knowledge based essentially on the idea we form of their greater or smaller independence by reference to the social conditions in which they have developed" (Perelman 1963, p. 154; see Ray 1978).

Communicology is by definition the human reflection that separates the process of human life from the events of nature. We are engaged in and by that reflection in an ongoing dialectic. The reflection is an ideology that we perform by conventionality. In the end we cannot escape the critical demand for phenomenological justification: to communicate is to be responsible, not merely responsive.

Appendix

Maurice Merleau-Ponty: A Biographical and Philosophical Sketch

Jean-Jacques Maurice Merleau-Ponty (1908–1961), French philosopher and psychologist identified with the existentialist movement, studied at the Ecole Normale Supérieure in Paris, taking his *agrégation* in philosophy in 1931. Subsequently, he taught in a number of *lycées* and at the Ecole Normale Superiéure. He was an army officer in World War II, after which he held academic appointments successively at the University of Lyons (professor of philosophy, 1945–49), the Sorbonne (Chair of Child Psychology and Pedagogy at the Institute de Psychologie, 1949–52), and at the Collège de France (after 1952) where he held the Chair of Philosophy. He was co-editor, with Jean-Paul Sartre, of the journal *Les Temps Modernes*, which they founded together with Simone de Beauvoir.

Occasionally overshadowed by the public visibility of Sartre, Merleau-Ponty had a distinguished academic career and a popular following in the intellectual life of Paris. He was a professional philosopher whose teaching and research focused on phenomenology and psychology. Yet he was a man of letters venturing to discuss politics and the arts in contributions to such publications as *Le Monde* and *L'Express*. His academic and popular exploration of existential and semiotic themes in phenomenology, a particular example of which is his essay "L'oeil et l'espirit" (1964a), displays an intellectual discipline and elegance that often surpass Sartre.

Merleau-Ponty's concern with semiotics is initially present in his first major work, in 1942, *La structure de comportement* (1963b), which is primarily a critique of positivistic psychological theories of sign production in human behavior. It is not until the 1945 publication of his second major book, *Phenomenologie de la perception* (1962), that we have a direct theoretical and empirical exploration of *parole*, *langue*, and *langage* with respect to the problem of perception. In particular, his concern is the role of expression in the constitution of perceived interpersonal reality. His examination focuses upon the unique place of gesture (*geste*) as a human embodiment of expression and perception in the signification of lived-reality (*être-au-monde*).

In Merleau-Ponty's essay on the phenomenology of language, in *Signes* (1964c), he specifically engages Saussure's diachronic/synchronic linguistic distinction. The result is the formulation of a *semiotic phenomenology* in which human communication displays a new, radical *cogito*. The Cartesian *cogito* of "I think, I feel, I am" displayed in Saussaure's *langue* distinction becomes for Merleau-Ponty a diachronic/synchronic conjunction in *parole*, which is the radical *cogito*, "I can, I am able to." The existential and social implications of this semiotic phenomenology and the process of sign production are surveyed in "An Unpublished Text by Maurice Merleau-Ponty: A Prospectus of his Work" (1964a) and in his inaugural lecture at the Collège de France (1963a).

Unfortunately, the promise of his growing interest in the relationship between phenomenology and semiotics was cut short by his death in 1961. The result is an incomplete record. We have a number of posthumous texts suggesting various directions. The course notes constituting "La conscience et l'acquisition du langage" (1973b), which indicate a focus on linguistic signs and psychological development, probably grew out of the research on "The Child's Relation With Others" (1964a). *La Prose du Monde* (1973a) points to Merleau-Ponty's concern with logico-linguistic elements in the phenomenology of communication, especially the place of discourse algorithms. Although this text bears the title of Merleau-Ponty's projected third major work, which was to concentrate on the *phenomenology of expression*, it is nonetheless a text apparently abandoned in favor of a new approach. This new direction is sketched an incomplete text and notes, which he was working on at his death, and are published as *Le visible et l'invisible* (1968). Although it is still directed toward the *phenomenology of communication*, it contains a more profound concern for the ontological status of the meaning and signification process.

In summary, it must be noted that Merleau-Ponty's work, with its central semiotic theme that unites his study of perception and expression (cf. Waehlens 1951; Silverman 1979b), is foundational to the philosophical grounding of both structuralism and phenomenology in the human sciences.

References

Ablamowicz, Halina (1984). An empirical phenomenological study of shame. (Ph.D. diss.; University Microfilms no. [in process]) Carbondale, Ill., Department of Speech Communication, Southern Illinois University.
Adorno, T.W., et al. (1976). *The positivist dispute in German sociology*. New York: Harper & Row (original work published 1969).
Advisory Commission (1968). Legitimation of violence; The Police. In *Report of the national advisory commission on civil disorders*. New York: The New York Times Co.
Alexander, Hubert G. (1972). *The language and logic of philosophy* (revised ed.). Albuquerque: University of New Mexico Press (original work published as "Language and thinking: A philosophical introduction" in 1967).
Alperson, B.L. (1975). In search of Buber's ghost: A calculus for interpersonal phenomenology. *Behavioral Science*, 20 179–90.
Anderson, James A. (1987). *Communication research: Issues and methods*. New York: McGraw-Hill Book Co.
Anon. (14 September 1981). Attica grimly marks anniversary of riot. Carbondale, Ill.: *Southern Illinoian*.
Anon. (21 August 1984). Tax rule prompts convention center name change. Carbondale, Ill.: *Daily Egyptian*, 3.
Apel, Karl-Otto (1967). *Analytic philosophy of language and the Geisteswissenschaften*. Dordrecht: D. Reidel.
———. (1972a). The a priori of communication and the foundation of the humanities. *Man and World*, 5, 3–37.
———. (1972b). Communication and the foundations of the humanities. *Acta Sociologica*, 15, 7–26.
———. (1975). The problem of philosophical fundamental-grounding in light of a transcendental pragmatic of language. *Man and World*, 8, 239–75.
———. (1980). *Towards a transformation of philosophy*. Boston: Routledge & Kegan Paul (original work published 1972).
———. (1981). *Charles S. Peirce: From pragmatism to pragmaticism*. Amherst: University of Massachussetts Press.
Austin, J.L. (1962). J.O. Urmson (ed.). *How to do things with words*. New York: Oxford University Press.
Banks, Ann (ed.) (1980). *First-person America*. New York: Alfred A. Knopf.
Barthes, Roland (1967). *Writing degree zero*. London: Jonathan Cape (original work published 1953).
———. (1968). *Elements of semiology*. New York: Hill & Wang (original work published 1964).

———. (1972). *Mythologies*. London: Jonathan Cape (original work published 1957).

———. (1982). Inaugural lecture, Collège de France, 1977. In S. Sontage (ed.), *A Barthes Reader*. New York: Hill & Wang. 457–78 (original work published 1978).

Bateson, Gregory. (1972). *Steps to an ecology of mind*. New York: Ballantine Books.

Beale, Walter H. (1978). Rhetorical performative discourse: A new theory of epideictic. *Philosophy and Rhetoric*, 11, 221–46.

Benveniste, Emile. (1971a). *Problems in general linguistics*. Coral Gables: University of Miami Press (original work published 1966).

———. (1971b). The correlations of tense in the French verb. In *Problems in general linguistics*. Coral Gables: University of Miami Press. 205–15. (original work published 1966).

Bernstein, Jeremy. (1978). A cosmic flow. *American Scholar*, 48, 1.

Bernstein, R.J. (1978). *The restructuring of social and political theory*. Philadelphia: University of Pennsylvania Press.

Bernstein, Basil B. (1971). Language and socialization. In N. Minnis (ed.), *Linguistics At Large*. London: Victor Gollanez.

Bertaux, Daniel (ed.) (1981). *Biography and society: The life history approach in the social sciences*. Beverly Hills, Calif.: International Sociological Association and Sage Publications, Inc.

Biskey, L. (1976). *Zur Kritik der bügerlichen Massenkommunikationsforschung*. Berlin, Ost: Deutscher Verlag der Wissenschaften.

Bisseret, N. (1979). *Education, class language, and ideology*. London: Routledge & Kegan Paul.

Bitzer, L.H., and Black, E. (eds.) (1971). *The prospect of rhetoric: Report on the national development project*. Englewood Cliffs, N.J.: Prentice-Hall.

Blackwell, Richard J. (1976). A structuralist account of scientific theories. *International Philosophical Quarterly*, 16, 263–74.

Blake, Cecil (1979). Communication research and African national development. *Journal of Black Studies*, 10, 218–29.

Bogdan, Robert, and Biklen, Sari K. (1982). *Qualitative research for education: An introduction to theory and methods*. Boston: Allyn and Bacon, Inc.

Bologh, R.W. (1979). *Dialectical phenomenology: Marx's method*. Boston: Routledge & Kegan Paul.

Bottomore, T.B., and Rubel, M. (eds.) (1963). *Karl Marx: Selected writings in sociology and political philosophy*. Harmondsworth, U.K.: Penguin.

Bourdieu, Pierre (1977). *Outline of a theory of practice*. New York: Cambridge University Press (original work published 1972).

Brandt, L. (1970). Phenomenology, psychoanalysis, and behaviorism: (E=ES) vs (E≠ES)? *Journal of Phenomenological Psychology*, 1, 7–18.

Brentano, Franz (1874). *Psychologie von empirischem Standpunkt*. Leipzig.

———. (1981). *The theory of categories*. Boston: Martinus Nijhoff (original work published 1937).

Brinkley, Alan B. (1960). The phenomenology of C.S. Peirce. (Ph.D. diss.; University Microfilms no. 60–5943) New Orleans: Tulane University.

Brooks, Deems M. (1968). Toward a synthesis of creative communication in the philosophy of Henry Nelson Wieman. (Ph.D. diss.; University Microfilms no. 69–06251) Carbondale, Ill., Department of Speech Communication, Southern Illinois University.
Brown, R.H. (1978). *A poetic for sociology: Towards a logic of discovery for the human sciences*. New York: Cambridge University Press.
Burgess, Parke G. (1968). The rhetoric of black power. A moral demand? *Quarterly Journal of Speech*, 54, 131.
Burnyeat, M.F. (27 September 1979). The virtues of Plato. *New York Review of Books*, 56–60.
Cahill, Corrine M. (1983). A phenomenology of feminism. (Ph.D. diss.; University Microfilms no. DA8326514) Carbondale, Ill., Department of Speech Communication, Southern Illinois University.
Chao, Yuen Ren (1970). *Language and symbolic systems*. Cambridge: Cambridge University Press.
Charbonnier, G. (1969). *Conversations with Claude Lévi-Strauss*. London: Jonathan Cape (original work published 1961).
Clavel, P., Forester, J., and Goldsmith, W. (eds.) (1980). *Urban and regional planning in an age of austerity*. Elmsford, N.Y.: Pergamon.
Coomarswamy, Anada K. (1956). *The transformation of nature in art*. New York: Dover Publications (original work published 1934).
Cotteret, J.-M. (1979). Televised debates in France. *Political Communication Review*, 4, 1–18.
Coward, R., and Ellis, J. (1977). *Language and materialism: Developments in semiology and the theory of the subject*. Boston: Routledge & Kegan Paul.
Culler, Jonathan (1976). *Ferdinand de Saussure*. London: Fontana & Collins.
———. (1977). In pursuit of signs. *Daedalus*, 106, 95–111.
Cushman, D.P., and Dietrich, D. (1979). A critical reconstruction of Jürgen Habermas holistic approach to rhetoric as social philosophy. *Journal of the American Forensic Association*, 16, 128–37.
Dallmayr, F.R., and McCarthy, T. (eds.) (1977). *Understanding and social inquiry*. University of Notre Dame Press.
Davies, I. (1976). Time, aesthetics, and critical theory. In J. O'Neill (ed.), *On Critical Theory*. New York: Seabury Press.
Deetz, S. (1973a). Words without things: Toward a social phenomenology of language. *Quarterly Journal of Speech*, 59, 40–51.
———. (1973b). An understanding of science and a hermeneutic science of understanding. *Journal of Communication*, 23, 139–59.
———. (1977). Interpretative research in communication: A hermeneutic foundation. *Journal of Communication Inquiry*. 3, 53–69.
———. (ed.) (1981). *Phenomenology in rhetoric and communication*. Washington, D.C.: The Center for Advanced Research in Phenomenology and University Press of America.
Derrida, Jacques (1976). *Of grammatology*. Baltimore: Johns Hopkins University Press (original work published 1967).
Descombes, Vincent (1980). *Modern French philosophy*. Cambridge: Cambridge University Press (original work published as "Le Même et L'Autre" in 1979).

Diekman, J.R. (1974). Speaking and being: A contemporary philosophical approach. (Ph.D. diss.; University Microfilms no. 75–00110) Carbondale, Ill., Department of Speech Communication, Southern Illinois University.

Dillon, Martin C. (1978). Merleau-Ponty and the psychogenesis of the self. *Journal of Phenomenological Psychology*, 9, 84–98.

Dreyfus, Hubert L. (1979). *What computers can't do: The limits of artificial intelligence* (revised ed.). New York: Colophon Books.

———. Rabinow, P. (1982). *Michel Foucault: Beyond structuralism and hermeneutics* (2nd ed.). University of Chicago Press (Afterword by Michel Foucault).

Eason, David L. (1977). Metajournalism: The problem of reporting in the nonfiction novel. (Ph.D. diss.; University Microfilms no. 77–24459) Carbondale, Ill., School of Journalism, Southern Illinois University.

———. (1978). New journalism and the image-world: Two modes of organizing experience (unpublished manuscript) (available from the author; Dept. of Communication, University of Utah).

Eckartsberg, Rolf von (1965). Encounter as the basic unit of social interaction. *Humanitas*, 1, 195–215.

Eco, Umberto (1976). *A theory of semiotics*. Bloomington: Indiana University Press.

Edie, James M. (1970). Can grammar be thought? In J.M. Edie et al. (eds.). *Patterns of the life world*. Evanston: Northwestern University Press. 315–45.

Ellul, Jacques (1975). *The new demons*. New York: Seabury Press.

Fales, Walter (1943). Phenomenology of questions. *Philosophy and Phenomenological Research*, 4, 60–75.

Falk, Eugene H. (1981). *The poetics of Roman Ingarden*. Chapel Hill: University of North Carolina Press.

Fauvel, J.G. (1975). Towards a phenomenological mathematics. *Philosophy and Phenomenological Research*, 36, 16–24.

Ferruolo, Stephen C. (1985). *The origins of the university: The schools of Paris and their critics*, 1100–1215. Standford, Calif.: Standford University Press.

Fisher, B.A., et al. (1977). The nature of complex communication systems. *Communication Monographs*, 44, 232–40.

———. (1978). *Perspectives on human communication*. New York: Macmillan.

Fiske, J., and Hartley, J. (1978). *Reading television*. London: Methuen.

Foucault, Michel (1965). *Madness and civilization*. London: Lowe and Brydone (original work published 1961).

———. (1970). *The order of things: An archaeology of the human sciences*. London: Tavistock (original work published 1966).

———. (1972). *The archaeology of knowledge, and The discourse on language*. New York: Pantheon Books, Random House. (original work published 1969).

———. (1974). Michel Foucault on Attica: An interview. *Telos*, 19, 157 (interviewer: John K. Simon).

———. (1977). *Language, counter-memory, practice*. Ithaca, N.Y.: Cornell University Press.

———. (1979). *Discipline and punish: The birth of the prison*. New York: Vintage Books, Random House (original work published 1975).

Frankfurt Institute for Social Research (1972). *Aspects of sociology*. Boston: Beacon Press (original work published 1956).

Freeman, Eugene (1934). *The categories of Charles S. Peirce*. Chicago: Open Court Publishing Co.

Frege, Gottlob (1948). Sense and reference (*Ueber Sinn und Bedeutung*). Max Black (trans.). *Philosophical Review*, 57, 207–30 (original work published 1892).

Gadamer, Hans-Georg (1975). *Truth and method*. New York: Seabury Press (original work published 1960).

Gardiner, Sir Alan (1951). *The theory of speech and language* (2nd ed.). Oxford: Clarendon Press.

Garvin, Paul (1954). Review of *Prolegomena to a theory of language* by Louis Hjelmslev. *Language*, 30, 69–96.

Gellner, Ernest (1974). *Legitimation of belief*. Cambridge: Cambridge University Press.

Geertz, Clifford (1973). *The interpretation of cultures*. New York: Basic Books, Inc.

———. (1983). *Local knowledge: Further essays in interpretive anthropology*. New York: Basic Books, Inc.

Giddens, Anthony (1976). *New rules of sociological method: A positive critique of interpretative sociologies*. New York: Basic Books.

Giglioli, P.P. (ed.) (1972). *Language and social contexts*. Harmondsworth, U.K.: Penguin.

Giorgi, A., et al. (eds.) (1971). *Duquesne studies in phenomenological psychology* (vol. 1). Pittsburgh: Duquesne University Press.

———. et al. (eds.) (1975). *Duquesne studies in phenomenological psychology* (vol. 2). Pittsburgh: Duquesne University Press.

———. et al. (eds.) (1979). *Duquesne studies in phenomenological psychology* (vol. 3.). Pittsburgh: Duquesne University Press.

Glassman, James K. (December 1969). SDS at Chicago. *The Atlantic*, 30–40.

Gomes, William B. (1984). Experiential psychotherapy and semiotic phenomenology: A methodological consideration of Eugene Gendlin's theory and application of focusing. (Ph.D. diss.; University Microfilms no. DA8414012) Carbondale, Ill., Department of Higher Education, Southern Illinois University.

Gordon, W.J.J. (1968). *Synectics: The development of creative capacity*. New York: Collier Books.

Grice, H.P. (1967). Meaning. In P.F. Strawson (ed.), *Philosophical logic*. London: Oxford University Press.

Grossberg, Lawrence (1978) Dialectics and rhetoric: An effort at definition (conference paper; Speech Communication Association, Minneapolis, Minn.).

———. (1979). Marxist dialectics and rhetorical criticism. *Quarterly Journal of Speech*, 65, 235–49.

Grotjah, Martin (December 1968). The psychoanalytic dialogue. In *A Center Occasional Paper*. Santa Barbara, Calif.: Center for the Study of Democratic Institutions.

Guba, E.G. (1981). Criteria for assessing the trustworthiness of naturalistic inquiries. *Educational Communication and Technology Journal*, 29, 75–91.

Gutherie, W.K.C. (1971). Rhetoric and philosophy. In *The sophists*. Cambridge: Cambridge University Press. 176–225.

Habermas, Jürgen (1970a). On systematically distorted communication. *Inquiry*, 13, 205–18.

———. (1970b). Towards a theory of communicative competence. *Inquiry*, 13, 360–75.

———. (1971a). *Knowledge and human interests*. Boston: Beacon Press (original work published 1968).

———. (1971b). *Towards a rational society: Student protest, science, and politics*. Boston: Beacon Press (original works published 1968 and 1969).

———. (1971c). Gauss lectures at Princeton university (unpublished manuscript; available at New School Library, New School for Social Research, New York).

———. (1973). *Theory and practice*. Boston: Beacon Press (original work published 1971).

———. (1975). *Legitimation crisis*. Boston: Beacon Press (original work published 1973).

———. (1976). Some distinctions in universal pragmatics: A working paper. *Theory and Society*, 3, 155–67.

———. (1979a). Aspects of the rationality of action. In T.F. Geraets (ed.), *Rationality today/Rationalité Aujourd'hui*. University of Ottawa Press.

———. (1979b). *Communication and the evolution of society*. Boston: Beacon Press (original work published 1976).

———. (1984a). *The theory of communicative action*: vol. 1, *Reason and the rationality of society*. Boston: Beacon Press (original work published 1981).

———. (1984b, in preparation). *The theory of communicative action*: vol. 2, *Lifeworld and system: A critique of functionalist reason*. Boston: Beacon Press (original work published 1981).

Hahn, E. (1968). *Historischer Materialismus und marxistische Soziologie*. Berlin, Ost.

Hall, Edward T. (1969). *The hidden dimension*. New York: Doubleday Anchor.

Halloran, J.D., Elliot, P., and Murdock, G. (1970). *Demonstrations and communications: A case study*. Harmondsworth, U.K.: Penguin.

Harms, L.S. (1980). Appropriate methods for communication policy science: Some preliminary considerations. *Human Communication Research*, 7, 3–13.

Havelock, Christine (1978). Art as communication in ancient Greece. In E. Havelock and J. Hershbell (eds.), *Communication arts in the ancient world*. New York: Hastings House, 95–118.

Hawkes, Terence (1979). *Structuralism and semiotics*. Berkeley: University of California Press.

Hay, Ian (1925). *Paid with thanks*. London: Hoddeler & Stoughton.

Haymond, Williams S. (1967). Merleau-Ponty on sensory perception. *Modern Schoolman*, 44, 93–111.

Hegel, G.W.F. (1967). *The phenomenology of mind*. New York: Harper Torchbook (original work published 1807; original translation 1910).

Heidegger, Martin (1962). *Being and Time*. New York: Harper & Row (original work published 1927).

———. (1972). *On time and being*. New York: Harper Tourchbooks (original work published 1969).

———. (1984). *The metaphysical foundations of logic*. Bloomington: Indiana University Press (original work published 1978).

Hickson, M., and Jandt, F.E. (eds.).(1976). *Marxian perspectives on human communication*. Rochester, N.Y.: PSI Publishers.

Hikins, James (1977) Discourse, dialectic and interpersonal rhetoric: A reinterpretation of Plato's rhetorical theory. (conference paper; Speech Communication Association, Washington, D.C.).

Hjelmslev, Louis (1961). *Prolegomena to a theory of language* (revised ed.). Madison: University of Wisconsin Press (original work published 1943).

———. (1970a). Langue et parole. In *Essais linguistiques* (*Travaux de cercle linguistique de Copenhague XII*) (deuxième éd.). Copenhague: Nordish Sprogog Kulturforlag (original work published 1943).

———. (1970b). Structural analysis of language. In *Essais linguistiques* (*Travaux de cercle linguistique de Copenhague XII*). Copenhague: Nordish Sprogog Kulturforlag (original work published 1948).

Holenstein, Elmar (1975). Jakobson and Husserl: A contribution to the genealogy of structuralism. *The Human Context*, 7, 61–83.

———. (1976). *Roman Jakobson's approach to language: Phenomenological structuralism*. Bloomington: Indiana University Press (original work published 1974).

Holzer, H. (1973). *Kommunikationssoziologie*. Reinbek bei Hamburg: Rowohlt.

Hooft, S. van (1976). Habermas communicative ethics. *Social Praxis*, 4, 147–75.

Horkheimer, M. (1972). *Critical theory: Selected essays*. New York: Seabury Press (original work published 1968).

Hörmann, Hans (1971). *Psycholinguistics: An introduction to research and theory*. New York: Springer-Verlag.

Hund, W.D., and Kirchhoff-Hund, B. (1980). *Soziologie der Kommunikation: Arbeitbuch zu Struktur und Funktion der Medien; Grundbergriffe und exemplarische Analysen*. Reinbek bei Hamburg: Rowohlt.

Hunt, Everett L. (1921). Dialectic—A neglected method of argument. *Quarterly Journal of Speech*, 1, 221–32.

Hunter, Floyd (1963). *Community power structures: A study of decision makers*. New York: Doubleday & Co.

Husserl, Edmund (1931). *Ideas: General introduction to pure phenomenology*. New York: Humanities Press (original work published 1913).

———. (1950–). *Husserliana, Edmund Husserl, Gesammelte Werke*. The Hague: Martinus Nijhoff.

———. (1960). *Cartesian meditations: An introduction to phenomenology*. The Hague: Martinus Nijhoff (original work published 1950).

———. (1964). *The idea of phenomenology*. The Hague: Martinus Nijhoff.

———. (1965). *Phenomenology and the crisis of philosophy*. New York: Harper & Row.

———. (1967). *The Paris lectures*. The Hague: Martinus Nijhoff (original work published 1950).

———. (1969). *Formal and transcendental logic*. The Hague: Martinus Nijhoff (original work published 1929).

———. (1970a). *Logical investigations* (2 vols.). New York: Humanities Press (original work published 1900–01, 1913, 1921).

———. (1970b). *The crisis of European sciences and transcendental phenomenology: An introduction to phenomenological philosophy*. Evanston: Northwestern University Press (original work published 1954).

Ihde, Don (1976). *Listening and voice: A phenomenology of sound*. Athens: Ohio University Press.

———. (1977). *Experimental phenomenology: An introduction*. New York: G.P. Putnam's Sons.

Ingarden, Roman (1964–66). *Der Streit um die Existenz der Welt* (3 vols.). Tübingen: Max Niemeyer Verlag (original work published 1947–48; 2 vols.).

———. (1973). *The literary work of art*. Evanston: Northwestern University Press (original work published 1931; 1965).

Isenberg, M.W. (1951). Plato's *Sophist* and the five stages of knowing. *Classical Philology*, 46, 201–32.

Israel, Joachim (1972). Stipulation and construction in the social sciences. In J. Isreal and H. Tajfel (eds.), *The context of social psychology*.

———. and Tajfel, H. (eds.) (1972). *The context of social psychology: A critical assessment*. New York: Academic Press.

Jacobson, R.E. (1980). Communication as complement: The practical gap. *Journal of Communication*, 30, 219–21.

Jakobson, Roman (1971a). Parts and wholes in language. In *Selected writings*. 2: 280–84.

———. (1971b). Linguistics and communication theory. In *Selected writings*. 2: 570–79.

———. (1971c). *Selected writings* (7 vols.). The Hague: Mouton.

Jameson, Fredric (1972). *The prison-house of language*. Princeton University Press.

Jaspers, Karl (1970). *Philosophy* (3 vols.). University of Chicago Press (2 vol. original work published 1932).

Jay, M. (1973). *The dialectical imagination: A history of the Frankfurt School and Institute of Social Research, 1923–1950*. Boston: Little, Brown.

Johnson, Richard, et al. (eds.) (1982). *Making histories: Studies in history writing and politics*. Minneapolis: University of Minnesota Press.

Jung, Hwa Y. (1979). *The crisis of political understanding: A phenomenological perspective in the conduct of political inquiry*. Pittsburgh: Duquesne University Press.

Kalmer, Howard (1983). *Communication: Sharing our stories of experience*. Seattle: Psychological Press.

Kerferd, George B. (1954). Plato's noble art of sophistry. *Classical Quarterly*, 48, 84–90.

———. (1981). *The sophistic movement*. New York: Cambridge University Press.

Klein, Jacob (1977). *Plato's triology: Theaetetus, the Sophist, and the Statesman*. University of Chicago Press.

Kockelmans, Joseph J. (1964). Merleau-Ponty's view on space-perception and space. *Review of Existential Psychology and Psychiatry*, 4, 69–105.

———. (1970). Merleau-Ponty on space perception and space. In J.J. Kockelmans and T.J. Kisiel (eds.). *Phenomenology and the natural sciences*.

——— and Kisiel, T.J. (eds.) (1970). *Phenomenology and the natural sciences: Essays and translations*. Evanston: Northwestern University Press.

Koestenbaum, Peter (1967). "Introduction" in Edmund Husserl, *The Paris Lectures*. The Hague: Martinus Nijhoff.

———. (1978). *The new image of the person: The theory and practice of clinical philosophy*. Westport: Greenwood Press. (Appendix: Simplified outline for the practice of clinical philosophy).

Kolakowski, Leszek (1968). *Positivist philosophy: From Hume to the Vienna Circle*. Harmondsworth, U.K.: Penguin Books.

Kress, G., and Hodge, R. (1979). *Language as ideology*. London: Routledge & Kegan Paul.

Krippendorff, Klaus (1977). Information systems theory and research: An overview. In B.D. Ruben (ed.). *Communication yearbook 1*. New Brunswick, N.J.: International Communication Association and Transaction Books. 149–71.

Kristeva, Julia (1975). *The system and the speaking subject*. Lisse: The Peter de Ridder Press.

Kuhn, Thomas S. (1962). *The structure of scientific revolutions*. University of Chicago Press.

———. (1970). *The structure of scientific revolutions* (2nd, enlarged ed.). University of Chicago Press.

Kwant, Remy C. (1969). *Phenomenology of expression*. Pittsburgh: Duquesne University Press.

Laing, R.D. (1967). *The politics of experience*. New York: Ballantine Books.

Langellier, Kristin (1980). The audience of literature: A phenomenological poetic and rhetoric. (Ph.D. diss.; University Microfilms no. 81–02388) Carbondale, Ill., Department of Speech Communication, Southern Illinois University.

Lanigan, Richard L. (1970). Merleau-Ponty's phenomenology of communication. *Philosophy Today*, 14, 79–88.

———. (1972). *Speaking and semiology: Maurice Merleau-Ponty's phenomenological theory of existential communication*. The Hague and Paris; Hawthorne, N.Y.: Mouton & Co.

———. (1973). The phenomenology of speech and linguistic discontinuity. *Degrés: revue de synthèse à orientation sémiologique*, 1, 1–7.

———. (1974). Enthymeme: The rhetorical species of Aristotle's syllogism. *Southern Speech Communication Journal*, 39, 207–22.

———. (1977). *Speech act phenomenology*. The Hague: Martinus Nijhoff.

———. (1979a). The phenomenology of human communication. *Philosophy Today*, 23, 3–15.

———. (1979b). A semiotic metatheory of human communication. *Semiotica*, 27, 293–305.

———. (1979c). Communication models in philosophy. In D. Nimmo (ed.), *Communication yearbook 3*. New Brunswick, N.J.: International Communication Association and Transaction Books.

———. (1979d) The objectivist illusion in therapeutic philosophy. (conference paper; The Merleau-Ponty Circle, State University of New York at Stony Brooks).

———. (1981a). A critical theory approach. In D. Nimmo and K. Sanders (eds.). *Handbook of political communication*. Beverly Hills: Sage Publications. 141–69.

———. et al. (1981b) Report on the "Task force on the phenomenology of communication and instruction: A Danforth Foundation Grant at S.I.U." (conference paper; Speech Communication Association, Anaheim, Calif.).

———. (1982a). Semiotic phenomenology: A theory of human communication praxis. *Journal of Applied Communication Research*, 10, 62–73.

———. (1982b). Semiotic phenomenology in Plato's *Sophist*. *Semiotica*, 41, 221–45.

———. (1983a). Talking: The semioitc phenomenology of human interaction. *International Journal of the Sociology of Language*, 43, 105–17.

———. (1983b). Merleau-Ponty on metajournalism: Signs, emblems, and appeals in the poetry of truth. *Communication*, 7, 241–61.

———. (1984). *Semiotic phenomenology of rhetoric: Eidetic practice in Henry Grattan's discourse on tolerance*. Washington, D.C.: The Center for Advanced Research in Phenomenology and University Press of America.

Larson, B.A., and Hensley, W.E. (1978). Convention evaluation: An examination of the uses of the past. *Central States Speech Journal*, 29, 3.

Leach, Edmund (1971). Language and anthropology. In N. Minnis (ed.), *Linguistics at large*. London: Victor Gollancz, 137–58.

———. (1976). *Culture and communication: The logic by which symbols are connected*. London: Cambridge University Press.

Leathers, Dale (1976). *Nonverbal communication systems*. Boston: Allyn & Bacon.

Ledermann, E.K. (1970). *Philosophy and medicine*. London: Tavistock.

Lefebvre, Henri (1968). *The sociology of Marx*. New York: Vintage Books (original work published 1966).

Lemert, Charles C. (1979). *Sociology and the twilight of man: Homocentricism and discourse in sociological theory*. Carbondale: Southern Illinois University Press.

———. (ed.) (1981). *French sociology: Rupture and renewal since 1968*. New York: Columbia University Press.

———. and Nielsen, Jr., Willard A. (1982). Structures, instruments, and reading in sociology. In Ino Rossi (ed.), *Structural sociology*. New York: Columbia University Press.

Levin, David (1979) Sanity and myth: Merleau-Ponty's understanding of human space. (conference paper; The Merleau-Ponty Circle, State University of New York at Stony Brook).

Lévi-Strauss, Claude (1967). *The scope of anthropology*. London: Jonathan Cape (original work published 1960).

———. (1969). R. Needham (ed.), *The elementary structures of kinship*. Boston: Beacon Press (original work published 1949).

Lewis, David K. (1969). *Convention: A philosophic study*. Cambridge: Harvard University Press.

Lingis, Alphonso (1979). Face to face: A phenomenological meditation. *International Philosophical Quarterly*, 19, 151–63.

Lotman, Ju. M. (1977). On the metalanguage of a typological description of culture. *Semiotica*, 14, 97–123.

Lyons, John (1963). *Structural semantics: An analysis of part of the vocabulary of Plato*. Oxford: Basil Blackwell.

———. (1969). *Introduction to theoretical linguistics*. Cambridge: Cambridge University Press.

———. (1977). *Semantics* (2 vols.). Cambridge: Cambridge University Press.

Manis, J.G., and Meltzer, B.N. (eds.) (1978). *Symbolic interaction: A reader in social psychology* (3rd ed.). Boston: Allyn & Bacon.

Marcus, Solomon (1974). Fifty-two oppositions between scientific and poetic communication. In Colin Cherry (ed.), *Pragmatics of human communication*. Dordrecht: D. Reidel. 83–96.

McCarthy, Thomas (1978). *The critical theory of Jürgen Habermas*. Cambridge: MIT Press.

McFeat, Tom (1974). *Small-group cultures*. New York: Pergamon Press.

McKeon, Richard (1940). Plato and Aristotle as historians: A study of method in the history of ideas. *Ethics*, 51, 66–101.

Merleau-Ponty, Maurice (1962). *Phenomenology of perception* (reprint, 1981). New York: Humanities Press (original work published 1945; trans. corrections 1981).

———. (1963a). *In praise of philosophy*. Evanston: Northwestern University Press (original work published 1953).

———. (1963b). *The structure of behavior*. Boston: Beacon Press (original work published 1942).

———. (1964a). *The primacy of perception and other essays*. Evanston: Northwestern University Press.

———. (1964b). *Sense and non-sense*. Evanston: Northwestern University Press (original work published 1948).

———. (1964c). *Signs*. Evanston: Northwestern University Press (original work published 1960).

———. (1968). C. Lefort (ed.), *The visible and the invisible; followed by working notes*. Evanston: Northwestern University Press (original work published 1964).

———. (1969). Phenomenology and Psychoanalysis, "Preface" to Hesnard's *L'oeuvre de Freud*. In A.L. Fisher (ed.), *The essential writings of Merleu-Ponty*. New York: Harcourt, Brace & World (original work published 1960).

———. (1970). *Themes from the lectures at the Collège de France 1952–1960*. Evanston: Northwestern University Press (original work published 1968).

———. (1973a). C. Lefort (ed.), *The prose of the world*. Evanston: Northwestern University Press (original work published 1969).

———. (1973b). *Consciousness and the acquisition of language*. Evanston: Northwestern University Press (original work published 1964).

Merton, R., and Gaston, J. (eds.) (1977). *The sociology of science in Europe*. Carbondale: Southern Illinois University Press.

Mićunović, D. (1979). Bureaucracy and public communication. In M. Marković and G. Petrović (eds.), *Praxis: Yugoslav essays in the philosopy and methodology of the social sciences*. Boston: D. Reidel.

Miller, C.A. (1980). A phenomenological analysis of literary experience. (Ph.D. diss.; University Microfilms no. 81–02397) Carbondale, Ill., Department of Speech Communication, Southern Illinois University.

Miller, G.R., and Simmons, H.W. (eds.)(1974)*Perspectives on communication in social conflict*. Engelwood Cliffs, N.J.: Prentice-Hall.

Morris, Charles W. (1938). *Foundations of the theory of signs*. University of Chicago Press.

———. (1971).*Writings on the general theory of signs*. The Hague: Mouton.

Morriston, Wesley (1979). Experience and causality in the philosophy of Merleau-Ponty. *Philosophy and Phenomenological Research*, 39, 561–74.

Mueller, Claus (1973). *The politics of communication: A study in the political sociology of language, socialization, and legitimation*. New York: Oxford University Press.

Natanson, Maurice (1965). The claims of immediacy. In M. Natanson and H.W. Johnstone, Jr. (eds.), *Philosophy, rhetoric, and argumentation*. University Park: Pennsylvania State University Press. 10–19.

———. (1969). Philosophy and psychiatry. In E.W. Straus et al. (eds.), *Psychiatry and philosophy*. New York: Springer-Verlag.

———. (ed.) (1973). *Phenomenology and the social sciences* (2 vols.). Evanston: Northwestern University Press.

———. (1974). *Phenomenology, role, and reason: Essays on the coherence and deformation of social reality*. Springfield, Ill.: Charles C. Thomas, Publisher.

National Public Radio. (1980). First-person America: Voices from the thirties. (Audio tape cassette and study guide no. SP–801109.S) Boston: WGBH Educational Foundation.

Nelson, Jenny Lee (1986). The other side of signification: A semiotic phenomenology of televisual experience. (Ph.D. diss; University Microfilms no. [in process]) Carbondale, Ill., Department of Speech Communication, Southern Illinois University.

Negt, O. (1978). Mass media: Tools of domination or instruments of liberation? Aspects of the Frankfurt School's communication analysis. *New German Critique*, 15, 61–80.

———. and Kluge, A. (1972). *Öffentlichkeit und Erfahung: Zur Organisationsanalyse von bürgerlicher und proletarischer Öffentlichkeit*. Frankfurt am Main: Suhrkamp.

Olmsted, Michael S. (1959). *The small group*. New York: Random House.

O'Neill, John (ed.). (1976). *On critical theory*. New York: Seabury Press.

Orth, Ernst Wolfgang (1973). Philosophy of language as phenomenology of language and logic. In M. Natanson (ed.), *Phenomenology and the social sciences*. 1, 323–59.

O'Sullivan, T., et al. (1983). *Key concepts in communication*. New York: Methuen.

Overfield, James H. (1984). *Humanism and scholasticism in late medieval Germany*. Princeton University Press.

Pace, Thomas J., et al. (1974). The situational analysis of urban communication: An extended-case study of racial tension. In K.G. Johnson (ed.), *Research designs in general semantics*. New York: Gordon & Breach Science Publishers. 95–105.

Paci, Enzo (1969). Vico, structuralism, and the phenomenological encyclopedia of the sciences. In G. Tagliacozzo and H. White (eds.), *Giambattista Vico: An international symposium*. Baltimore: Johns Hopkins University Press.

Palmer, Richard E. (1969). *Hermeneutics: Interpretation theory in Schleiermacher, Dilthey, Heidegger, and Gadamer*. Evanston: Northwestern University Press.

Pateman, Trevor (1976). Habermas and the critique of communication: An introduction. (unpublished manuscript; available from the author, Education Area, University of Sussex, Falmer, Brighton BNI 9RG, U.K.).

———. (1980).*Language, truth, and politics: Towards a radical theory for communication* (2nd ed.). Sussex, U.K.: Jean Stroud Publisher.

Peirce, Charles Sanders (1953). I. Leib (ed.), *Charles S. Peirce's letters to Lady Welby*. New Haven: Yale University Press.

———. (1931–35; 1958). Charles Hartshorne, Paul Weiss, and Arthur Burks (eds.), *The collected papers of Charles Sanders Peirce* (8 vols.). Cambridge: Harvard University Press.

Perelman, Chaim (1963). *The idea of justice and the problem of argument*. Atlantic Highlands, N.J.: Humanities Press (original work published 1963).

———. and Olbrechts-Tyteca, L. (1971). *The new rhetoric: A treatise on argumentation*. University of Notre Dame Press (original work published 1958).

Peterson, Eric E. (1980). A semiotic phenomenology of performing. (Ph.D. diss.; University Microfilms no. 81–02411) Carbondale, Ill., Department of Speech Communication, Southern Illinois University.

Piatigorsky, A.M. (1974). On some theoretical presuppositions of semiotics. *Semiotica*, 12, 185–87.

Plato (1961). Sophist. In E. Hamilton and H. Cairns (eds.), *Plato: The collected dialogues including the letters*. New York: Pantheon Books.

Plochmann, George K. (1954). Socrates, the Stranger from Elea, and some others. *Classical Philology*, 49, 223–31.

Poole, Roger C. (1966). Indirect communication: 2. Merleau-Ponty and Lévi-Strauss. *New Blackfriars*, 47, 594–604.

Poster, M. (1979). *Critical theory of the family*. New York: Seabury Press.

Potter, David (1957). Some aspects of speaking in the town meeting of colonial New England. *Southern Speech Communication Journal*, 22, 157–63.

Presnell, Michael L. (1983). Sign, image, and desire: Semiotic phenomenology and the film image. (Ph.D. diss.; University Microfilms no. DA8326559) Carbondale, Ill., Department of Speech Communication, Southern Illinois University.

Prior, William (1979) Plato's account of being and non-being in the *Sophist*. (conference paper; American Philosophical Association, Western Division Conference, Denver).

Psathas, George (ed.) (1973). *Phenomenological sociology: Issues and applications*. New York: Wiley.

Ray, J.W. (1978). Perelman's universal audience. *Quarterly Journal of Speech*, 64, 361–75.

Reid, H.G., and Yanarella, E. (1974). Toward a post-modern theory of American political science and culture: Perspectives from critical Marxism and phenomenology. *Cultural Hermeneutics*, 2, 91–166.

Reynolds, P. A. (1971). *A primer in theory construction*. Indianapolis: Bobbs-Merrill.

Ritter, Harry (1979). Science and the imagination in the thought of Schiller and Marx. In J.Fink and J.W. Marchand (eds.). *The quest for the new science*. Carbondale: Southern Illinois University Press. 28–40.

Roche, Maurice (1973). *Phenomenology, language, and the social sciences*. Boston: Routledge & Kegan Paul.

Rogers, E.M. (1981). The empirical and the critical schools of communication research. In M. Burgoon (ed.), *Communication yearbook 5*. New Brunswick, N.J.: International Communication Association and Transaction Books.

Rosenfield, L., et al. (1976). *The communicative experience*. Boston: Allyn & Bacon.

Rosenthal, Sandra B. (1977). Pragmaticism, scientific method, and the phenomenological return to lived experience. *Philosophy and Phenomenological Research*, 38, 55–66.

Rossi, Ino (1982). Relational structuralism as an alternative to the structural and interpretative paradigms of empiricist orientation. In Ino Rossi. (ed.), *Structural Sociology*. New York: Columbia University Press.

Ruesch, Jürgen (1972). *Semiotic approaches to human relations*. Paris: Mouton.

Runciman, W.G. (1973). What is structuralism?. In A. Ryan (ed.), *The philosophy of social explanation*. London: Oxford University Press. 189–202.

Russell, Bertrand (December 1967). On fanaticism (radio interview). London: British Broadcasting Corporation.

Sadock, J.M. (1974). *Toward a linguistic theory of speech acts*. New York: Academic Press.

Sagan, Carl (1978). *The dragons of Eden: Speculations on the evolution of human intelligence*. New York: Ballantine Books.

Sallis, John (1975). *Being and logos: The way of Platonic dialogue*. Pittsburgh: Duquesne University Press.

Sandywell, B., et al. (1975). *Problems of reflexivity and dialectics in sociological inquiry: Language theorizing difference*. London: Routledge & Kegan Paul.

Sartre, Jean-Paul (1956). *Being and nothingness*. New York: Philosophical Library (original work published 1949).

Saussure, Ferdinand de (1966). C. Bally and A. Sechehaye, with A. Riedlinger (ed.), *Course in general linguistics*. New York: McGraw Hill (original work published 1915).

Savan, David (1952). On the origin of Pierce's phenomenology. In P.P. Wiener and F.H. Young (eds.), *Studies in the philosophy of Charles Sanders Peirce*. Cambridge: Harvard University Press. 185–94.

———. (1976). *An Introduction to C.S. Peirce's semiotics: Part 1*. Toronto: University of Toronto Semiotic Circle (prepublication monograph).

Schmidt, R. (1967). Phenomenology. In P. Edwards (ed.), *The encyclopedia of philosophy* (1972 reprint ed.) (8 vols). New York: Macmillan and The Free Press.

Schnapp, A., and Vidal-Naquet, P. (1971). *The French student uprising November 1967–June 1968: An analytical record*. Boston: Beacon Press (original work published 1969).

Schrag, Calvin O. (1980). *Radical reflection and the origin of the human sciences*. West Lafayette, Ind.: Purdue University Press.

Schroyer, T. (1975). *The critique of domination: The origins and development of critical theory*. Boston: Beacon Press.

Schutz, Alfred (1967). *The phenomenology of the social world*. Evanston: Northwestern University Press (original work published 1932).

———. (1973). Maurice Natanson (ed.), *Collected papers* (3 vols) The Hague: Martinus Nijhoff.

———. (1973). Symbol, reality, and society. In M. Natanson (ed.), *Collected papers* (3 vols.). The Hague: Martinus Nijhoff. 1: 287–356.

Seamon, David (1979). *A geography of the life world: Movement, rest, encounter.* London: Croom Helm.

Searle, John R. (1967). Human communication theory and the philosophy of language: some remarks. In F.E.X. Dance (ed.), *Human communication theory: Original essays.* New York: Holt, Rinehart & Winston.

———. (1969). *Speech acts: An essay in the philosophy of language.* New York: Cambridge University Press.

———. (29 April 1982). The myth of the computer. *The New York Review of Books.* 3–6.

———. (1983). *Intentionality: An essay in the philosophy of mind.* New York: Cambridge University Press.

———. (1985). *Minds, brains, and science.* Cambridge: Harvard University Press.

Sebeok, Thomas A. (1977). *How animals communicate.* Bloomington: Indiana University Press.

———. and Rosenthal, R. (eds.) (1981). *The Clever Hans phenomenon: Communication with horses, whales, apes, and people.* New York: The New York Academy of Sciences.

Shinner, Larry (1969). A phenomenological approach to historical knowledge. *History and Theory*, 8, 260–74.

Silverman, Hugh J. (1979a). For a hermeneutic semiology of self. *Philosophy Today*, 23, 199–204.

———. (1979b). Merleau-Ponty's human ambiguity. *Journal of the British Society for Phenomenology*, 10, 23–38.

Smart, B. (1976). *Sociology, phenomenology and Marxian analysis: A critical discussion of the theory and practice of a science of society.* London: Routledge & Kegan Paul

Smith, Andrew R. (1977). A phenomenology of confinement (M.S. thesis). Department of Speech Communication, Southern Illinois University.

Smith, D.R., and Williamson, L.K. (1977). *Interpersonal communication: Roles, rules, strategies, and games.* Dubuque, Iowa: Wm.C. Brown Co.

Smythe, Dallas W. (1977). Communications: Blind spot of Western Marxism. *Canadian Journal of Political and Social Theory*, 1, 1–27.

Sobchack, Vivian C. (1984). The address of the eye: A semiotic phenomenology of cinematic embodiment. (Ph.D. diss.; University Microfilms no. DA8510068; forthcoming from Princeton University Press) Carbondale, Ill., Department of Speech Communication, Southern Illinois University.

Sochat, Nancy A. (1978). Teaching medical diagnostic interviewing skills: An application of semiotic theory and principles. (Ph.D. diss.; University Microfilms no. 79–08084) Carbondale, Ill., Department of Speech Communication, Southern Illinois University.

Sontag, Frederick (1969). *The existentialist prolegomena: To a future metaphysics.* Chicago, Ill.: University of Chicago Press.

Spengler, J.C. (1975). A phenomenological explication of loneliness. (Ph.D. diss.; University Microfilms no. 76–13291) Carbondale, Ill., Department of Speech Communication, Southern Illinois University.

Spiegelberg, Herbert (1956). Husserl's and Peirce's phenomenologies: Coincidence or interaction [?]. *Philosophy and Phenomenological Research*, 17, 164–85.

———. (1975). *Doing phenomenology*. The Hague: Martinus Nijhoff.

———. (1982). *The phenomenological movement: A historical introduction* (3rd revised and enlarged ed.). The Hague and Boston: Martinus Nijhoff (original work, 2nd ed., published 1979 in 2 vols.).

Spitzack, Carole J. (1984). The subjects of weight consciousness: A discursive analysis of experiential unity. (Ph.D. diss.; University Microfilms no. DA8526735 Carbondale, Ill., Department of Speech Communication, Southern Illinois University.

Strasser, Stephan (1974). *Phenomenology and the human sciences: A contribution to a new scientific ideal*. Pittsburgh: Duquesne University Press.

Strawson, P.F. (1971). *Logico-linguistic papers*. New York: Barnes & Noble.

Strobl, Rudolf L. (1980). Recent European critical thought: Emergence of a theory of communication. (conference paper; Seminar on Communication Theory from Eastern and Western Perspectives, Institute of Communication and Culture, East-West Center, Honolulu).

Sullivan, W.M. (1978). Communication and the recovery of meaning: An interpretation of Habermas. *International Philosophical Quarterly*, 18, 69–86.

Taylor, A.E. (1956). *Plato: The man and his works*. New York: World Publishing Co.

Thompson, Paul (1978). *The voice of the past: Oral history*. New York: Oxford University Press.

Toulmin, Stephen (1977). From form to function: Philosophy and history of science in the 1950s and now. *Daedalus*, 106, 143–62.

Tragesser, R.S. (1977). *Phenomenolgy and logic*. Ithaca, N.Y.: Cornell University Press.

Tsuda, Yukio (1985). Language inequality and distortion in intercultural communication: A critical theory approach. (Ph.D. diss.; University Microfilms no. [in process]; forthcoming from Benjamins Publ.) Carbondale, Ill., Department of Speech Communication, Southern Illinois University.

U.S. Department of Commerce (1969). We the black people of the United States (pamphlet). Washington, D.C.: Government Printing Office.

Verón, E. (1971). Ideology and social sciences: A communicational approach. *Semiotica*, 3, 59–76.

Virasoro, Manuel (1959). Merleau-Ponty and the world of perception. *Philosophy Today*, 3, 66–72.

Vise, Pierre de (1967). *Chicago's widening color gap*. Chicago: Interuniversity Social Research Committee.

Waehlens, Alphonse de (1951). *Une philosophie de l'ambiguïté: L'Existentialisme de M. Merleau-Ponty*. Louvain: Publications Universitaires de Louvain.

Watson, L.C. and Watson-Franke, M-B. (1985). *Interpreting life histories: An anthropological inquiry*. New Brunswick, N.J.: Rutgers University Press.

Weiss, Robert (1978). The emergence and transformation of private detective industrial policing in the United States, 1850–1940. *Crime and Social Justice*, 9, 35–48.

Wellmer, A. (1976). Communication and emancipation: Reflections on the linguistic turn in critical theory. In J. O'Neill (ed.), *On critical theory*. New York: Seabury Press.

———. (1971). *Critical theory of society*. New York: Herder & Herder.

Whitsett, Gavin C. (1979). A phenomenology of human sexuality. (Ph.D. diss.; University Microfilms no. 80–04104) Carbondale, Ill., Department of Speech Communication, Southern Illinois University.

Wicker, Tom (1975). *A time to die*. New York: Quadrangle; New York Times Book Co.

Wilden, Anthony (1972). Analog and digital communication: On the relationship between negation, signification, and the emergence of the discrete element. *Semiotica*, 6, 50–82.

———. (1987). *The rules are no game: The strategy of communication*. New York: Routledge & Kegan Paul.

———. (1980). *System and structure: Essays in communication and exchange* (2nd ed.). New York: Tavistock Publications and Methuen.

Wilson, James Q. (1965). *Negro politics: The search for leadership*. New York: The Free Press.

Worth, Louis (1964). A.J. Reiss (ed.), *On cities and social life*, University of Chicago Press.

Zaner, Richard M. (1975). On the sense of method in phenomenology. In Edo Pivcevic. (ed.), *Phenomenology and philosophical understanding*. New York: Cambridge University Press.

Znaniecki, Florian (1969). The principles of selection of cultural data. In R. Bierstedt (ed.), *On humanistic sociology*. University of Chicago Press.

Index

I

J

K

L

M

N

O

P

Q

R